BUDDHIST
&
MASTERS
AN INTRODUCTION
(An account of metal statues made by Nepalese artisans)

Conceptualized, Compiled and Edited by
CHANDRA B SHAKYA

INTRODUCTION TO BUDDHIST
DEITIES & MASTERS
BY : CHANDRA B SHAKYA

© ADARSH BOOKS 2009
Reprint 2017

ISBN 10 : 81-8363-071-5
ISBN 13 : 978-81-8363-071-9

Published by :
ADARSH BOOKS
New Delhi - 2

Distributed by :
ADARSH ENTERPRISES
4393/4 Tulsidas Street, Ansari Road,
Daryaganj, New Delhi-2
Phone : 23246131-32, 41009940
Fax : 91-011-23246130
e-mail : adarshbooks@vsnl.com

Laser typesetting : Jay Mata Graphics

Printed at : Saurabh Printers Pvt. Ltd., Noida

Visit us at : www.adarshbooks.com

*for Lucy
with love from
Simon - Jenny
Christmas 2019*

CONTENTS

v

viii

ix

PREFACE

It is needless here to mention about the popularity of Nepalese arts and crafts in the world. Among various craftworks, metal statues have their specific importance due to several reasons. Since long time ago, Nepal had been a site for renowned Buddhist/Spiritual Masters to practice meditation and dharma teaching. Nepali artisans had gone to far off countries like China, Mongolia, Tibet, Bhutan, etc., to create masterpieces of craftworks, even in those days. Princess Bhrikuti had taken Nepali artisans with her to work in constructing monasteries and statues in Tibet, way back in 7th century. Later, Guru Rinpoche had taken Nepali artisans to Tibet, to work at Samye Monastery. During 12th century, Balbahu (Arniko) had gone to China to make temples at the invitation of the Emperor Kublai Khan. Guru Shandrung Ngawang Namgyal of Bhutan also took Nepali artisans to construct several fortresses and monasteries there in 16th century. Within Nepal also, especially in Newar community, the practice of Mahayana Buddhism along with involvement of people in arts and crafts relating to the same as their ways of livelihoods have had been greatly instrumental in flourishing such fine craftsmanship that we see today.

Actually, the casting of bronze, brass and copper statues in Nepal dates back to the 13th century. Usually, a *lost wax method* is followed for casting different deities. Apart from the activity of casting, there are series of works that need to be done to prepare a completed piece of statue such as engraving, gold plating, face painting, etc. Improved modes and techniques have evolved lately in making a beautiful and durable statue. With the spread of Mahayana Buddhism in various parts of the world, including the West, there have been increased demands of Buddhist statues. Today, we find many buyers coming from different parts of the world mostly from Asian countries. However, Tibetan masters and practitioners constitute the main job givers to these hardworking, laborious artisans of Nepal. With the arrival of Buddhist masters and practitioners from different sects of Mahayana Buddhism, the artisans are exposed to additional array of Buddhist deities. Consequently, newer and better statues can be seen in the statue shops around Kathmandu and Patan especially. Because of the multitude of varieties of such deities and Buddhist masters' statues, it is natural that people get bewildered and sometimes confused as to which deity represents what activity or essence.

Mahayana Buddhist pantheons have so many deities, that too belonging to different sects; it would be a very difficult task if not impossible, to list them out. Let the readers be reminded here that this book deals with those Buddhist deities and Masters, whose metal statues are being made by Nepalese artisans and which are comparatively popular. Endeavor is made here to present a general introduction, iconographic details and related doctrine about the respective deity. In case of Masters, a brief history with the mention of specific mastery and contribution is presented in this book. Considering the vastness and complexity of the subject, the readers would be considerate towards the writer in case there happens to be any flaws or mistakes of any kind.

Thanks are due to statue business houses and artisans for providing access to photographing some statues. Acknowledgements are also due to some web sites from where the photographs have been drawn.

It is hoped that this book will serve statue makers, shop keepers, tourists and all those interested persons. Any comment or suggestion is highly welcome in order to improve the future endeavors. The author can be easily contacted through email :
chandrashakya@yahoo.com or SMS to 9841-534364.

– Author

HISTORY OF METAL STATUE MAKING IN NEPAL

Since long time ago, Nepal had been a site for renowned Buddhist/ Spiritual Masters to practice meditation and dharma teaching, for its tranquil and naturalistic geographic setting of mountains, Himalayas and valleys. Perhaps, for that reason, the art of statue making might have flourished in this region since very old times. There have been remarkable sculptures since as early as 5th century i.e Lichhavi period (330 - 700 AD). As found in an inscription, the ruler Amshuvarma had ordered a metal crest for the Changu Narayan Temple in 607 AD, shows that there was well developed metal craft works at that time. The fact that Princess Bhrikuti had taken Nepali artisans with her to work in constructing monasteries and statues in Tibet, also points to the same. Famous Chinese traveler Huang Tsang in 648 AD, had greatly appreciated Nepalese crafts. Guru Padmasambhava had taken Nepali artisans to Tibet to work at Samye Monastery in the 786 AD.

It is said that during the Pala dynasty (750 - 1150 AD), the metal statue art works had highly flourished. Know-how of such art works was believed to have introduced from the developed plains of the Indian subcontinent. Many metal workers at that time were considered to be Buddhist monks working for vihara or religious schools and institutions. Metal workers used copper and bronze as well as other metals for casting. With increased outside influences from Indian subcontinent in terms of technology, the Buddhist masters from Tibet and China, as well as the metal workers in Nepal became busy making more and more deities. The number of gods and goddesses also increased with increased introduction of legends and scriptures by newly arrived masters. It is believed that metal art work was at its peak demand during 10th century, as compared to other craft works especially from Tibet side.

There had been Muslim influence around 12th century in Nepal following the invasion that took place in Indian subcontinent during 1094 AD. New skills, styles and technical expertise were introduced by refugees that entered Nepal. There was variation in shape and forms of statues that followed thereafter. It was during 13th century, a Nepali artist by the name of Balbahu (Arniko) (1245 - 1306 AD) was invited to Tibet and then China to build monasteries and statues.

The artistic creations during the early Malla period (1200 - 1400 AD) were numerous deities of both religions. There was more influence of tantrism at that time. The statues were embellished with semi precious stones.

The best of metal statue making was yet to come. During 14th and 15th century, further development in statue making took place mainly within Kathmandu valley. In 1484 AD, after the death of Yaksa Malla, the Kathmandu valley was divided into three kingdoms. Later, these three kingdoms became great rivals in producing better art works. As a result, finer art works of metal, wood, stone and other forms of art flourished which greatly decorated monuments, palaces, temples, etc. With the rise in Tantrism during Malla period, the metal workers had to work hard to make and supply new series of statues and images. Tantric images challenged the artists to look up for new ways of imagining and bringing forth innovative and richer ways of expression, jewelry, clothing and other accessories.

In this way, metal art work reached its zenith during the late Malla period (1400 - 1768 AD). Bronze statues were increasingly traded to Tibet. Some of the excellent examples of metal work at that time are the Buddha in Hiranya Varna Mahavihar monastery and the gilted figure of Garuda in front of the Krishna temple in Patan.

In 17th century, Guru Shandrung Ngawang Namgyal of Bhutan had taken Nepali artisans to construct several fortresses and monasteries there.

With the coming of the Shah dynasty (1768 AD), there had been dramatic changes in socio-cultural settings in Nepal thus affecting the previous culture and business situations. There was much turmoil politically like fight with China in Tibet, fight with British army in India and Rana rule (1847 - 1951). By that time, Tibet was ruled by the Buddhist religious leader, the Dalai Lama. Buddhist metal works were being produced in Tibet in greater quantities. Along with other cultural texts and influences, Buddhist art was flowing from Tibet to Kathmandu, which was opposite to what had been happening earlier. However, there were numbers of artisans, especially Newars from Kathmandu valley who were in Tibet and engaged in such art works.

After the invasion of Tibet by China in 1959, there had been much movement of Tibetan masters and practitioners in Nepal as well. With the resulting spread of Mahayana Buddhism in various parts of the world including the West, there have been sharp increase in the demand of metal statues. In fact, the making of statues has been remarkable since the seventies in Nepal. With the increased interaction with more and more Buddhist masters and practitioners from different sects of Mahayana Buddhism, the artisans are introduced to newer array of deities. Consequently, newer and better statues can be seen in the statue shops around Kathmandu and Patan especially. Booming tourism and access of internet technology also helped in proliferation of statue making and selling business.

ACTUAL MAKING OF
A STATUE

In Nepal, the metal statues are made in two ways. One is wax model followed by metal casting and another is called working out from metal sheet called *repousse*.

WAX MODEL AND METAL CASTING

A wax model is prepared by artisan by hand. Some times, duplicates are made out of original wax model. In this way, wax models may be one of a kind or replicas. Replicas are made by pressing a warm harder wax around an original model, of wax, or metal, or other material. When the hard wax is removed it becomes a mold into which soft wax is pressed to replicate the original.

Casting is done by the "lost wax" method. In this process, a wax model is prepared at first and then encased in clay and dried. Then it is melted out by pouring molten metal. After the metal hardens, the clay mold is broken revealing a metal replica of the wax model. A solid wax model produces a solid casting; a hollow wax model with a clay core produces a hollow cast. Usually small statues are solid cast while bigger ones are cast hollow as required.

REPOUSSE METHOD

The technique of hammering sheet metal into relief is called embossing or *repousse*. The latter is a French term translated as "pushed again", referring to an alternate front and back hammering the technique. Because of irreversible nature of the hard metal, it is difficult to rectify mistakes here. As this practice is difficult, it is relatively rare worldwide. Nepal is an exception. This tradition is still followed and in a way flourishing in Nepal. Many sacred and notable images are made in this style. Several other objects and architectural embellishment are also made through this technique. Large hollow images of dovetailed sheet metal are sometimes supplemented with solid cast limbs and other accessories.

TYPES OF METAL USED FOR CASTING

In ancient time, it was mostly the bronze metal that was used to cast statues. But, there were some uses of copper as well. For some small and important statues, gold and silver were also used. However, there was gradually increased use of copper for casting. It was because the artisans were gradually exposed to knowing of techniques of generating needed heat to melt copper. Artisans preferred copper as the engraving and smooth finishing was better.

TYPES OF FINISH

With the exposure to innovative and newer techniques, artisans came up with better statues with different kind of *finish (or look)*. Statues are made with (i) fully gold coated (ii) partly gold coated. Gold coating can be in shining fashion or just dull looking or ancient looking style also. For silver coating also, it can be in shining color or dull and antique looking one.

Sometimes, the statues are given an oxidized look or copper colored. The color can be varied at the test of the buyers or practitioners. Sometime, there can be multicolors with varied colors to different parts of the statues.

Then the intensity of engraving can differ very much among statues. Some statue can have very intriguing and rich carvings while other may be quite plain enough.

Some statues may have gold dust face painted. But some may have just plain face. Sometimes, different color pigments are used to highlight the various paraphernalia.

DIFFERENT SIZES

Statues are made in various sizes. It can be small as 2 or 3 inches in height or it can be several feet. Usually, statues are made in 6 inches, 9 inches, 12 inches, 18 inches, 24 inches, 30 inches, 36 inches, 42 inches, 48 inches, 60 inches, etc.

DIFFERENT POSTURE, HAND GESTURE AND HOLDING OBJECTS

This is a very important aspect of the statue. A given deity needs to have the correct posture, hand gesture and holding objects. Even, the color and proportionate size matters here. An artist cannot have his/her liberty to change or alter such things on his/her own.

Some prominent postures are *dhyanasana, lalitasana, paryankasana, alidasana,* etc. Similarly, the popular hand gestures which are called *mudras* are *abhaya mudra, bhumisparsha mudra, dharmachakra mudra, varada mudra, vitarka mudra,* etc. Similarly, some of the customary holding objects are *vajra, kapala, phurba, amoghapasa, utpala,* sword, *kartika, khatvanga,* trident, vase, etc.

ACHALA
(CHANDAMAHAROSANA)

Photo no 1. : *Achala (a fully gold-plated statue)*

INTRODUCTION

Âchala (also called Acala, Achalanath, Chandamaharosana, and Krodaraja; Tib: *Mi yo wa*) is the best known of the Five Wisdom Kings of the Womb Realm in Vajrayana Buddhism,. (Other wisdom kings are Trilokavijaya, Kundali, Yamantaka and Vajrayaksa).

Achala means "The Immovable One" in Sanskrit. Achala is the destroyer of delusion and the protector of Buddhism. His immovability refers to his ability to remain unmoved by carnal temptations. Despite his fearsome appearance, his role is to aid all beings by showing them the teachings of the Buddha and leading them into self-control.

He is seen as a protector and aide in attaining goals. Temples dedicated to Achala depicts a periodic fire ritual in devotion to him. Locally, he is also known by the name of Shankata, one who save beings from problems.

Achala is also the name of the eighth of the ten stages of the path to Buddhahood.

The Buddha Akshobhya, whose name also means 'the immovable one', is sometimes merged with Achala. However, Achala is not a Buddha,

Achala is also called *Chandamaharoshana*, an appellation by which he is known in the *Chandamaharoshana Tantra*, a text that Tibetans classified among the Anuttarayoga Tantras. He is the enlightened exponent of truth.

Achala is considered one of the Thirteen Buddhas in Japan.

ICONOGRAPHY

Achala is typically depicted with a sword for subduing demons in his right hand and a rope for catching and binding them in his left hand. He wears a tantric crown and jewelry, and an animal skin around his thighs. A scarf draped loosely around his shoulders flay sideways. He has a fearsome blue visage and is surrounded by flames, representing the purification of the mind. He is often depicted seated or standing on a rock to show his immovability. His hair commonly has seven knots and is draped on his left side, a servant hairstyle in Buddhist iconography. He is frequently depicted with two protruding fangs. One tooth points down, representing his compassion to the world, and one tooth points up, represent his passion for truth.

Sometimes, he is shown with his consort, Dveshvajri. In that case, she holds a kartrika in her right hand while embracing by her left hand.

DOCTRINE AND OTHERS

Photo no 2 : *Achala in standing position*

Krodharaja Achala is found in two Tantras from the Kriya classification alongwith the Siddhaikavira Tantra, catalogued by the Sakyas as a Charya Tantra, also known as the White Manjushri Tantra. It is from here that he takes on his role as a remover of obstacles and the special protector for the practices of Manjushri. In Anuttarayoga, there are three Tantras specifically for Achala. The Chandamaharoshana is the most famous of these. The Kriya Tantra practice of Achala was popularized by Lord Atisha (982-1054) the founder of the Kadampa School and also by Lobpon Sonam Tsemo (1142-1182) of Sakya School.

Achalanatha embodies sitting still amid the three fires of greed, hate and delusion. His vow is to subdue all disturbances that might distract trainees from their meditation. His especial concern is to protect the training of women against those who would disparage their spiritual ability and to dispel all obstacles to their training—whether internal, in the form of doubts or external, in the form of men or women, who denigrate the capacity of women to become Buddha. In Buddhism, the attitude of mind that denigrates the spiritual ability of women is regarded as a serious obstacle in training. Indeed in some Buddhist texts this attitude is called a "root cause of spiritual downfall." In the earliest Buddhist scriptures, it is the voice of Mara that tries to cause doubt by saying that the highest stages of realization are closed to women.

Mantra : *Namah samanta-vajranam chanda-maharosana sphotaya hum trat ham mam*

Above is the general mantra, but there are four types of mantra dedicated to Achala. They are:

1. Mantra of Ferocious Eating (*namah samanta vajranam trat amogha chanda maha rosana sphataya hum tramaya hum trat ham mam*)
2. Mantra of the Fire Realm (*namah sarva tathagatebhyah sarva mukhebhyah sarvatha trat chandamaha rosana kham khahi khahi sarva vighanam hum trat ham mam*)
3. Mantra of Compassionate Rescue (*namah samanta vajranam canda maha rosana sphataya hum traka ham mam*)
4. The Heart Mantra: (*namah samanta vajranam ham*)

These mantras represent the various qualities of Achala. The Mantra of Ferocious Eating invokes his power to eat away all our karmic obstacles. The Mantra of the Fire Realm is able to burn away all our defilements. The Mantra of Compassionate Rescue represents his ability to protect all sentient beings, and the Heart Mantra brings out the immovable aspect in our Buddha-nature. Achala's sadhana (method) belongs to the carya tantra of the Vajrayana tradition and it is a powerful one. If a person of the right aptitude is initiated into this sadhana, it is believed that a constant practice will quickly lead one to enlightenment.

AKSHOBHYA BUDDHA

Photo no 3 : *Akshobhya Buddha (a partly gold plated statue)*

INTRODUCTION

Akshobhya Buddha (Tib: Mikyop) is one of the Five Wisdom Buddhas or Pancha Buddhas in Vajrayana Buddhism. The other Budddhas are Vairocana Buddha, Ratnasambava Buddha, Amitabh Buddha and Amoghasiddhi Buddha.

Akshobhya Buddha is located in the east of the Diamond Realm and is the lord of the Eastern Pure Land Abhirati His consort is Locana. He is normally accompanied by two elephants. His color is blue. Akshobhya Buddha's blue color is closely linked to the mirror-like deep awareness and the aggregate of all types of consciousness.

Akshobhya Buddha is sometimes merged with Achala, whose name also means 'immovable one' in Sanskrit. However, Achala is not a Buddha, but one of the Five Wisdom Kings of the Womb Realm in Vajrayana.

ICONOGRAPHY

Akshobhya Buddha is depicted in blue color which is closely linked to the mirror symbolism. Blue is the color of water, and water has the capacity to act as a clear mirror.

He is seen in bhoomisparsha mudra (earth touching gesture). This mudra suggests confidence, deep-rootedness, and the same kind of determination which carried the Buddha to his enlightenment, in spite of the numerous hurdles that stood in his path.

Akshobhya Buddha's emblem is the vajra, the symbol of Vajrayana, or tantric Buddhism. The vajra essentially signifies the immovable, immutable, indivisible, and indestructible state of enlightenment. Thus is Akshobhya Buddha touching the earth with the fingertips of his right hand, the earth too being a symbol of the immutable, the solid, and the concrete.

Akshobhya Buddha's mount is the elephant. An elephant places its foot upon the earth with unshakeable certainty. It has the same unalterable quality as the Buddha's fingers touching the ground, and the same determination that carried Buddha through his tribulations.

He represents the primordial cosmic element of Vijnana (Consciousness). When represented in the Stupa, he always faces the east.

Akshobhya Buddha's paradise is Abhirati, the Land of Exceeding Great Delight. Buddhists believe that whoever is reborn there cannot fall back to a lower level of consciousness. Akshobhya Buddha's bija is Hum.

DOCTRINE AND OTHERS

Akshobhya Buddha appears in the "Scripture of the Buddha-land of Akshobhya", which dates back to 147 AD and is the oldest known Pure Land text. According to the scripture, a monk wished to practice the Dharma in the eastern world of delight and made a vow to think no anger or malice towards any being until enlightenment. He duly proved "immovable" and when he succeeded, he became the Buddha Akshobhya.

Akshobhya Buddha is believed to transform the human failing of anger into a clear, mirror-like wisdom. With this wisdom, one sees things just as they are, impartially and unaffectedly. (Five wisdom Buddhas are identified with five different negative delusions of human beings viz. ignorance, anger, pride, attachment and jealousy).

The Buddha Akshobhya established the enlightened intention that all sentient beings could purify any degree of non-virtue. Even the extreme non-virtues of hatred, violence, and killing can be cleansed through relying on him as the focus of meditation, acknowledging and abandoning non-virtuous actions, and invoking his blessings of purification. In the *Akshobhya sutra*, the Buddha Sakyamuni himself extolled the perseverence of Akshobhya in actualizing this intention so powerfully that countless beings have been saved from the intense suffering of lower states of existence.

Akshobhya meditation can liberate not only the practitioner him or herself from the fear of inauspicious rebirth, but other beings as well. The merit generated by reciting one-hundred-thousand of

Akshobhya Buddha's long dyani mantra and creating an image of him could be dedicated to another person, even someone long deceased, and they would be assured of release from lower states of existence and rebirth in spiritually fortunate circumstances. Likewise, people practice mantra of Akshobhya for their pets or for animals to release them from the animal realm.

Mantra : *Om Akshobhya Hum.*

In short, particulars of Akshobhya Buddha are as following :

Particular	For Akshobhya Buddha
Meaning of the Name	Immovable or Unshakable Buddha
Direction	East
Color	blue
Mudra	bhoomisparsa (witness)
Vija (Syllable)	Hum
Symbol	Vajra (thunderbolt)
Embodies	steadfastness
Type of wisdom	mirror like
Cosmic element (skandha)	Vijnana (consciousness)
Earthly element	water
Antidote to	anger and hatred
Sense	sound
Vehicle	Elephant
Spiritual son	Vajrapani
Consort	Locana
Paradise	Abhirati, the Land of Great Delight

AMITABHA BUDDHA

Photo no 4 : *Amitabha Buddha (a partly gold plated statue)*

INTRODUCTION

Amitâbha Buddha (Tib: *Opame*) is one of the Five Wisdom Buddhas or Pancha Buddhas in Vajrayana Buddhism. The other Budddhas are Vairocana Buddha, Akshobhya Buddha, Ratnasambava Buddha, and Amoghasiddhi Buddha.

According to Mahayana school of Buddhism, Amitabha Buddha is a celestial Buddha who possesses infinite merits resulting from good deeds over countless past lives as a bodhisattva named Dharmakara and who created Sukhavati (Pure land) Buddha field.

Amitabha Buddha is known as Amitayus in Tibet as a deity who renders longevity and prevents from an untimely death.

Amitabha Buddha is one of the thirteen Buddhist deities in Japanese Vajrayana, or Shingon Buddhism.

The *nembutsu* used in Pure Land Buddhist schools is incorporated into Shingon, but Shingon also uses special devotional mantras for Amitabha as well.

Amitabha Buddha is also one of the Buddhas featured in the Womb Realm Mandala used in Shingon practices.

ICONOGRAPHY

Amitâbha Buddha is portrayed as Sâkyamuni Buddha. But, usually, he is often depicted seated in meditation mudrâ while earth-touching mudrâ is reserved for a seated Sâkyamuni Buddha alone.

When standing, Amitâbha is often shown with his left arm bare and extended downward with thumb and forefinger touching, with his right hand facing outward also with thumb and forefinger touching. The meaning of this mudra is that wisdom (symbolized by the raised hand) is accessible to even the lowest beings, while the out-

Photo no 5 : *Amitabha Buddha in standing pose*

stretched hand shows that his compassion is directed at the lowest beings, who cannot save themselves. Amitâbha Buddha is often portrayed with two assistants: Avalokitesvara on right and Mahâsthâmaprâpta on his left.

In Tibetan Buddhism, Amitâbha is red in color (red being the color of love, compassion, and emotional energy). His direction is west and so he is envisioned as the (red) setting sun. He is seen as the supreme power and energy of nature, cast on an earthly plain, accessible to all sentient beings. He is being known to protect beings from the negative emotions of attachment. His unique emblem is the lotus. He is thus associated with the attributes of the lotus: gentleness, openness, and purity.

DOCTRINE AND OTHERS

According to the *Larger Sûtra of Immeasurable Life* Amitâbha Buddha was, in very ancient times and possibly in another realm, a monk named Dharmakâra.

In some versions of the sûtra, Dharmakâra is described as a former king who, having come into contact with the Buddhist teachings through the Buddha Lokesvararaja, renounced his throne. He then resolved to become a Buddha and came into possession of a *buddhakcetra* ("buddha-field", a world produced by a Buddha's merit), possessed of many perfections. These resolutions were expressed in his forty-eight vows, which set out the type of buddha-field he aspired to create, the conditions under which beings might be born into that world, and what kind of beings they would be when reborn there.

The sutra goes on to explain that Amitâbha, after accumulating great merit over countless lives, finally achieved Buddhahood and created Sukhavati (Pure Land).

He is still alive in this land of Sukhâvatî. By the power of his vows, Amitâbha has made it possible for all who call upon him to be reborn into this land and to undergo instruction by him about the dharma and ultimately become bodhisattvas and Buddhas in their turn (the ultimate goal of Mahâyâna Buddhism). From there, these bodhisattvas and Buddhas return to this world to help yet more beings.

The basic doctrines concerning Amitâbha and his vows are found in three canonical Mahâyâna texts: (1) The Larger Sukhâvatîvyûha Sûtra (2) The Smaller Sukhâvatîvyûha Sûtra and (3) The Amitâyurdhyâna Sûtra (Sutra on the Meditation on Amitâyus). The openness and acceptance of all kinds of people has made the Pure Land belief one of the major influences of Mahâyâna Buddhism. Pure Land Buddhism seems to have become popular first in northwest India/Pakistan and Afghanistan, from where it spread to Central Asia and China, and from China to Vietnam, Korea and Japan.

In the versions of the sutra widely known in China, Vietnam, Korea and Japan, Dharmakâra's eighteenth vow was that any being in any universe desiring to be born into Amitâbha's Pure Land and calling upon his name even as few as ten times will be guaranteed rebirth there. His nineteenth vow promises that he, together with his bodhisattvas and other blessed Buddhists, will appear before those who call upon him at the moment of death.

In Vajrayana Buddhism, Amitâbha Buddha is believed to be the most popular deity among the Pancha Buddhas. He is associated with the freeing of beings from attachment and desire. In conformity with his hand mudra, the essential message of Amitabha is that of meditation. His association with the setting sun (west direction) suggests the withdrawal of the external sense perceptions inwards, into higher states of meditative concentration. Amitabha Buddha, thus, provides the beings with infinite wisdom that helps them to transmute the negative trait of obsessive attachment into a discerning awareness. By realizing discerning wisdom, the enlightened mind is experienced and one becomes united with the Buddha Amitabha.

Mantras : *Amitabha Buddha is the center of a number of mantras in Buddhist Vajrayana practices. The mantra of Amitâbha is Om Amitabha Hri.*

In short, the particulars of Amitabh Buddha are as following :

Particular	For Amitabh Buddha
Meaning of the Name	Buddha of Infinite Light
Direction	West
Color	red
Mudra	dhyana
Vija (Syllable)	Hrih
Symbol	lotus
Embodies	light
Type of wisdom	discriminating
Cosmic element (skandha)	sanjna (name or perception)
Earthly element	fire
Antidote to	malignity
Sense	taste
Vehicle	peacock (because of eyes on its plumes)
Spiritual son	Avalokiteshvara
Consort	Pandara
Paradise	Sukhavati, Western Paradise, or Pure Land

AMOGHAPASA LOKESHVARA

Photo no. 7 : *A statue of Amoghapasa Lokeshvara with parwa in   metal finsih*

INTRODUCTION

Amoghapasa Lokeshvara is one of the several forms of Avalokiteshvara, the Bodhisattva of Compassion, the most popular deity in the Buddhist pantheon. Amoghapasa is named after the important emblem, *amoghapasa* (an infallible noose) that he carries in one of his right hands. By virtue of this noose, devotees are inspired to follow the path of truth, sever the bonds of illusion, thus, helping them to achieve enlightenment.

ICONOGRAPHY

Amoghapasa Lokeshvara has one face and three eyes. He is depicted to be completely white. He wears a saffron dress. He has eight arms. The first right hand is in *abhaya-mudra*. The second right hand is in *varada-mudra*. The third hand holds *amoghapasa* (infallible noose). The fourth hand holds a rosary. Similarly, the first left hand holds a *kamandalu* (water pot). The second left hand holds a lotus flower. The third left hand holds a trident and the fourth left hand holds a scripture.

The meaning of these emblems is as following :

- He has three divine eyes looking on triple worlds.
- His first right hand shows the gesture of fearlessness. It symbolizes that one who practices *astami vrata* sincerely would be protected from falling into lower realms.
- Second right hand displaying gesture of *varada-mudra* shows that those who practice *astami vrata* generating compassion and bodhicitta would receive all desirable objects.
- Third right hand holding *amoghapasa* suggests that Amoghpash Lokeshvara has infallible skill in means in converting ignorant sentient beings to the path of dharma.
- Fourth right hand holding rosary signifies that by recitation of six syllable mantra of Avalokiteshvara one frees oneself from the bondage of *samsara*.
- The first left hand holds *kamandalu* signifying that he has the capacity of initiating all the sentient beings into *Tathagata*

- Second left hand holding a lotus signifies that he frees the sentient beings residing in hell realm from the suffering of intense heat and cold.
- Third left hand holding trident signifies that he purifies three poisons of sentient beings.
- Fourth left hand holding a scripture signifies that he gives *prajna* (wisdom) to the devotees and thereby attaining liberation from cyclic existence.

DOCTRINE AND OTHERS

Photo no 8 : *An old statue of Amoghapasa Lokeshvara*

According to *Amoghpasa Hrdya nama Dharani sutra,* Avalokiteshvara Bodhisattva received the transmission of this *Dharani* from Lokeshvararaja Tathagata ninety one *kalpas* ago in the realm of Loka-avalokana. Since then, he used that *Dharani* to teach countless sentient beings.

The special feature of this dharani is that it purifies the evils of wrong doings of slandering noble Bhikshu Sanghas, Pratyeka Buddhas, Bodhisattvas, Buddhas. Otherwise such wrong doings could be the causes of falling into lower realms such as *Avici Hell.* The purification becomes effective if someone after confessing one's down-falls observes *Uposadha Vrata* of Amoghapasa Lokeshvara holding eight precepts and recites this dharani many times.

It is believed that those who recite this dharani seven times correctly in the eighth day of lunar calendar will receive twenty other meritorious qualities such as freeing from diseases, prosperity, joyfulness, equanimity, kind heart, protection from evils, freeing from fears, etc.

The worshipping of Amoghapasa Lokeshvara has been popular in Nepal since the middle ages. Newar Buddhists regularly perform rituals of sadhana of Avalokiteshvara during half-moon days and full-moon days which are called Uposadha Vrata or Astami Vrata. The Uposadyha Vrata of Amoghpasa Lokeshvara is perhaps the most popular one.

Amoghapasa Lokeshvara is not only popular in Nepal but also in several other countries where Mahayana Buddhism had spread. The images of Amoghpasa can be found in Java, China and Japan.

AMOGHASIDDHI

Photo no 9 : *Amoghasiddhi Buddha (a partly gold plated statue)*

INTRODUCTION

Amoghasiddhi Buddha (Tib: *Donyo Drupa*) is one of the Five Wisdom Buddhas or Pancha Buddhas in Vajrayana Buddhism. The other Budddhas are Vairocana Buddha, Akshobhya Buddha, Ratnasambhava Buddha and Amitava Buddha. Amoghasiddhi Buddha is the Buddha of Unfailing Accomplishment; Lord of the Karma Family, associated with the wisdom that achieves all. Amoghasiddhi Buddha is associated with the north of the ground of Prakuta Buddha, or Karmasampat. His power and energy are both subtle, their dynamics often hidden from conscious awareness. Amoghasiddhi is Lord of the Supreme Siddhi—the magic power of enlightenment which flowers in Buddha Activity. In this way the inner and outer world, the visible and invisible are united as body is inspired and the great spirit of bodhicitta spontaneously embodies.

ICONOGRAPHY

Amoghsiddhi Buddha is represented in the stupa facing to the north. His recognition symbol is viswa-vajra or the double thunderbolt. He is green in color. He rides on Garuda symbolizing that he can detect the presence of serpent-like delusion from a distance. He is depicted with a serpent with seven hoods and an umbrella in the background. He exhibits abhayamudra showing that by following bodhisattva path fearlessness is gained.

Amoghsiddhi Buddha alone has a canopy of snakes over his head. He sometimes resembles Shakyamuni Buddha with nine headed nagas. According to tantric text, this Buddha is said to be originated from seed syllable green Kham. He is also said to be the embodiment of volition (Skt. Sanskara) and Air element (*Skt. Vayu*).

DOCTRINE AND OTHERS

Amoghasiddhi is the Buddha of the north, and he aids in the release of jealousy and envy. His right hand is in the mudra of fearlessness, which one needs in all aspects of life especially that of the spirit. The same mudra also represents protection, again, what we all need throughout our life, not only from others, but from ourselves as well, as ignorance and delusion have a way of manipulating our perceptions to suit our needs instead of seeing the truth to benefit others. With that in mind, Amoghasiddhi is the guide that leads one to the Bodhisattvas path, with fearlessness and protection from adversary.

Like Ratna Sambhava Buddha, the vows, activity and deeds of Amogh Siddhi Buddha are not extant in Mahayana Buddhist literature. It is however said that cultivators relying on this Buddha's protection will achieve accomplishments in Buddhist affairs and worldly matters and will perfect the work benefiting sentient beings.

Mantra : The mantra is, *"Om Amoghasiddhi Ah"*.

In short, the particulars of Amoghasiddhi Buddha are as following :

Particular	For Amoghasiddhi Buddha
Meaning of the Name	Almighty Conquerer or Lord of Karma
Direction	North
Color	green
Mudra	abhaya (fearlessness)
Vija (Syllable)	Ah
Symbol	double thunderbolt
Embodies	dauntlessness
Type of wisdom	all-accomplishing
Cosmic element (skandha)	samsakara (volition)
Earthly element	air
Antidote to	envy and jealousy
Sense	touch
Vehicle	garuda (half-man, half-bird)
Spiritual son	Vajrapani
Consort	Green Tara
Paradise	Amoghavati

APARMITA

Photo no 10 : *A fully gold plated statue of Aparamita*

INTRODUCTION

Aparmita (also called Amitayus, Tib: *Tse-pameh)* is the name given to Amitabha Buddha in his characteristic role of a bestower of longevity. Aparmita is called a "Crowned Buddha" sometimes. Amitayus is considered the samboghakaya form of Amitabha Buddha. Amitayus is a popular figure in the Tibetan tantric tradition.

ICONOGRAPHY

Aparmita is depicted in *dhyanamudra* like a Buddha and his hands are kept on his lap holding the ambrosia vase. He is shown in red colour. He is shown wearing thirteen ornaments. His hair is painted blue and falls on either side to his elbows.

DOCTRINE AND OTHERS

Amitayus, the Buddha of Eternal Life, is often interchangeable with Amitabha, especially in East Asia and Tibet. Amitayus had acquired a separate identity in Tibetan worship as the Buddha for the attainment of long life. Amitayus and Amitabha are both associated with the cardinal direction west, the color red, the lotus flower, and the transmutation of lust into discriminating wisdom. Their abode is Sukhavati, the Pure Land in the west. Amitayus is traditionally pictured holding a vase said to contain the Elixir of Life: water, saffron, and nectar pills which confer immortality. His worship

Photo no 11 : *Aparimita (a statue in oxidized finish)*

takes many forms. In Tibet, Amitayus is a *yidam* or personal guiding deity as well especially in New Kadampa Tradition. His short mantra is given as *Om Amarani Jiwantiye Swaha.*

In context of Nepal, Aparmita Buddha is more pronounced. He is the Buddha of long life, good fortune and wisdom.

Mantra: The mantra of Aparmita is widely read which is *"Om Namo Bhagavate Aparimita Ayu Jnana Suvini Citta Tetso Ratsaya Tathagataya Arahate Samyak Sambuddhay/ Tadhyata Om Punye Punye Mahapunye Aparamita Punnye Aparamita Jnana Sambharo Patsite Om Sarva Samskara Parishuddha Dharmate Gagana Samudgate Svabhava Vishuddhe Mahanaya Parivare Swaha"*.

ATISHA

Photo no 12 : *Atisha (Dipamkara Srijnana) (an antique finish statue)*

INTRODUCTION

Atisha (AD 982-1054) was the great Indian Buddhist Master who was instrumental in formulating Kadampa lineage. His contribution in practice of Bodhichitta has been greatly acknowledged. Atisha remains an important figure in the Tibetan Buddhist tradition.

BRIEF BIOGRAPHY

Atisha was born in Vikramapur, the northeastern region of Bengal (in modern day Bangladesh). Like Sakyamuni Buddha, he was born in a royal family. His childhood name was Chandragarbha. There were signs of enlightened nature since his childhood. He was inclined to learning and practicing dharma from the very early age. He was taught by several instructors and yogis as well. It was at the eve of his wedding time that Atisha experienced a momentous encounter with the Vajrayana goddess Tara, who explained to the prince that in his past lives he had been a devout monk. Thereafter, his devotion to dharma greatly increased.

Atisha came across a renowned Brahmin Buddhist teacher Jetari, who taught him to take refuge in the Three Jewels of Buddha, Dharma and Sangha and to practice bodhichitta. After teaching the young Atisha in the basic principles of Mahayana Buddhism, Jetari advised him to go to Nalanda, a Buddhist center. In Nalanda, Atisha received once again brief instruction regarding the Bodhisattva vows under the spiritual guide of Bodhibhadra, who in turn advised him to seek out a teacher renowned for the perfect meditation of perceiving emptiness, Vidyakokila.

Atisha's acquisition of the wisdom to perceive emptiness was particularly significant. It was during this stage of study that Atisha became aware of pure human nature and the fundamental freedom inherent to every sentient being's existence; a freedom from physical attachment and mental bondage. Upon completing his training for meditation on emptiness, Atisha was advised to go to study with Avadhutipa, a Vajrayana master. Though Avadhutipa consented to teach young Atisha, he wished that the prince first consult the Black Mountain Yogi. The Black Mountain Yogi tested Atisha in several ways and then imparted teaching on Hevajra lineage for thirteen days bestowing him with the code name *Indestructible Wisdom*. Finally, the Black Mountain Yogi insisted that before Atisha continue his studies, he would need to secure permission from his parents to be formally acquitted of royal responsibility.

Returning to the royal palace, Atisha explained to his parents that his pursuit of Dharma was for the greater benefit of all sentient beings. After understanding his reasons and remembering the religious signs that accompanied the prince's birth, Atisha's mother willingly gave her consent and approved her son's decision to pursue the Dharma. Atisha's father, on the other hand, was much harder to convince and, like the Shakyamuni Buddha's own father, only conceded after multiple requests.

Upon his parent's approval, Atisha went back to Avadhutipa to continue his studies and learnt the Madhayamka middle way and various tantra practices. At an age of twenty-ninth, Atisha was formally declared a monk under an ordination of the great Silarakshita, and he was given a new name of Dipamkara Srijnana, meaning *"He whose deep awareness acts as a lamp."*

Even as a monk, Dipamkara Srijnana yearned for the fastest and most direct means of attaining perfect enlightenment. He made a pilgrimage to Bodhigaya. At that time, he happened to have a vision through Tara that "the practice of bodhichitta, supported by loving kindness and great compassion is most important". Thereafter, Atisha dedicated himself to refining his understanding and practice of bodhichitta. At the age of thirty-one, the monk arranged for a perilous journey, traveling for thirteen months to Sumatra in order to study under the reputable Suvarnadvipi Dharmarakshita, known in Tibet as Serlingpa, a supposed master of bodhichitta. Under the guidance of Dharmarakshita, Atisha remained on the island of Sumatra for twelve years studying bodhichitta and exclusive mind training techniques of oral origination. Finally, after over a decade of intensive training, Dharmarakshita advised Atisha to "go to the north, the Land of Snows". Dharmarakshita was referring to Tibet, a region with a Buddhist tradition, which changed forever after the arrival of Atisha Dipamkara Srijnana.

SPECIFIC MASTERY AND CONTRIBUTION

Atisha remains an important figure in the Tibetan Buddhist tradition for several reasons. First, he refined, systematized, and compiled an innovative and thorough approach to bodhichitta known as "mind training" (Tib. *lojong*), in such texts as *A Lamp for the Path to Enlightenment*, and established the primacy of bodhichitta to the Mahayana tradition in Tibet. In other words, Atisha not only postulated a scholarly model for bodhichitta but also lived as a human example himself.

Secondly, after King Langdarma's tyrannical reign, the monastic Buddhist tradition of Tibet had been nearly wiped out. Atisha's efforts had come to rescue the same in Tibet. It was Dromtönpa, Atisha's closest disciple, who later became the founder of the Kadampa School, which later evolved into the Geluk, one of the four main schools of Tibetan Buddhism. Although monasticism and the lojong teachings were of greatest importance to the Kadam/Geluk, they were incorporated into other three schools as well viz. Nyingma, Kagyu, and Sakya.

Atisha's devotion to Tara was well established through his script of Praise to Tara and the 21 Taras. His own practice of Tara has been largely instrumental in popularizing the spreading of Tara in Tibet and other countries.

Also, Atisha mobilized his influence in India in reforming the impurities and redirecting the development of Buddhism. For these reasons also, Atisha remains a central figure in the history and religious study of Buddhism.

After Atisha, the Kadampa lineage was passed down through a succession of great Kadampa Teachers like Dromtönpa, Geshe Potowa,

Geshe Sharawa, and Geshe Chekhawa from generation to generation until the fourteenth century when it reached the great Buddhist Master Je Tsongkhapa who further clarified all the teachings of Kadam Dharma and made them very accessible to the people of that time. In particular, he showed how to combine Lamrim, and Lojong with Mahamudra Tantra in a unified daily practice.

After Je Tsongkhapa, the New Kadampa lineage flourished for hundreds of years, down to the present day. In recent years, it has been promoted widely throughout the world by the contemporary Buddhist Master, Venerable Geshe Kelsang Gyatso.

AVALOKITESHVARA

Photo no 13 : *A fully gold plated statue of Avalokitesvara (Chenrezig)*

INTRODUCTION

Avalokiteshvara (Tib: Chenrezig) is the bodhisattva who embodies the compassion of all Buddhas. He is the most widely revered bodhisattva in Buddhism. Avalokiteshvara is considered the earthly manifestation of the self born, eternal Buddha, Amitabha. In the Tibetan Buddhist pantheon of enlightened beings, Chenrezig is renowned as the embodiment of the compassion of all the Buddhas, the Bodhisattva of Compassion. As Chenrezig, he is considered the patron Bodhisattva of Tibet, and his meditation is practiced in all the great lineages of Tibetan Buddhism.

ICONOGRAPHY

There are several forms of various emanations of Avalokiteshvara. However, the most common form of Avalokiteshvara is the four-armed one in vajra-mudra. His first pair of hands is folded and there lies a jewel in those folded hands. The jewel symbolizes Bodhichitta which is the treasure of supreme merits. The folding of hands near the heart symbolizes supplicating the Buddhas and Bodhisattvas of the ten directions. He holds a crystal rosary in his second right hand which symbolizes liberating sentient beings from cyclic existence with ideal means and aspirations. He is holding a white lotus flower in his second left hand symbolizes his profound wisdom that realized the nature of emptiness.

In one of the teaching on the Chenresig Sadhana, it is mentioned that "The four arms and hands signify the four immeasurables: immeasurable loving kindness, immeasurable *compassion*, immeasurable *joy*, and immeasurable *equanimity*.

The skin of the deer draped over his left chest symbolizes his compassionate heart towards all sentient beings. (This particular deer is said to live in mountains among rocks and snow. It has incomparable physical strength, but is extremely compassionate by nature. One of the hunters' tactics is to enter its territory and pretend to fight among themselves with swords. Seeing this, the deer becomes overwhelmed with compassion and emerges to mediate between them, which render the hunters an opportunity to capture it. Merely touching its skin with one's feet calms the mind).

DOCTRINE AND OTHERS

Photo no 14 : *A partly gold plated statue of Avalokitesvara (Chenrezig) with colored parwa*

Mahayana sutras associated with Avalokitesvara include the *Heart Sutra* and the *Lotus Sutra*, particularly the 25th chapter, which is sometimes referred to as the *Avalokitesvara Sutra*. According to the Lotus Sutra, Shakyamuni Buddha had said that if a suffering being hears the name of Avalokiteshvara Bodhisattva and earnestly calls out to him, Avalokiteshvara will hear the call and relieve that being from his suffering. Avalokiteshvara Bodhisattva transforms himself into forms that suit the nature of those to be helped. His manifestations or transformation bodies are thus countless. His skilful means are limitless and he can appear in any form in all the six realms of existence to relieve the suffering of the sentient beings.

Some popular forms of Avalokiteúvara are :

1. Amoghapâúa Lokeshvara
2. Padmapani Lokeshvara
3. Thousand-hands and thousand-eyed lokeshvara
4. Hayagriva
5. Chundi
6. Chakrasamvara, etc.

There are several other forms of Avalokitesvara which are named lokeshvaras. But, all lokeshvaras are not the emanations of Avalokiteshvara.

Chenrezig's six-syllable mantra is *Om Mani Padme Hum*. Thus, Chenrezig is also called Shadakshari ("Lord of the Six Syllables"). The connection between this famous mantra and Avalokiteœevara is mentioned in the Karandavyuha Sutra.

The Great Compassion Mantra is an 82 syllable mantra spoken by Avalokiteœevara to the assembly of Buddhas and Bodhisattvas, and extolling the merits of chanting the mantra. This mantra is popular in almost all Eastern countries.

Perhaps, the quote of Bokar Rinpoche about Avalokiteshvara is very correct—"Every person whose heart is moved by love and compassion, who deeply and sincerely acts for the benefit of others without concern for fame, profit, social position, or recognition expresses the activity of Chenrezig." This very nature, when manifested in physical emanations according to the merit of the disciples, assumes the forms of spiritual teachers, deities, Buddhas, Bodhisattvas, yogis, *dakinis*, religious protectors and so forth. It assumes the various forms of peaceful and wrathful deities of mundane and transcendental classes. In human form, it is manifested as ordained novices and *bhikshus*; and as laymen such as kings and ministers, householders, and so forth; besides these it assumes even the forms of birds, animals, boats, bridges and so forth, to help sentient beings in the most appropriate way.

Mantra : *Om Mani Padme Hum*

CHAKRASAMVARA

Photo no 15 : *Chakrasamvara with four faces, 12 arms and embracing his consort Vajravarahi (a statue with antique gold finish)*

INTRODUCTION

Chakrasamvara (Tib: *Korlo Demchog*) is the principal yidam and heruka of the Kagyu sect of Tibetan Buddhism, considered to be of the mother class of the *anuttarayoga tantra*.

Chakrasamvara is considered as the tantric emanation of Avalokiteshvara.

Chakrasamvara is one of important deity meditated by 84 mahasiddhas as well as one of primary Buddha in six yogas of Naropa.

ICONOGRAPHY

Chakrasamvara is typically depicted with a blue colored body, four faces, and twelve arms, and embracing his consort Vajravarahi. Other forms of the deity are also known, with varying numbers of limbs. Chakrasamvara and consort are not to be thought of as two different entities, as an ordinary husband and wife are two different people; in reality, their divine embrace are a metaphor for the union of great bliss and emptiness, which are one and the same essence. Chakrasamvara stands on minor deities. The deity under his right foot is Kalaratri, the Night of Time, who is said to represent nirvana. Under the left is Bhairava, the Terrifier, who is said to represent samsara. Chakrasamvara has transcended these extremes, so he stands atop them in the warrior's pose, with the left knee bent and the right extended at an angle.

He also wears garlands of skulls about his neck and waist, one of which hangs between the two figures. His expression is intense. Two eyes look down at his consort, and the third, which always sees reality directly, looks upward.

Each of his twelve arms holds a ritual object, which symbolize the "experience of overcoming the specific obstructions inherent in self-centered consciousness." In the hands that embrace his consort, Vajravahari, Chakrasamvara holds the *vajra* and bell in the HUM-sound gesture. They symbolize the union of wisdom and skillful means, and the destruction and transmutation of egotistic processes.

In his other left hands, from top to bottom, he holds the *Khatvanga* staff, indicating the "blissful thought of enlightenment;" the skull cup, showing that he has cut away the discrimination between existence and nonexistence; the *vajra* lasso, which binds beings to wisdom from life to life; and the severed four-faced head of Brahma, which represents his triumph over the temptation to become a god. In his right hands, he holds the *damaru* drum, to symbolize his joyous voice; the *vajra* chopper, which cuts off "the six defects, pride and the rest"; the axe, which "cuts off birth and death at the roots;" and the trident, showing that he has overcome the evil of the threefold world.

In other representations, Chakrasamvara typically holds the flayed skin of the elephant of ignorance behind his back. This is another symbol of the obstacles to enlightenment which he has overcome.

Photo no 16 : *Eight-armed Chakrasamvara (an oxidized finish statue) with consort*

Chakrasamvara's consort, Vajravahari, is herself an important deity symbolizing wisdom. Here, she stretches her left leg to rest her foot on Chakrasamvara's right foot. Her right leg is folded over his thigh. She wears a small crown and holds a skull cup and a vajra chopper, both behind Chakrasamvara. She also wears an ornate girdle and has bracelets of human bone on her wrists and ankles.

Actually, there are many different forms of Chakrasamvara appearing with different number of faces, hands, and number of surrounding retinues. In the Drigung Kagyu lineage, the most popular and common Chakrasamvara deity practice is in the form of the Five-deity Chakrasamvara. The Five-deity Chakrasamvara includes the central deity of the two-armed, single-faced male Chakrasamvara deity in union with the female Vajravarahi deity (these two in union are taken as a single deity) and four surrounding dakinis in the four directions.

DOCTRINE AND OTHERS

Photo no 17 : *Single face and two-armed Chakrasamvara with consort (an antique finish statue)*

In general, Buddhists categorize two types of sentient beings: those which have physical bodies and those, such as spirits, which don't have physical bodies. All sentient beings live in three worlds: the celestial world, the human world and the Nag's world. Once upon a time, eight members of each world came to the earth. They are recognized as eight space goers, eight ground walkers and eight underground dwellers. These twenty four non-human beings occupied twenty-four different territories on the earth. Their evil presence caused great suffering to everyone on earth. Therefore, according to the tantric tradition of Buddhism, the historical Buddha Shakyamuni from the state of Dharmakaya manifested sambhogakaya in the most wrathful Chakrasamvara (Tib. Palkhorlo Dompa) and subdued all the invaders. Since then, those twenty-four sites have been converted into palaces of Chakrasamvara.

By practicing Heruka Tantra one gains the profound realization of the emptiness of all phenomena and beings. This realization is descried as the greatest bliss of mind.

The mantra of Heruka is : *Om Shri Vajra He He Ru Ru Kam Hum Hum P'hat Dakini Dzala Shambaram Soha*

CHUNDI

Photo no 18 : *A comparatively old design statue of Chundi with three faces.*

INTRODUCTION

Chundi is one of the emanations of Avalokitesvara. She is said to have been the manifestation of the World Honored One entering into the Samadhi of Spiritual Power of Transformation of Space and Ocean. The word Chundi means Supreme Purity. Being the mother of all the deities of the Lotus class, she is, therefore, known as the Mother of Buddha, the Mother of Seven Kotis of Buddhas and Bodhisattvas.

ICONOGRAPHY

Chundi appears with eighteen arms and three faces. (She is depicted in one face as well). She is adorned with a jeweled crown which is mounted with a figure of a manifested Buddha. Her body is light yellow in color, adorned with all kinds of ornaments. She wears a white celestial garment. Seated on a lotus throne, her eighteen arms, with the original two hands forming the Root Mudra, hold different implements, in a clockwise direction: a wish-fulfilling banner, a lotus, a vase, a lasso, an eight-spiked wheel, a conch, a precious vase, a wisdom chest, a head-dress, a vajra scepter, a hook, an axe, a heavenly fruit, a rosary, a sword, and the Fearless Mudra. She is attended by two dragon (*naga*) kings who stand guard by her lotus throne. These two dragon kings are Nanda and Upananda. Her Tantric epithet is the Most Victorious Vajra, or Subjugation Vajra.

DOCTRINE AND OTHERS

Chundi Bodhisattva is the source of all the Buddhas of past, present and future whose secret name is Great Victorious Vajra and has unimaginable power of blessings. Those who practice this, bodhisattva will attain wisdom, victory in debate, harmonious and respectful family, and improved relations with others, longevity, healed sicknesses, removal of negative karmas, and other wishes fulfilled.

The eighteen arms of Chundi are said to express the eighteen merits of attaining Buddhahood. These are the eighteen uncommon qualities. Her arms are the symbolic expression of these secrets, endowed with the significance of profound principles. They are able to eliminate all the negative karma of sentient beings, hence, the name Most Victorious Vajra. One who practices this deity yoga is able to eradicate all past negative karmas and avoid all calamities. All that he or she wishes for in this lifetime, and all *siddhis* of worldly and transcendental practices, would be manifested swiftly.

Photo no 19 : *A fully gold plated statue of Chandi with color parwa*

As Chundi is also known as the Subjugation Vajra, and the practice of Chundi constitutes a special practice of Tantrayana, this practice is regarded as supreme. It is wish-fulfilling and can subjugate all maras and heretics. It embodies infinite power and merits, and through this practice, the practitioner would gain a round and perfect aura.

The Symbolism and Meaning of the Eighteen Arms of Chundi are as following :

1. The original 2 hands forming the root Mudra of Expounding the Dharma represents the fluency of elucidating all Dharma.
2. The wondrous precious banner represents the ability to build a most magnificent, great monastery.
3. The Fearless Mudra represents the ability to deliver sentient beings away from all terror and fears.
4. The lotus flower represents the purification of the six senses which, untainted, are as pure as the lotus flower.
5. The sword of wisdom represents the severing of the entanglements of afflictions and the three poisons of greed, anger and ignorance.
6. The empowerment vase represents the flowing of nectar to nurture all sentient beings so that they may receive the empowerment of the Buddhas.
7. The wonderful jeweled headdress represents the wish to be linked to wonderful dharma art.
8. The vajra lasso represents the ability to attract all into the yoga tantra.
9. The wonderful celestial fruit represents the accomplishment of the fruition of enlightenment, and the extensive cultivation of good karma.
10. The eight-spoke wheel represents the constant turning of the great dharma wheel, radiating its magnificent lights over the three lower realms.
11. The battle axe represents the elimination of all evil practices and the severing of attachment to oneself and others.
12. The large dharma shell represents the expounding of pure Dharma which shakes the universe.
13. The vajra hook represents the skill to magnetize and attract all phenomena within one's view.
14. The wish-fulfilling vase represents the function of manifesting all treasures and scriptures at will.
15. The vajra represents the collective convergence of support given by the eight classes of celestial beings and dragons. It

also represents the subjugation of stubborn sentient beings.
16. The wisdom sutra represents the self-cognition of knowing the profound and wonderful truth without any guidance from a teacher.
17. The Mani or wish-fulfilling pearl represents the vibrant and luminous state of mind which is flawless, pure and perfect.
18. The two original hands, beginning with the first hand, are held in the Dharma Expounding Mudra.

Some images of Chundi depict different gestures, such as forming the root mudra or holding mala beads. The meaning remains the same, regardless.

Heart Mantra is : *Om Cale Cule Cundi Svaha*

DHRITARASHTRA

Photo no 20 : *A partly gold plated statue of Dhritarastra*

INTRODUCTION

Devaraja Dhritarashtra (Tibetan: *yul khor srung*) is one of the four heavenly guardian kings (others being Virudhaka, Virupaksa and Vaisravana). He is the guardian of the Eastern Direction and lord of the Gandharva - celestial musicians. His kingdom is located on the eastern side of Mount Sumeru (the axial mountain of the Universe and where the gods live). Dhritarashtra uses music to help spread the dharma and subdue evil forces. He holds a stringed instrument. He is worshipped as a protector.

ICONOGRAPHY

In a regal appearance, white in colour, he has a broad square face with grey eyebrows, moustache and a beard. The fingers of the right hand strum the golden strings of a lute (Sanskrit: veena) having a wide green body and dark blue neck held above with the left hand. Adorned with a crown of gold studded with jewels, and earrings, tassels and ribbons, he is richly attired in brocade garments, trousers, and boots of various colours. The head is encircled by an irregular dark green areola edged with licks of red and orange flame. Seated on a maroon coloured mat above a rocky bench, in a relaxed posture, the right foot presses on the stomach of a reclining figure - fair and smiling, with the right hand cupped to the ear enjoying the celestial music. The left foot is held up by a demon figure, pink of colour, kneeling in an acquiescent posture. The background is filled with swirling smoke, grey and black, and the level foreground is sparse and green.

DOCTRINE AND OTHERS

The stories of the Four Guardian Kings are mentioned in early Buddhist sutras and became fully developed with the later Mahayana. They are common to all schools of Tibetan Buddhism. Each of these guardian kings watches over one cardinal direction of the world. They battle against evils and the Asuras who are ever trying to disrupt the peace and contentment of heaven. Each sits atop a mountain peak that is the highest point of their continent. They are said to guard Buddhist temples. They are also known to have protected the Buddha at the moment of conception in his mother's womb.

These guardians are also regarded as Recorders of the happenings in the Devas' assemblies. On the eighth day of the lunar half-month, they send their councilors out into the world to discover if men cultivate righteousness and virtue; on the fourteenth day, they send their sons, on the fifteenth day, they themselves appear in the world, all these visits have the same purpose. Then, at the Devas' assembly, they submit their report to the gods of Távatimsa, who rejoice or lament according to whether men prosper in righteousness or not.

DIPANKARA BUDDHA

Photo no 21 : *A statue of Dipankara Buddha in antique style*

INTRODUCTION

Dipankara Buddha (Tib: *mi slob*) is the name of the first Buddha of 24 mythological Buddhas mentioned in Pâli sources. It is said that it was during the time of Dipankara Buddha that Sakyamuni Buddha (then the ascetic Sumedha) made a vow to become a Bodhisattva and seek the enlightenment which he ultimately attained.

According to some Buddhist traditions, Dipankara was a Buddha who reached enlightenment aeons prior to Shakyamuni, the historical Buddha. Generally, Buddhists believe that there has been a succession of many Buddhas in the distant past and that many more will appear in the future; Dipankara, then, was one of numerous previous Buddhas, while Shakyamuni was the most recent, and Maitreya will be the next Buddha in the future.

He is sometimes equated with Adibuddha, the "original Buddha." Since the 17th century, his sect has been popular with Nepalese Buddhists who consider him a protector of merchants and associate him with alms-giving and he is popularly known as *Samyak Buddha*

ICONOGRAPHY

Buddha Dipankara is generally represented as a sitting Buddha, but his depictions as a standing Buddha are common in China and Thailand; with the right hand he generally forms a protection mudra (abhaya mudra), and often he forms it with both hands.

He is generally depicted with two Bodhisattvas either Manjusri and Vajrapani (as found in Java) or Avalokitesvara and Vajrapani (as found in Sri Lanka); or with the Buddhas who come after him viz Sakyamuni and Maitreya.

DOCTRINE AND OTHERS

Buddha Sakyamuni had told about 554 episodes of past life stories during the 45 years of teaching life (*Jaathaka Kathas*). One story accounts a meeting between Dipankara Buddha and Shakyamuni many lifetimes before Shakyamuni's eventual enlightenment. Sakyamuni Buddha was born as a bodhisattva in the time of Dipankara Buddha. He was rich but gave away all his wealth to become a Monk. When Dipankara told Shakyamuni he would become a Buddha one day, Shakyamuni replied, "I am to become a Buddha, awakened to enlightenment; may you tread with your feet on my hair - on my birth, old age, and death." Dipankara Buddha then said, "Freed from human existence, you will become an effective teacher, for the sake of the world. Born among the Shakyas, as the epitome of the Triple World, the Lamp of all Beings, you will be known as Gautama. You will be the son of King Suddhodana and Queen Maya. Shariputta and Moggallana will be your chief disciples. Your caretaker will have a name as Ananda". It is said that as Bodhisattva, he had received his first *Niyatha Vivarana* from Dipankara Buddha. This meeting of Shakyamuni Buddha with Dipankar Buddha can be found in the Mahayana text, the Sanghata Sutra.

Photo no 22 : *Samyaka Festival at Nagbahal, Lalitpur where Dipankara Buddha's statues are displayed from different places.*

It was in 17th century that Dipankara Buddha became a figure of veneration in Nepalese Buddhist communities. The followers consider him a protector of merchants and associate him with alms-giving. Dipankara Buddha has come to be associated with the virtues of Buddhist alms giving. The principal scripture related to Dipankara Buddha is the Kapisarvananda. It stresses the importance of feeding and giving alms to the monastic community. Buddhist monks cannot claim anything from the laymen, yet, it is considered as the laymen's duty and privilege to provide monks with food, clothes, lodging and whatever else they might legitimately need. It is the most obvious and easy method for laymen to acquire religious merit. Shamyak festivals are organized in Kathmandu valley at different places at different occasions.

Buddha Dipankara is also considered the protector of the sailors. Sometimes statues of Dipankara Buddha are found on the coastline to guide and protect the ships in their route.

One of the Buddhas of Bamiyan, destroyed by the Talibans in Afghanistan in 2001, was said to portray Dipankara Buddha.

DORJE DROLLO

Photo no 23 : *A fully gold gilded statue of Dorje Drollo.*

INTRODUCTION

Dorje Drollo is the one of the two wrathful emanations of Guru Padmasambhava from the set of eight main manifestations.

Guru Padmasambhava was an Indian saint, who traveled mostly Northern Indian and Nepalese territories especially mountainous caves practicing tantric Buddhism. He had achieved highest wisdom during retreats in Nepalese caves. He was called upon to Tibet to revive the Buddhism in seventh century. He was mainly known for teaching and spreading tantric Buddhism in Tibet and other Himalayan regions including Bhutan.

ICONOGRAPHY

As with all the other emanations of Guru Rinpoche, Dorje Drollo is a wisdom form, a rainbow body, not a solid or concrete object. Transforming from a sphere of bright red light, he is visualized with one face, two arms and two legs. His body color is dark red. His right hand holds a nine-pointed vajra and his left a phurba, a mystic dagger made of meteoric iron or sky metal. Dorje Drollo is very wrathful, displaying fangs, an overbite and three eyes. He is wearing Tibetan boots, a chuba and monk's robes, two white conch shell earrings and a garland of severed heads. His hair is bright red and curly, giving off sparks. He is shown dancing on the back of a fiery tigress, surrounded by wisdom flames.

DOCTRINE AND OTHERS

Guru Rinpoche remained in Tibet for 55 years and six months; 48 years while the king Trisong Deutsen was alive and seven years and six months afterwards. He visited almost all nook and corner of Tibet such as the 20 Snow Mountains of Ngari, the 21 places of practice in Central Tibet and Tsang, the 25 sacred places of Dokham, the three hidden valleys, and numerous other places, etc. Anticipating an act of destruction of Buddhism by future kings, he started vigorous activities of preparing the sacred and secret scriptures and concealing them at various secret places all over the country. At the same time, he also predicted when and who would discover them in future as the appropriate time would prevail.

Dorje Drollo emanated right before Guru Rinpoche's departure from Tibet as a way of confirming his legacy of these actions. This emanation happened about five years before he left. During this time, he gave many teachings and Yeshe Ts'ogyal had been very instrumental in transcribing them. Following her guru's instructions, she hid many of these texts throughout the land.

Photo no 24 : *Taktsang Gompa (Tiger's Nest Monastery, Paro, Bhutan)*

Dorje Drollo had flown to thirteen different caves in Tibet by riding on tigress back. (It is said that the tigress was no other than his own consort and student Tashi Kyedin, whom Guru Padmasambhava converted). Yeshe Ts'ogyal and Tashi Kyedin had helped Guru Rinpoche carry out his wisdom activities over numerous places. All those places where they have visited and where they have concealed *termas* were termed Tiger's Nests. It is said that such emanations of thirteen Dorje Drollo took place all at the same time.

The most renowned Tiger's Nest of all was in a place located at a steep mountain rock which is about 1000 meter high above Paro valley. It lies now in Bhutan and called *Taktsang* which means Tigers Nest and in there, a beautiful monastery was built in 1692 AD.

Guru Rinpoche said that in the future, all Tibetan men would be influenced by a demonic force called *Gyal-po*, the Tibetan women would be possessed by a demon called *Sen-mo*, and all the young Tibetans would be affected by an evil spirit called *Ti-mug*. *Gyal-po* symbolizes anger and jealousy and *Sen-mo* represents attachment. *Ti-mug* is an unclear, confused mind, without the ability to focus, center or direct attention. These three demons are metaphors. Guru Padmasambhava had explained that a degenerative era is characterized by such strong forms of anger, jealousy and attachment. These would be the major obstacles confronting practice of dharma and meditation. In order to transform such situations, the emanation of Dorje Drollo had occurred.

It is said that the practice of Dorje Drollo brings to help clear away and dispel complex loops of mental and emotional obstacles.

SPECIFIC MASTERY AND CONTRIBUTION

Guru Padmasambhava is accepted as the Second Buddha. It is impossible to evaluate his contribution. If Sakyamuni Buddha taught Buddhism through sutras, then Padmasambhava taught Buddhism through teaching of tantras.

DORJE LEGPA

Photo no 25 : *Dorje Legpa in "majestic yogi form"*

INTRODUCTION

Dorje Legpa (Skt: *Vajrasadhu*) is held to be one of the highest ranking "oath-bound" guardian deities of the Nyingma "old" sect of Tibetan Buddhism. He is often called Damchen Dorje Legpa to mean oath-bound.

Dorje Legpa is one of the native deities subdued by *Padmasambhava* and bound by oath to serve the *dharma*.

According to the Nyingma tradition, he is one of four treasure guardians who resides in the South and guards the treasures and appears at times as a guide to help practitioners to find hidden *dharma* teachings.

ICONOGRAPHY

Like other protective deities he has a variety of forms and is sometimes indistinguishable from his chief officer Garba Nagpo ("the dark-hued blacksmith," who is venerated by Tibetan blacksmiths as the protector of their craft).

Damchan Dorje Legpa is portrayed in three forms. In one, he is shown riding a snow lion and this form is called the 'majestic yogi form'. The snow lion carries Dorje Legpa on her back in a graceful yet precise manner. While in another, he is shown riding a goat and wields a hammer and bellows. In third form, he is depicted as a yidam – a long bearded yogi sitting on a goat's skin as a manifestation of *Guru Padmasambhava*. He holds a nine-pronged *vajra*, which is said to be made of meteoric iron, in his right hand above his head and he holds a string of prayer beads made of miniature skulls in his left hand. His feet are naked. He is shown with a hat. In latter case, he wears his hair in a yogi's topknot wrapped around a nine-prong vajra.. He wears a gown of a tantrika - a red, white, and blue shawl; and, a mélong hangs at the level of his heart. A mélong is a symbol of his function as a protector of the Dzogchen teachings.

DOCTRINE AND OTHERS

Guru Padmasambhava while meditating in seclusion in a cave at a mountain called Yarigong in India is said to have subdued Dorje Legpa. He had oath-bounded him by putting the texts of the pledge on his head. He, on his part vowed never to deviate from his oath. He offered Guru his life-heart and pledged to protect the Dharma. Later, when Guru came to Tibet, Dorje Legpa received him. Since that time Dorje Legpa is considered one of the main guardians of Nyingma (the Old School).

The snow lion represents youthful energy enlivened by humour as well. It is said that mental weakness including neuroses simply runs from the gaze of the Dorje Legpa on his snow lion. Dorje Legpa is a benign thunderbolt who reminds one of one's vows. He is a great helper to practitioners when their time is at risk. He is seen as the most encouraging and kindly of the protectors.

EKAJATI

Photo no 26 : *A statue of Ekajati in Oxidized finish*

INTRODUCTION

Ekajati (Tib: *Tse-chik-ma* or *Ral-chik-ma* meaning Single-plaited Mother, also known as *Ngag Sung-ma* meaning Mother Protectress of Mantra) is considered to be an emanation of Samantabhadri, the female primordial buddha, and she also manifests as Vajrayogini, a pre-eminent female deity or yidam. She is the highest of protectors.

Ekajati is the supreme protectress of the Dzogchen Atiyoga teaching, and a guardian of the tantric path, protecting it from the unworthy.

Within the Nyingma lineages, Ekajati which is known as Mamo Ekajati (*man mo e mKha dza*) is the most prominent among the three protectors of the Nyingma tradition.

In Tibetan mythology, Ekajati is one of the most powerful and fierce goddesses which is a modification of the old Tibetan goddess of heaven. She is the protector of secret mantras. Also, she is considered the mother of "the mothers of all the Buddhas," and represents the ultimate unity.

First Dalai Lama was said to engage in secret mantra of Ekajati during his earlier time and he considered her to be the personal protector.

ICONOGRAPHY

The iconography of Ekajati is unusual in itself. She has single open eye of wisdom upon her forehead, while her two eyes are sunken and dried, symbolizing the exhaustion of dualistic perception. She has a single plait of hair that flows straight upward, symbolizing the single unified path of the Ati Great Perfection. She has a single tooth in the middle of her mouth, projecting down below the rest of her teeth which is the realization of the single nature. She has a single breast that nutures the pure practioner upon the spiritual attainments of the single essence of ultimate truth. She is of a blue skin tone, with a high, red chignon. She wears a cloud as a garment to indicate that she dwells within the expanse of the sky.

In her right hand, she wields a human corpse as a symbol that duality destroys by itself. In her left hand, she holds a ripped out human heart considered to be symbolizing aggressive self-justification. With her right foot, she steps upon corpses, symbols of the ego. She wears the human bone cemetery ornaments and the tiger skin skirt showing her mastery of all enlightened activities.

However, she is wrathful and can assume a number of different forms and colors. She can hold various implements and weapons. She is also depicted with varying body parts; up to twelve heads and twenty-four arms, with different tantric attributes (viz. khatvanga, knife, blue lotus, axe, vajra, skull cup). In her chignon, there is a picture of *Akshobhya*. She sits in the vajra position on a lotus and is surrounded by flames representing wisdom.

DOCTRINE AND OTHERS

Photo no 27 : *A fully gold coated Statue of Ekajati*

Ekajati is a principal female protector in both the Nyingma (Old) and Sarma (New: Sakya, Kagyu, Gelug) Schools of Tibetan Buddhism. In the Nyingma School, she is the chief protector for the 'Revealed Treasure' traditions and manifests in numerous forms, often appearing with only one eye and one tooth, sometimes with only one leg as in the red manifestation from the Longchen Nyintig tradition of Jigme Lingpa. The different forms and descriptions of Ekajati are found in the various 'Revealed Treasure' texts of the Nyingma School.

In the Sarma Schools, she is the mother of Shri Devi (*Palden Lhamo*) and has a more typical appearance with one face, three eyes, and two breasts, always in a semi-wrathful visage and with one braid of hair. She is found in the various Mahakala Tantra texts (*anuttaryoga* class) originating from India. Ekajati is also found in the lower kriya tantra texts and more commonly in association with the important figure of Tara where she is often seen as an attendant figure standing on the left while the goddess *Brikuti* stands on the right side.

Ekajati removes obstacles to the life and accomplishment of those who do practice on the Secret Mantra path. She is a guardian of mantras who keeps them from those who are unworthy of using them. Her ascribed powers are removing the fear of enemies, spreading joy and removing personal hindrances on the path to enlightenment.

She is a symbol of feminine fearlessness.

Dzogchen and Nyingma Gurus give Ekajati related mantras and empowerments to only serious practitioners.

GAMPOPA

Photo no 28 : *A partly gold plated statue of Gompopa*

INTRODUCTION

Gampopa Sonam Rinchen (1079-1153), was the founder of the monastic order of the Kagyu School and the lineages that branch out from him is known as the Dhakpo Kagyu. Gampopa was also known as Dakpo Rinpoche.
Gampopa was Milarepa's foremost student.

SHORT BIOGRAPHY

Gampopa Sönam Rinchen was born in a small village Dakpo, in the southern region of Tibet, near the border of Nepal. His father was Nyiwa Sangye Gyalpo and mother was Shomo Zatse. He was named Dharma Drak. His father was a renowned medical doctor. He had a smaller brother as well. As a child, Gampopa was extremely clever. When he was about fifteen years old, he started studying Nyingma scriptures and leant about Nyingma tradition. He became a famous medical doctor. But, he pursued many spiritual studies as well. He got married to a lady named Chogney at the age of twenty-two. He became a father of a son and a daughter. Following an outbreak of a contagious disease in the village, his wife and children died. Thereafter, he was more involved in seeking *dharma*. At the age of twenty-six, Gampopa received the fully monastic ordination of the Kadam order. The teacher by the name, Shawa-lingpa gave him this ordination name of Sonam Rinchen. As a monk, he practiced intensively with a series of Kadampa Geshes, meditating and studying with these great masters. He often spent days without food or a drop of water, absorbed in the blissful mental and physical feeling of perfect concentration. Gampopa reached such a level of attainment of *samadhi* concentration that he was able to sit for seven days completely absorbed in meditation. He was known far and wide by the name of Dakpo Rinpoche.

Hearing of the fame of the Lord of Yogins, Milarepa, he decided to search for him. He already had a great deal of insight and confidence in his Dharma practice. He had mastered the complete Kadam teachings and had extraordinary dreams, such as that he was a tenth-level bodhisattva. He frequently dreamt that a blue yogi with a walking stick placed his right hand over his head and would sometimes spit at him. Thinking that this strange dream was an indication of a harmful spirit who was trying to cause him a great deal of interference and obstacles for his Dharma practice, he did an intense retreat on Achala (*Mi-g.yo-ba*), the Immovable One. Achala is a fierce-looking figure specially meditated on in the Kadam tradition to eliminate all obstacles to practice.

After a long and difficult search and journey, finally he met Milarepa at Trode Tashigang. After testing all the empowerments, teachings and blessings Gompopa had received from his previous masters. Milarepa at first initiated him into the practice of Vajrayogini. Gampopa immediately immersed himself in the practices and quickly developed the experiences and insights of these teachings. Each day his insights grew and grew, just like a sprout coming out of the ground. He meditated on tummo, and each day he had a new experience. One extremely cold winter night, he was meditating completely naked in a cave to test the inner heat that he had developed. He remained warm throughout the night, but in the morning when he stopped doing the tummo practice, he froze completely. He did this meditation for a week and, at the end of the week, had visions of the five Dhyani Buddhas. He used to continue the meditation and ask about his findings with Milarepa. Once, during meditation, Gompopa had the vision that Avalokitesvara penetrated through the top of his head and dissolved and merged within him. During the meditation, Gampopa underwent a series of internal physical changes. He felt a violent wind and a flow of hot air going up and down along his spine. Another time he had a complete vision of all of the various states of the divine beings, the gods. He had a pure vision of the higher gods pouring white nectar over and initiating the gods of the lower states. At times, Milarepa gave Gampopa many yogic exercises to do, mudra hand gestures and movements of the body to open up the other subtle energy-centers in the body. In this way, he made great progress in meditation upto the satisfaction of Milarepa and finally, came to Tibet.

SPECIFIC SKILLS AND CONTRIBUTIONS

Gampopa had many Kadampa masters who taught him the practices and views of their lineage. After Gompopa received the teachings and traditions of mahamudra from his guru, Milarepa he combined the two streams of teachings into. He wrote *Jewel Ornament of Liberation* which is the combined streams of the Kadam and mahamudra traditions. He had written many others as well.

He had founded the Dhaklha Gampo Monastery, where he continued his activities of teaching, meditation and benefiting beings.

The four prominent disciples of Gampopa have founded the "four great" schools of the Kagyupa. Then there were eight students of Dogyal, who also spread the teachings in the "eight lesser" schools of the Kagyupa. The four schools of the Kagyupa are not very different from each other except in very little ways, all having the same origin. The various forms of teachings only make them more available to many.

In total, there are twelve traditions, twelve schools of Kagyupa, (four greater and eight lesser), all deeply rooted and cultivated in the soil of Tibet, and spread very effectively in China.

Among many disciples of Gampopa, Karmapa Düsum Khyenpa was the one who became the Golden Rosary lineage heir of Gampopa, the First Karmapa.

GREEN TARA

Photo no 29 : *A fully gold plated statue of Green Tara*

INTRODUCTION

Green Tara (Tib: *Pagma Drolma*), is one of the principal forms of Arya Tara. In general, the mention of the name Tara would mean Green Tara.

Green Tara is also regarded as the consort of Buddha Amoghasiddhi.

The practice of Green Tara helps to overcome fear and anxiety, but devotees also believe that she can grant wishes, eliminate suffering of all kinds and bring happiness.

ICONOGRAPHY

Green Tara is typically pictured in dark green in color. Green Tara is depicted in seating position as her right foot being extended a little and rested on a small lotus flower. Her right hand is in the gesture of granting refuge, while holding the stem of a lotus plant that waves over her shoulder. Her left hand is in the gesture of the Three Jewels, with the thumb and ring finger touching and the other three fingers stretched upward. These three fingers represent the Three Jewels. On Tara's crown is Amitabha Buddha. She is adorned with all sorts of ornaments.

DOCTRINE AND OTHERS

Tara represents the entire enlightened activities of all Buddha and hence she is called the mother of the Buddhas. According to a sutra, Avalokiteshvara Bodhisattva had been saving and ferrying out from the ocean of suffering enumerable beings. But when he found further countless beings still plunged into this ocean of suffering and still to be saved, his heart ached so much out of compassion and tears dropped from his eyes. It is said that those tears turned into lotus flowers, wherein White Tara and Green Tara appeared. They vowed before Avalokiteshvara that they would help in liberating living beings

The practice of Green Tara helps to overcome eight fears. They are :

(1) lions and pride
(2) wild elephants and delusions

(3) forest fires and hatred

(4) snakes and envy

(5) robbers and fanatical views

(6) prisons and avarice

(7) floods and lust, and

(8) demons and doubt.

According to another lineage, there are sixteen fears that are removed through plasticizing of Tara mantra. They are—the fear of earthquakes, floods, wind, fire and lightening, fear of tyrannical authority/state injustice, war/riot/struggle, robbers/thieves, ghosts/spirits, animals, poisons, conflicts/bad dreams, sickness, misfortune, untimely death, and poverty. In fact, Green Tara is meditated to bring forth fulfillment of all kinds of wish, elimination of suffering and acquisition of happiness in life.

Photo no 30 : *Fully gold coated statue of Green Tara with artistic parwa*

According to another legend, many eons ago in a different universe, a princess named Yeshe Dawa lived. Based on her own investigation and experience, she came to have great confidence in the Three Jewels - the Buddhas, Dharma, and Sangha. She understood the unsatisfactory nature of cyclic existence and thus, determined to be free from all sufferings. Thinking that all living beings were like her in wanting happiness and not wanting suffering, Princess Yeshe Dawa developed genuine, impartial love and compassion for each and every living being. She was not enchanted by the luxuries of palace life; instead, she vowed to show the way to liberation to millions of beings each day before eating breakfast, to millions more before eating lunch, and to even more before going to sleep at night. When religious authorities suggested that she pray to be born a man in future lives, Tara refused, pointing out that many Buddhas had already manifested in male bodies and vowing to attain full awakening in a woman's body and continuously return in female form in order to benefit others.

THE MANTRA OF TARA

Tara's mantra is *Om Tare Tuttare Ture Swaha.*

Om represents Tara's holy body, speech and mind.

Tare means liberating from true suffering, the sufferings of *samsara*, our aggregates being under the control of delusion and karma.

Tuttare means liberating from the 8 fears, the external dangers, but mainly from the internal dangers, the delusions, and also karma.

Ture means liberating from the ignorance of the absolute nature of the "I"; it shows the true cessation of suffering.

Swaha means "may the meaning of the mantra take root in my mind."

Also, in the context of the Lam Rim, *Tare* refers to the graduated path of the lower capable being; *Tuttare* refers to the path of the middle capable being; *Ture* refers to the path of the higher capable being. So the meaning is that by taking refuge in Tara and doing Tara practice, we can achieve the fully enlightened state with the four *Kayas*, which is the state of cessation of, or liberation from, the two obscurations.

GUHYASAMAJA

Photo no 31 : *A partly gold plated statue of Guhyasamaja*

INTRODUCTION

Guhyasamaja's name means "Secret Union" or "Assembly of the Secret Ones (Tib. *Sangwa-dupa*). Guhyasamaja is also known as "King of Tantras". In Tibet, he is particularly favored by the Geluk Order, most likely for the antiquity of his texts.

ICONOGRAPHY

Photo no 32 : *Another statue of Guhyasamaja of metal finish.*

Guhyasamajas is dark blue in color. He has three faces: the central one is blue and fierce, the right face is peaceful white; and the left one is red. He is considered Lord of the Diamond Body, Speech, and Mid of All the *Tathagatas*. He gently holds his consort, Sparshavajra, in an intimate embrace. The goddess has six hands and three faces, and is "like her consort," in the words of an early ritual. Sparshvajra gazes upward in rapture, meeting Guhyasamaja's downward glance.

The goddess protects an energy and ferocity that contrasts with the serene countenance of her mate. Being "of the same nature," the divine pair possesses similar hand implements. The central pair of hands hold, right and left, a vajra scepter and a bell, the upper pair, a wheel and a blazing jewel; the lower pair, a lotus and a sword. The vajra scepter and the bell symbolize, among other things, the vajra Buddha clan of Akshobhya. The wheel symbolizes the mirror wisdom clan of Vairochana, the lotus the discriminating wisdom clan of Amitabha, the jewel the equality wisdom clan of Ratnasambhava, and the sword the all-accomplishing wisdom clan of *Amoghasiddhi*. Thus, Guhyasamaja Budha symbolically represents the union of all the Buddha clans.

DOCTRINE AND OTHERS

Translated in the 8th century, the *Guhyasamaja Tantra* was one of the first Sanskrit works to be translated into Tibetan. One tradition has it that Shakyamuni Buddha himself proclaimed the tantra, the morning after his enlightenment. Other traditions claimed that Maitreya taught the tantra in the Tushita Heaven, and that the Indian scholar Asanga brought it to the human world in the 4th century. Like other deities of the Unexcelled Yoga tantra tradition, Guhyasamaja is associated with the Buddha Akshobhya. Many texts, including the Guhyasamaja Tantra itself, simply call him *Akshobhya* or *Akshobhyavajara*.

HARIHARIHARIVAHAN
LOKESHVARA

Photo no 33 : *Harihariharivahan Lokeshvara.*

INTRODUCTION

Harihariharivahan Lokeshvara is one of the several forms of Avalokiteshvara, the Bodhisattva of Compassion and the most popular deity in the Buddhist pantheon.

ICONOGRAPHY

Harihariharivahan Lokeshvara is depicted white in color. He has six arms. The first right hand displays witness gesture. The second right hand holds a rosary. The third right hand displays a bodhyanga mudra. The three left hands hold a staff, a krishnajina and a vase. He is seated on a vehicle of naga, lion, garuda and Narayan.

DOCTRINE AND OTHERS

According to *Swayambhu Purana*, when *Manjushree Bodhisattva* drained the lake called Nagadah (now Kathmandu Valley) numerous aquatic animals including serpents were washed out. The king naga called Takshala was very angry. It killed many people and animals. Later, this king naga was afflicted with leprosy due to the evil karma that he did. He repented for his evil actions and prayed Arya Avalokiteshvara for mercy and recovery from the disease. Eventually, he was cured. One day, while he was basking in a nearby ground, a hungry garuda saw him. It alighted and tried to capture the naga king. They engaged in a ferocious battle. The naga king dragged garuda to the river and was about to kill it. The garuda at that time prayed to Lord Vishnu, its protector for help. Lord Vishnu came immediately and was about to cut the head of naga king with the *sudarshan-chakra* (devine whirling disc), the naga king prayed Avalokiteshvara for help. Avalokiteshvara came there instantly riding on his vehicle, lion. Vishnu was humbled to see Avalokiteshvara there and instantly bowed before him after placing his *sudarshan-chakra* in its safe place.

Thereafter, the naga king and the garuda also retreated from their fighting and joined Lord Vishnu in paying homage to Arya

Avalokiteshvara. After that, Vishnu offered himself to Avalokiteshvara to be his vehicle. In the mean time, the lion also offered to be the vehicle of Garuda. The naga king also offered to be the vehicle of lion.

Thus, Harihariharivahan Lokeshvara is depicted seating on Vishnu, then Vishnu on Garuda, then Garuda on lion, and then Lion on the naga king. This is a very interesting form of Lokeshvara.

Sculptures of this Lokeshvara can be seen in Changu Narayan in Bhaktapur, and Golden temple in Lalitpur

HAYAGRIVA

Photo no 34 : Hayagriva

INTRODUCTION

Hayagriva is a primary emanation of Avalokiteshvara, the Bodhisattva of absolute compassion. In Tibetan Buddhism, Hayagriva is a wrathful manifestation of Avalokiteshvara. There are believed to be 108 forms of Hayagriva. Avalokiteshvara's compassion manifests itself in various angry, energetic deities who serve as his acolytes, attending to the needs of afflicted devotees. Hayagriva is of the Padma family of enlightened speech and an emanation of Buddha Amitabha in wrathful form. Buddha Amitabha in peaceful form is Chenrezig, but in order to benefit those not tamable by peaceful means, Chenrezig appears in wrathful aspect as the supreme lord of wrathful kings Hayagriva.

Specifically, In Tibet, Hayagriva is one of the primary *yidam*, or chosen meditational deities. Essentially, the *yidam* deities are visualization devices that force the realization of a devotee's own potential for religious attainment. Thus, Hayagriva provides a means through which a practitioner recognizes his or her own innate altruistic compassion. Subsequently, this awareness leads the devotee towards the final religious goal.

ICONOGRAPHY

Several forms of Hayagriva exist in Mahayana Buddhism. He is represented as the *Krodha Atiguhya* (meaning—angry and most secretive) Hayagriva. He is depicted as a powerful, three-headed, paired-deity in union with his Prajna, or female counterpart. According to Sadhanamala, Hayagriva is red in color. He wears a garland of skulls with teeth and lips. Hayagriva is crowned with his Jata and a figure of Amitabha. His second face is that of a horse, which is blue in color and neighs continuously. He tramples on the top of the world. He wears the snake ornaments. He is short and dwarfish and is clad in tiger skin. He threatens all the deities and asuras and holds the Vajra and staff in his two hands.

The characteristic neighing horse's head is visible in Hayagriva's hair, above his central crown. Each of his six arms hold specific attributes. In his upper right and left hands, he holds an elephant goad and a noose respectively. In his lower right hand, he holds a club. A sword is held in his lower left hand. He holds a lotus and a skull cup in his primary left and right hands while supporting his Prajna. Large meteoric iron wings expanding behind Hayagriva's arms suggest that, as Krodha Atiguhya, he possibly belongs to the Heruka, or fully enlightened peaceful/wrathful class of highly esoteric deities. Heruka figures define religious attainment through detachment from delusion and ignorance.

Photo no 35 : *A statue of Hayagriva without consort.*

In his simplest form, Hayagriva is depicted with one face, two arms and two legs. Everything about him is angry - a scowling face with three glaring eyes, a roaring mouth with protruding fangs, a pose of warrior's aggressiveness, a broad belly bulging with inner energy, a sword raised threateningly in his right hand, his left hand raised in a threatening gesture and snake ornaments. This terrifying aspect expresses compassion's fierce determination to help us overcome inner egotism and outer obstructions.

The most distinguishing characteristic of Hayagriva is the representation of a horse's head above his own. Frequently, as many as three horses' heads are depicted. This is particularly common in multiple-headed representations of the deity. The horse is significant for its neigh is believed to cut through false attachments, revealing the reality of enlightenment.

The Hayagriva's terrific appearance is directed towards ego grasping and outer obstructions. His wrathfulness is said to be fierce compassion directed towards a self-cherishing attitude.

DOCTRINE AND OTHERS

Hayagriva's special ability is to cure diseases, especially skin diseases even as serious as leprosy, which is said to be caused by the *Nagas* (water spirits with serpent bodies).

It is said that Tibetan horse-dealers worshipped Hayagriva because he could frighten away demons by neighing like a horse. When invoked, he announces his coming by neighing, the sound of which pierces false appearances and disguise.

To thoroughly pacify all eight classes of negative beings, Hayagriva arose in an even more wrathful form as black Hayagriva. It is said that Guru Rinpoche – himself none other than Hayagriva – transmitted this practice to Yeshe Tsogyal and King Trisong Deutsen, and prophesied that this practice, extracted from the cycle of trantric texts known as 'Taming the Nagas', would be very important in the future.

When in times of darkness royal families become like ordinary people and ordinary people behave like kings, when the virtuous experience great suffering and punishment while evil-doers prosper and flourish – these are the degenerating times when the practice of Hayagriva will be of such significance. When dharma practitioners are reviled and criminals are highly regarded, when engaging in wars, robbery, murder becomes normal, and even within families cheating and harming is commonplace, and king demons, nagas and negative non-human spirits become powerful and spread many kinds of rare and unknown diseases, then beings can turn to the powerful practice of Hayagriva to tame all these negativities. This particular practice was revealed by Dudjom Lingpa, who then practiced it secretly and attained highest realization and powers. He kept it hidden for 33 years before opening it at the appropriate time at the request of protectors and dakinis. Jigme Rinpoche received this transmission from His Holiness Dudjom Rinpoche.

HEVAJRA

Photo no 36 : *Hevajra*

INTRODUCTION

Hevajra ((Tib. *Kye Dorje*) is one of the eight Yidams. Hevajra belongs to the *Anuttara Yoga Tantra* class of deities) and is considered a deity of the non-dual type of tantras. This tutelary yidam is described in the Hevajra tantra with all the ceremonies used in his worship as well as his sadhana.

Hevajra means "Secret Union" (Tib. *Sangwa-dupa*). Hevajra is also known as "King of Tantras".

Hevajra is a meditational deity closely associated with the Sakya school of Tibetan Buddhism especially in the core method of Lamdre cycle of teachings.

ICONOGRAPHY

As described in Hevajra Tantra, Hevajra has different forms. They are as following:

Kaya Hevajra—The two armed Body (Kaya) Hevajra stands in an advancing posture on a multi-coloured lotus, corpse, and sun disk. He is dark blue in colour. His right hand holds a vajra, and his left hand holds a vajra-marked skull cup. He embraces his consort Vajranairatma. A khatvanga staff rests on his left shoulder and he is adorned with the six symbolic ornaments. In the Sadhanamala, this form of Hevajra is shown in a single (*ekavira*) - without a consort.

Vak Hevajra – The four armed Speech (Vak) Hevajra stands in an advancing posture on a multi-coloured lotus, corpse, and sun disk. He is dark blue in colour. One right hand holds a vajra and one left hand a skullfull of blood, the other pair of arms embrace his consort Vajravarahi.

Citta Hevajra – The six armed Mind (Citta) Hevajra stands in an advancing posture with right leg extended and left bent on a multi-coloured lotus, corpse, and sun disk. He is dark blue in colour with three faces – central face blue, right face white and left face red. Each face has three blood shot eyes and four bared fangs, and frowns with knotted brows. His tawny hair streams up surmounted with a crossed vajra. Two right hands hold a vajra and a knife, two left a trident and a bell; the remaining pair of arms embraces his consort *Vajrasrnkhala*. Hevajra is imbued with the nine dramatic sentiments and adorned with a crown of five dry skulls, a necklace of fifty fresh heads and the six symbolic ornaments or 'seals'.

HRDAYA HEVAJRA

The sixteen-armed, four-legged eight-faced Heart (Hrdaya) Hevajra stands with two legs in ardha-paryanka and the other two in alidha posture (left bent, right extended) on a multi-coloured eight petalled lotus, the four Maras in the forms of yellow Brahma, black Vishnu, white Shiva (*Mahesvara*) and yellow Indra and a sun disc resting on their hearts.

Photo no 37 : *A statue of 16 arms Hevajra.*

His central face is black, the first right white, the first left red, the upper face smoke-colored and ugly; the outer two faces on each side, black. All have three round blood shot eyes, four bared fangs, a vibrating tongue, and frowning with knotted brows. His lustrous tawny hair streams upward crowned with a crossed vajra. He is adorned with a diadem of five dry skulls. The sixteen hands hold sixteen skull cups. The central pair of arms skull contain a white elephant and the yellow earth-goddess *Prithvi*, and embrace his consort Vajranairatma whose two legs encircle his body. Her right hand holds a curved knife, while the left is wrapped around the neck of her lord and holds a skull cup. In the other seven skull cups, held in Hevajra's outer right hands are: a blue horse, a white-nosed ass, a red ox, an ashen camel, a red human, a blue sarabha deer, and an owl or cat. In the skull cups in the outer seven left hands are the white water-god Varuna, the green wind-god *Vayu*, the red fire-god *Agni/Tejas*, the white moon god Candra, the red sun god *Surya* or *Aditya*, blue *Yama* lord of death and yellow *Kubera* or Dhanada lord of wealth. Hevajra is adorned with the six symbolic ornaments: circlet, earrings, necklace, bracelets, girdle armlets and anklets and smeared with the ashes of the charnel ground. He wears a necklace of fifty freshly severed human heads.

DOCTRINE AND OTHERS

In Tibet, Hevajra is particularly favored by the Geluk Order, most likely for the antiquity of his texts. Translated in the 8th century, the Hevajra Tantra was one of the first Sanskrit works to be translated into Tibetan. One tradition has it that Shakyamuni Buddha himself proclaimed the tantra the morning after his enlightenment. Other traditions claimed that Maitreya taught the tantra in the Tushita Heaven, and that the Indian scholar Asanga brought it to the human world in the 4th century. Like other deities of the Unexcelled Yoga tantra tradition, Hevajra is associated with the Buddha Akshobhya.

Hevajra is the most important archetype deity of the Sakya Order. The Hevajra Tantra is considered the basic Mother tantra, and its contemplation is particularly excellent in creating the conditions for the blazing of the inner fury-fire [Tib.: *tummo*] so important to Himalayan yogis, such as Milarepa. The Hevajra Tantra teaches the *Union of Skillful Means and Profound Cognition;* and states that such union is helpful in achieving the powers known as *siddhis*. The text belongs to the higher or Inner Tantras.

The Hevajra Tantra is a non-dual, Yogini tantra of the late Mantrayana tradition of Buddhism which was composed in north-eastern India during the 8th century A.D. It was one of the principal later tantric cycles which were first introduced into Tibet during the late 10th century A D. in a general reintroduction of the Buddhism, thereafter the persecutions of the previous century. The method of the Hevajra Tantra was especially evolved from the views on the trantric Buddhist method found in the Guhya Samaja Tantra, the Manjusri Mulakalpa, the Tattva Samgraha and other Yoga tantra works.

Only the chosen practitioners can practice Hevajra. One has to learn and practice all virtuous conducts then the Vaibhasya teachings and then the Sautrantika, after that the Yogacara and then the Mayamika. When they know all mantra-methods, they would be allowed to start upon Hevajra.

KUBERA

Photo no 38 : *Kuvera*

INTRODUCTION

Kubera (also called Vaishravana or Jambala) is the guardian of the North, the most powerful of the four Buddhist kings or *Lokapalas,* protecting the four directions of the compass. He presides over the *Yaksas,* and over riches, war, etc. Vaisravana is often identified as a 'proprietor of the grand depository of treasures' and he is popularly known as *Kuvera,* a deity of wealth mainly in Tibet and Nepal.

In China and Japan, Vaishravana is commonly known as an armored warrior and he is shown symbolically holding a baton in one hand and a stupa in another hand.

ICONOGRAPHY

Photo no 39 : *Jambala with a banner*

In many Tibetan and Nepalese images of Kubera, the deity is shown as a plump figure wearing a crown, ribbons and jewelry, and holding a wish fulfilling gem in right hand and a mongoose in left hand depicting spewing gems. The mongoose is also said to represent this god's victory over the naga (snake deities), who symbolize greed. As God of Wealth, Vaishravana/Kubera squeezes the mongoose and causes the creature to spew out jewels. He is primarily black in color and has the stunted, thick form of a dwarf with a potbelly. He is seated sideways on a dragon with his right foot down and his knee up.

In the white form, he holds a banner of victory in his right hand and a mongoose in his left hand showing both wealth and protection. Sometimes, he is shown seated on the powerful celestial dragon which again signifies power and good fortune.

Sometimes, he is shown in yellow color also. There, he sits on a white lion with green Mane, holding a dvaja in the right hand and carrying a mongoose that spews a wish fulfilling gem under the left arm. He wears the crown and jewels particular to his rank.

Photo no 40 : *Kuvera on lion*

In fact, there are many other forms of Kubera. Some are depicted mounting on different animals such as lion, dragon, etc. Kubera is also shown with his consort. Actually, Kubera or Vaisaravana is worshipped in several countries such as Tibet, China, Japan, Thailand, Mangolia and other eastern countries and he is depicted in various postures.

DOCTRINE AND OTHERS

Photo no 41 : *Kuvera on a dragon*

According to some legend, Vaishravana is the Buddhist form of the earlier Hindu deity, Kubera who was the son of an Indian sage, Vishrava, hence the name, Vaishravana. According to Hindu legend, Kubera performed austerities for a thousand years, and was rewarded for this by the greater god, Brahma, who granted him immortality and the position of God of Wealth, and guardian of the treasures of the earth. Later, he has received the mission of Buddha himself with his 91 sons who traverse the ten directions, mounted on animals, men, women, and with the *yaksas, raksasas, kumbhandas, pretas, pisacas, nagas, devas,* constellations who form his army. He defends Buddhism and reprimands the bad; to the pious he assures five advantages: increment of life, of riches, of health, of pleasure, of fame.

Photo no 42 : *Kuvera with consort*

AS A GOD OF WAR

Primarily, Vaisravana is venerated in China and Japan as a god of war. There is a dharani entitled 'Dharani of Devaraja' of the north, Vaisramana, who watches over armies for protecting the *Dharma* and if one pronounces this dharani before an image of Vaisravana — which represents the Devaraja under his terrible aspect, dressed in armour plate, holding a lance in his left and his right resting on his hip, a *stupa* which he offers to Buddha Sakyamuni, and treading on two black *yaksinis* — he sends his third son Nada to the side of those who direct their troops for the protection of their country; or still, if one covers the armour plate of his image with the powder of gold and offers him perfumes, flowers and other offerings while pronouncing the dharani a hundred thousand times, he himself takes the command of his celestial troops and goes to support his devotees, to whom he assures victory; or furthermore, if one recites nonstop day and night, he delegates his heir-prince Dokken at the head of celestial troops; or still one can hang his image on a staff and carry it as a banner fifteen paces in front of the army which will render the enemy ineffectual.

As a god of wealth – Awakening of Vaisravana, often identified with Kubera, suppresses the suffering of poverty.

KALACHAKRA

Photo no 43 : *Kalchakra*

INTRODUCTION

Kâlachakra is a term used in Tantric Buddhism that means "time-wheel" or "time-cycles". It refers both to a Tantric deity (Tib. yidam) of Vajrayana Buddhism and to the philosophies and meditation practices contained within the Kalachakra Tantra and its many commentaries. The Kalachakra Tantra is more properly called the Kalachakra Laghutantra, and is said to be an abridged form of an original text, the Kalachakra Mulatantra which is no longer extant. Some Buddhist masters assert that Kalachakra is the most advanced form of Vajrayana practice. Certainly, it is one of the most complex systems within tantric Buddhism.

ICONOGRAPHY

Photo no 44 : *Kalachakra, single face & two arms*

Kalachakra tantra is usually depicted in a mandala form. In this, most elements (if not all) of the mandala refer to the universe (outer Kalachakra), the body and mind (inner Kalachakra) and the practice (initiation, generation and destruction).

The Kalachakra deity can be represented in several forms. The simplest one is only Kalachakra with one face and two arms. Others can include his consort, Vishvamata. But most commonly used one is a full fledged deity with four faces, twenty-four arms and two legs, embracing Visvamata. As is usual, the male deity Kalachakra symbolizes method/bodhicitta/bliss and the consort represents the wisdom of emptiness. They embrace each other to show the ultimate combination of method and wisdom, or bliss and emptiness. In the Kalachakra context, it refers to the Body of Empty Form and Immutable Bliss. Vishvamata also symbolizes the wrathful aspect of Kalachakra.

To name only some of the symbols contained in the arms and hands of the deity:

- The six collar-bones refer to (in the outer Kalachakra) the six seasons (spring, hot season, monsoon, fall [harvest], early winter and late winter, as well as the six periods of the day and the night.
- The twelve shoulders symbolize the two times six cycles of the breath.
- The 24 arms refer to the 12 black and 12 white phases of a year (the 12 waxing and the 12 waning phases of the moon), and the 24 half periods of the breath
- Analogous to the 360 days of the year and - inner - analogous to the 360 periods of the day which contain 60 draws of the breath each, Kalachakra has 360 bones and joints and also 360 finger parts (three in each of the 5 fingers of the 24 hands).

Photo no 45 : *Fully gold-plated statue of Kalchakra.*

Even the colors of each finger have a deeper meaning: the yellow color of the outside of the thumbs refers to the element earth, the white index finger refers to water, the red middle finger refers to fire, the black ring finger to air and the green pinks to space. The colors of the inside of the joints refer to the trinity of mind (black), speech (red) and body (white).

The main deity stands on *Mara* and *Rudra* to symbolize his victory over delusions: Here, the aspects of Mara can be divided into: inner delusions; the aggregates; death; and the "outer Mara" - the desire god Karma Deva. Mara is holding 5 flower arrows in the first right hand, which have interesting meanings: making happy; making to want again; making confused; emaciating and killing. In his second right hand, is a hook, like Kalachakra is holding; in his first left hand, a bow and in the second left hand, a lasso. Rati is the goddess of Mara and symbolizes the female organ and sexual desire; she is trying to lift Kalachakra's foot to put less weight on her consort.

Rudra is also called Ishvara, Mahadeva or Shiva. Rudra literally means "dreadful or terrible one". Uma, the consort of Rudra, (in Tibetan "the middle way") is also known as: Parvati (Lord Shiva's wife), *Durga, Kali Ishvara* or *Palden Lhamo.*

The deities stand in the centre of a lotus which represents amongst other things, renunciation. On top of the lotus are four discs; the white moon disc for bodhicitta; the red sun disc for the realization of emptiness, the black rahu disc for immutable bliss, the yellow kalagni disc for the empty form body.

DOCTRINE AND OTHERS

The Kalachakra tradition revolves around the concept of time (*kâla*) and cycles (*chakra*): from the cycles of the planets, to the cycles of human breathing. It teaches the practice of controlling the most subtle energies within one's body on the path to enlightenment. The Kalachakra deity represents a Buddha and thus omniscience. Since Kalachakra is time and everything is under the influence of time, he knows all.

The Kalachakra Tantra is divided into five stages – the first two of which are considered the "ground Kalachakra." The first chapter deals with what is called the "outer Kalachakra"—the physical world– and in particular the calculation system for the Kalachakra calendar, the birth and death of universes, our solar system and the workings of the elements.

The second stage deals with the "inner Kalachakra," and concerns processes of human gestation and birth, the classification of the functions within the human body and experience, and the vajra-kaya— the expression of human physical existence in terms of channels, winds, drops and so forth. Human experience is described as consisting of four mind states: waking, dream, deep sleep, and a fourth state, which is sexual orgasm.

The last three stages describe the "other" or "alternative Kalachakra," and deal with the path and fruition. The third stage deals with the preparation for the meditation practices of the system: the initiations of Kalachakra. The fourth stage explains the actual meditation practices of the Six Yogas. The fifth and final stage describes the state of enlightenment (fruition) that results from the practice.

The Kalachakra initiations empower the disciple to practice the Kalachakra tantra in the process of attaining Buddhahood. There are two main sets of initiations in Kalachakra, eleven in all. The first set concerns preparation for the generation stage meditations of Kalachakra. The second set concerns preparation for the completion stage meditations known as the Six Yogas of Kalachakra. Attendees who don't intend to carry out the practice are generally only given the lower seven initiations.

According to the Kalachakra Tantra, King Suchandra (Tib. *Dawa Sangpo*) of the Kingdom of Shambhala requested teaching from the Buddha that would allow him to practice the dharma without renouncing his worldly enjoyments and responsibilities. In response to his request, the Buddha taught the first Kâlachakra root tantra in Dhanyakataka in a small town in Andhra Pradesh. (At the same time, Buddha was also delivering the Prajnaparamita sutras at Vulture Peak Mountain in Bihar). Along with King Suchandra, ninety-six minor kings and emissaries from Shambhala were also said to have received the teachings.

The Kalachakra thus passed directly to Shambhala, where it was held exclusively for hundreds of years. Later Shambhalian kings, Manjushrikirti and Pundarika, are said to have condensed and simplified the teachings into the *"Sri Kalachakra"* or *"Laghutantra"* and its main commentary the *"Vimalaprabha"*, which remain extant today as the heart of the Kalachakra literature.

There are presently two main traditions of Kalachakra, the Ra lineage (Tib. Rva-lugs) and the Dro lineage (Tib.'Bro-lugs). Although there were many translations of the Kalachakra texts from Sanskrit into Tibetan, the Ra and Dro translations are considered to be the most reliable (more about the two lineages below).

Today Kalachakra is practiced by all four Tibetan schools of Buddhism, although it appears most prominently in the Gelug lineage. It is the main tantric practice for the Jonang school.

The chief Kalachakra lineage holder for the Kagyu lineage was H.E. Kalu Rinpoche (1905-1990), who gave the initiation several times in Tibet, India, Europe and North America. Upon his death, this mantle was assumed by his heart son the Ven. Bokar Rinpoche (1940 - 2004), who in turn passed it on to Ven. Khenpo Lodro Donyo Rinpoche. Bokar Monastery, of which Donyo Rinpoche is now the head, features a Kalachakra stupa and is a prominent retreat center for Kalachakra practice in the Kagyu lineage. Ven. Tenga Rinpoche is also a prominent Kagyu holder of the Kâlachakra; he gave the initiation in Grabnik, Poland in August, 2005. Chogyam Trungpa Rinpoche, while not a noted Kalachakra master, became increasingly involved later in his life with what he termed Shambhala teachings, derived from the Kalachakra tradition, in particular, the mind term which he claimed to have received from the Kulika.

The Dalai Lamas have had specific interest in the Kâlachakra practice, particularly the First, Second, Seventh, Eighth, and the current (Fourteenth) Dalai Lamas. The present Dalai Lama has given thirty Kalachakra initiations all over the world, and is the most prominent Kalachakra lineage holder alive today.

KARMA PAKSHI

Photo no 46 : *Karma Pakshi.*

INTRODUCTION

Karma Pakshi (1203–1283) was the second Gyalwa Karmapa. He had attained mastery of the tantric teachings and was considered the embodiment of the highest expression of Mahamudra wisdom.

ICONOGRAPHY

Powerful and contented, gazing forward, he is adorned with a short black goatee. Both arms are extended with the hands resting across the knees in the mudra of earth witness. Atop the head, is the small black vajra crown, a gift of the dakinis, invisible to those not spiritually developed. Wearing the orange and red patchwork robes of a fully ordained monk, he is further covered with a red meditation cloak. With the legs folded in vajra posture, right over left, he sits above an ornate cushioned throne decorated with a backrest of carved dragons.

BRIEF BIOGRAPHY

Born in Kyil-le Tsakto in eastern Tibet to a noble family of yogins, the young boy was named Chözin. He was a child prodigy who had already acquired a broad understanding of Dharma philosophy and meditation by the age of ten. His teacher, Pomdrakpa, had received the full Kagyu transmission from Drogon Rechen, the first Karmapa's spiritual heir. Pomdrakpa realized, through certain very clear visions, that the child in his charge was the reincarnation of Dusum Khyenpa, as indicated in the letter given to Drogon Rechen.

The young Karma Pakshi is said to have assimilated the deepest teachings effortlessly and required only one reading of a text to be familiar with it, as he was already enlightened. Nevertheless, Pomdrakpa made a point of formally passing on all the teachings through the traditional empowerments, so that the stream of the empowerment lineage would be unbroken. This has been the case ever since: despite their innate clarity, young Karmapas receive all the transmissions formally.

The second Karmapa spent much of the first half of his life in meditation retreat in caves and retreat homes, mostly in the Tolung valley near Tsurphu. He also visited and restored the monasteries established by the first Karmapa and is famous for having introduced to the Tibetan people communal chanting of the Om Mani Padme Hung mantra of compassion.

At the age of forty-seven he set out on a three-year journey to China, in response to an invitation from Munga Khan, a brother of Kublai Khan, and the grandson of Genghis Khan. He performed many miracles, ending wars and traveling for over ten years in the different parts of China, Mongolia and Tibet. Munga Khan adored the Karmapa. But, Kublai Khan was not in good terms with his brother. So he had animosity with the Karmapa as well. After Munga Khan passed away, Kublai Khan tried to ridicule the Karpama at different occasions. In one of his first attempts, the Khan invited the 2nd Karmapa to the imperial court. He arranged a throne and placed copies of the scriptures inside of it. The 2nd Karmapa arrived and seated himself upon the throne, to the delightment of the Khan and his ministers. The imperial court joyfully condemned the Karmapa for sitting on the sacred words of the Buddha. However, the Karmapa stated there were no words under him and after checking, to the amazement of the Imperial Court, the scriptures were blank of any script known to man.

The legend tells that each attempt to capture, or even kill, the Karmapa was thwarted by the latter's miracles. At one point, the Karmapa 'froze' a battalion of 37,000 soldiers on the spot, by using the power of *mudra,* yet all the time showing compassion, he eventually let himself be captured and put in exile, knowing that his miracles and compassion would eventually lead to Kublai Khan having a change of heart—which did in fact happen. Later, Kublai Khan also became very much devoted to him. Kublai Khan, bestowed on him the Chinese title of *Pakshi* "highest spiritual leader". He requested the Karmapa to reside there permanently, but the Karmapa declined, not wishing to be the cause of sectarian conflicts with the Sakyapas, whose influence was strong in China at that time. Instead, the Karmapa wished help to build 50 feet tall statue of Buddha at his hown town Tsurphu, to which the Khan readily agreed. Returning to Tibet towards the end of his life, he made that enormous statue of the Buddha built at Tsurphu, to fulfill a dream he had had long before. The finished work was slightly tilted; it is said that Karma Pakshi straightened it by sitting first in the same tilted posture as the statue and then righting himself. The statue moved as he moved. Before dying, he told his main disciple, Urgyenpa, details concerning the next Karmapa's birth.

Karma Pakshi passed away at eighty years old and the instructions to find his next incarnation were relayed to Drubtop Urgyenpa, his foremost disciple.

SPECIFIC SKILLS AND CONTRIBUTIONS

Karma Pakshi had attained mastery of the tantric teachings and was considered the embodiment of the highest expression of Mahamudra wisdom. He was the teacher to the Mongol emperor of China and the first publicly acknowledged incarnate Lama of Tibet.

Yongey Mingyur Dorje had developed a guru sadhana based on Karma Pakshi, called a *gong ter*, "mind treasure" which is in every retreat centres of Karma Kagyu and has made compulsory for Lamas to complete this retreat before proceeding to the next practice. It is also a daily practice of all the Karma Kagyu Lamas as a form of Guru Yoga together with the Yidam and Protector practices in one. As per Kagyu tradition, Mahamudra realization is very much dependant on the perfection of Guru devotion and the true devotion can be developed by the person who practices Guru yoga regularly and who knows that the Guru is the union and embodiment of all the enlightened ones. It is believed that by practicing regularly the visionary Karma Pakshi Guru yoga, one will receive immeasurable blessings that eliminate all the outer and inner karmic forces and accumulate merits and wisdom to create every favorable causes of happiness and ultimately the realization of Great Mahamudra.

His Holiness, the Sixteenth Karmapa often recommended *Karma Pakshi Guru Sadhana* for students who completed their *ngondro* because this sadhana includes Karmapa guru yoga as well as yidam and protector practice.

In general, Karma Pakshi was renowned both, for the depth of his realization and for his powers, and he consequently had students throughout Tibet, Mongolia and China.

KURUKULA

Photo no 47 : *Kurukula*

INTRODUCTION

Kurukula (Tib. *Rigjyedma*) is a dakini, very popular in Tibetan Buddhism. Her worship is said to bring wealth, well-being and power to the devotees.

ICONOGRAPHY

There are five forms of the deity Kurukula. But the most important form is called Tarodbava Kurukula.

Kurukula is depicted in red color with red garments, red ornaments and seated on a red lotus. She is usually represented in dancing attitude. If she stands, she stands on her left foot and her right leg is raised. She either wears a crown of skulls or a band surmounted by ornaments. She has four arms. Two hands show charging a flowery arrow on a flower bow ready to strike at and other two hands show a flowery elephant hawk and a flowery lasso.

Moreover, there exists a sadhana text for the red Kurukula in her eight-armed form. Whether she had, eight arms or four arms, but she is known as the Uddiyana Kurukula.

According to the texts, Kurukulla is described to be a sixteen years old girl with perfect beauties. Her face is beautiful and alluring, because of her magical function of enchantment and magnetism. She has a single face which indicates the non-dual wisdom beyond conventional distinctions of good and evil. She has four arms indicating the four immeasurable states of mind, namely, love, compassion, joy, and equanimity. She holds the bow and arrow entwined with flowers showing that she can give rise to thoughts of desire in the minds of others. In her other two hands, she holds the hook that attracts and summons them into her presence and the noose by which she binds them to her will. The ornaments of human bone she wears signify the five perfections, whereas she herself embodies the sixth perfection, that of wisdom. She wears a necklace of fifty severed human heads symbolizing her vanquishing of fifty negative emotions. She is dancing showing that she is active and energetic, her compassionate activity manifesting in both Samsara and Nirvana. She dances, treading upon a male human corpse indicating that she enchants and subjugates the demon of ego. She stands upon a red sun disc because her nature is hot and enflamed with passion and upon a red lotus blossom because she is a pure vision of enlightened awareness. In the practitioner's meditation, such is the recollection of the purity of the vision of the goddess Kurukulla in the Nyingmapa tradition.

Photo no 48 : *Silver statue of Kurukula.*

Other Forms of Kurukula—There is one form of Kurukulla depicted red and with four arms and she is known as Uddiyana

Kurukulla or Uddiyanodbhava, since she comes from Uddiyana. There is another form that is said to be formed from Tara and hence called Tarodbhava Kurukula. She may have two-arms and eight-arms.

Then there is *Ashtabhuja Kurukula* with eight arms that appear in a sadhana attributed to King Indrabhuti in the Tangyur and also in a sadhana mentioned in Sadhanamala collection. Her first two hands make the gesture of *Trailokyavijaya-mudra* or "victory over the three worlds", while her other right hands hold the iron hook, an arrow, and make the gesture of supreme generosity, *varada-mudra*. Her other left hands hold the noose, the bow, and the red lotus. Her two legs are in *vajrasana* position. Moreover, she is surrounded by a retinue of eight goddesses resembling herself, but with four arms: in the east *Prassana Tara*, in the south *Nishpanna Tara*, in the west *Jaya Tara*, in the north *Karna Tara*, in the southeast *Aparajita*, in the southwest *Pradipa Tara*, in the northwest *Gauri Tara*, and in the northeast *Chunda*.

There is also a two-armed white form of Kurukulla known as Shukla Kurukula as mentioned in the Sadhanamala. She has a single face which is calm and beautiful and the Buddha Amitabha adorns her crown. Her two hands hold a rosary and a bowl full of lotus flowers. Her two legs are in *vajrasana* position. She adorns her body with serpents who are the great Naga kings: *Ananta* is her hair ribbon, *Vasuki* is her necklace, *Takshaka* is her ear rings, *Karkotaka* is her sacred thread, *Padma* is her girdle, and Mahapadma is her anklet, and so on.

DOCTRINE AND OTHERS

The practice of Kurukula is found in all four Buddhist schools, especially in rituals associated with the enchanting or subjugating magical function.

In the Terma cycle of Dudjom Lingpa (1835-1904), Kurukulla represents the inner aspect of Dechen Gyalmo, the yogini form of Yeshe Tsogyal, the consort of Guru Padmasambhava. Kurukula is very popular among the Sakyapa Schools.

Kurukula also appears at times in the retinues of other deities. For example, in the mandala of the wealth god, the red Jambhala, she appears in her usual four-armed form. Also, in the mandala of the four-armed Mahakala according to the system of Shantigupta, she appears in the southwest in a red two-armed form.

She embodies non-dual wisdom beyond conventional distinctions of good and evil. Her four arms represent the four immeasurable states of mind: love, compassion, joy, and equanimity. Her bow and arrows are intertwined with flowers allowing her to place thoughts of desire in the minds of others. She has a hook to summon people towards her and a noose to bind them.

It is believed that she assists unhappy lovers. Her activity as a yidam concerns the transformation of obsessive craving. She transforms dualistic desire into non-dual desire.

Kurukula appears to have become popular because of the magical function of enchantment or the bewitching of people in order to bring them under one's power. More than any other figure in the Buddhist pantheon, Kurukula is one of the most popular deities concerning love. In a real sense, she represents the empowerment of the feminine in a patriarchal milieu. In Tibet, Kurukula was also called upon when commencing the building of a new monastery, when undertaking a new business or enterprise, when going into court in order to win a law case, and other such activities, because she can subdue and subjugate the demonic and the human forces that stand in one's way. She, together with Manjushri and Sarasvati, might even be called upon when a student faces a difficult examination in school.

A text like the *Arya Tara Kurukula Kalpa* contains many ritual practices of lower magic to accomplish specific goals. or example: 1. amulets for enchanting and bringing others under one's power, 2. spells to frighten away poisonous snakes, 3. methods for a dissatisfied wife to subjugate her husband, 4. amulets for protection from evil spirits and bad luck, 5. spells for acquiring wealth and gaining power, 6. the use of cowries shells in divination and ritual, 7. divinations to find a treasure, 8. methods for walking on water, 9. methods to avoid getting gray hair, 10. cures for frigidity and impotence.

Photo no 49 : *Partly gold-plated statue of Kurukula*

In one Kurukula Sadhana found in the Sadhanamala, there occurs a list of eight great siddhis or magical powers acquired through her practice:

1. Khadga-siddhi, the power to be invincible in battle with a sword (khadga);

2. Anjana-siddhi, the power to remove ordinary lack of sight by using a magical ointment that enables the user to see Devas, Nagas, and other spirits;

3. Padalepa-siddhi the power to be swift of foot by using a magical ointment that, when applied to the feet, allows the user to run with incredible swiftness;
4. Antardhana-siddhi the power to become invisible;
5. Rasayana-siddhi, the power of rejuvenation and long life through obtaining the elixir of life by way of an alchemical process;
6. Khechara-siddhi, the power to levitate or to fly through the sky;
7. Bhuchara-siddhi, the power to move freely through the earth, mountains, and solid walls; and
8. Patala-siddhi, the power to have command over the spirits of the underworld (*patala*).

Mantra : *'Om kurukule hum hrin svaha'* is the mantra when muttered ten thousands times is said to fulfill every one's desires.

MAHAKALA

Photo no 50 : *Six armed Mahakala*

INTRODUCTION

Mahakala (Tib: *Gonpo Phyag*) is a dharmapala i.e. a protector of dharma in all sects of Mahayana Buddhism.

Mahakala is relied upon in all schools of Tibetan Buddhism.

ICONOGRAPHY

However, he is depicted in a number of variations, each with distinctly different qualities and aspects.

Photo no 51 : *Six-armed standing White Mahakala.*

The most notable variation in Mahakala's manifestations and depictions is in the number of arms, but other details can vary as well. For instance, in some cases there are Mahakalas in white, with multiple heads, without genitals, standing on varying numbers of various things, holding various implements, with alternative adornments, and so on.

Six-Armed Mahakala—The Six-Armed Mahakala is favored by the Gelug order of Tibetan Buddhism, and in this manifestation is considered to be a fierce and powerful emanation of Avalokiteœvara.

There is also a White Six-Armed Mahakala popular among Gelugpas. In this case, he is a "wealth deity", specifically supporting the comfort and economic well-being of tantric practitioners. As such, his iconography differs in form and symbolism, with his skull bowl containing various jewels rather than the typical mortal remains of his victims, and a crown of jewels instead of skulls. The following description is found in his sadhana: "His body is white. His face is wrathful and he has three eyes. He has six arms. His main right hand holds a wish-fulfilling jewel (cintamani) mounted on a jewel-tipped handle, in front of his chest."

Four-Armed Mahakala - Various Four-armed Mahakalas are the primary protectors of the Karma Kagyu and Drikung Kagyu schools of Tibetan Buddhism. One of the Four-Armed versions is an emanation of Cakrasamvara and the main protector of Karma Kagyu; a four-armed Mahakala is also found in the Nyingma School, although the primary protector of the Great Perfection teachings which are the pinnacle of the Nyingma system is Ekajati. The four arms of this manifestation of Mahakala perform one of the following four positive karmas or actions, which are said to be his specific boon to his worshippers :

- Pacify sickness, hindrances, and troubles.
- Increase life, good qualities and wisdom.
- Attract whatever Dharma practitioners need and bring people to the Dharma.
- Destroy confusion, doubt, and ignorance.

Photo no 52 : *Four armed Mahakala.*

Two-Armed Mahakala—The two-armed Mahakala called Bernakchen an emanation of Samantabhadra, is a protector of the Karma Kagyu school. It is often thought to be the primary protector, but it is actually the main protector of the Karmapas specifically.

Panjaranatha Mahakala, 'Lord of Charms" or "Lord of the Pavilion", an emanation of Manjushree is a protector of the Sakya order.

Symbolism of Mahakala in the six-armed Manifestation :

The Protector's body is midnight blue, symbolic of the changeless Dharmakaya.

- His three eyes symbolize his knowledge of the past, present and future, and also the manifestation of the three bodies of Buddha.
- The crown adorned with five skulls symbolizes the transformation of the five poisons of anger, desire, ignorance, jealousy and pride into the five wisdoms.

Photo no 53 : *A partly gold plated statue of Panjaranatha Mahakala*

- His six arms symbolize the attainment of the six Perfections: generosity, patience, morality, diligence, meditation and wisdom. The kartika or triku [or trigu, pron. tigu] the ritual curved knife, cuts attachment to ego.
- The kapala or skull bowl filled with blood symbolizes the subjugation of the maras or evil ones. (An alternate interpretation can be found in other contexts.)
- The rosary symbolizes his continuous activity for the benefit of beings.
- The damaru or hand-drum symbolizes his power over the dakinis. (Also, different interpretations in other contexts.)
- His trident symbolizes his power over the three kayas — the spheres of desire, form and formlessness. (An alternate interpretation can also be found.)

Photo no 54 : *Two armed Mahakala*

The lasso binds those who break their vows.

- His two feet are the means and the wisdom to accomplish his task. That his left leg is straight and his right leg bent which symbolizes his accomplishment of the benefit to oneself and to others. He tramples on a *vinayaka*, to symbolize his destruction and dispersal of great obstacles.
- The sun on which he stands symbolizes his illumination of the darkness of ignorance.
- His lotus seat symbolizes purity undefiled by *samsara*.
- The surrounding blazing fire symbolizes his activity that consumes neurotic states.
- The tiger skin stands for purification of desire; the elephant skin for purification of pride, and the snake, for the purification of anger.

DOCTRINE AND OTHERS

Origin of Mahakala—The compassion of the red Buddha Amitabha manifested as Avalokiteshvara who took a vow to forgo his own enlightenment until all the realms of *samsara* had been emptied. This vow required a renewal of determination, and so with Amitabha's blessing, Avalokiteshvara next assumed a form with eleven heads and a thousand arms. Still he had been unable to benefit even a few beings. Therefore after reflecting for one whole week, he determined that by assuming a wrathful form he would be able "to subdue the degenerate beings of this Age of Darkness." Also he saw that even beings who practiced Dharma were unable to escape from the Bardo realms (time between rebirths where beings may face great anxiety and terrifying experiences) and he thought that in wrathful form he could also protect them in that way. And lastly, he thought that the beings in this Dark Age were poor and needy, experiencing only suffering after suffering, and that in wrathful form he could provide them an antidote to that suffering so that by simply making the wish (for protection) their needs could be met.

These three motives made his determination even greater than before and so from the heart of Noble Avalokiteshvara emerged a dark blue *hung* syllable that immediately became the Instantaneous Protector of Wisdom, Mahakala. The foundations of all the Pure Lands shook with six kinds of earthquakes, and the Conquering and Transcending One of Immeasurable Light (Amitabha) and all the other Tathagatas of the ten directions proclaimed with one voice: "Son of the family, it is well that you have made this resolution. You shall have the empowerment of all the wisdom dakinis. You shall have the strength of the wrathful Yama, Lord of Death. You shall have the mountain spirits, the yakshas, the devils and the demonesses as your messengers. You shall embody the great wrathful empowerments of the Body, Speech, Mind, Qualities and Activity of all the Buddhas throughout the three times." Ever since, bodhisattva Mahakala is the Dharma (Buddha's Doctrine), Protector of all Buddha fields.

Mantra : *Om, Shri Mahakala Yaksha Betli, hung dsa.*

MAHAPRATISARA

Photo no 55 : *Mahapratisara.*

INTRODUCTION

Mahapratisara is the principal female deity of Pancharakshya. Others are Mahasahasra Pramardani, Mahamayuri, Mahasitavati, and Mahamantranusarini. Pancharakshya is very popular in Nepal.

The characteristic feature of each deity is that Mahapratisara protects against sin, illness and other dangers. Similarly, Mahasahasra Pramardani protects against evil spirits. Mahamayuri protects against the venomous snakes and cobras, wild animals and poisonous insects. Mahasitavati protects against all sorts of harmful influences from the evil deities, planets, Yakshas, non-human beings, and others. And Mahamantranusarini protects against illness.

ICONOGRAPHY

Mahapratisara has four heads and eight arms. She is white in color and her heads are successively yellow, white, red and green. She is seated on a lotus throne in vajraparyanka posture. She wears the diadem. In her right hands, she holds a vajra, an arrow, a sword and in her left hands holds a trident, a bow and an axe while her two principal hands hold a wheel and a garment.

Mahasahasra Pramardani has four heads and is awesome in appearance. The heads are successively white, blue, red and yellow. The deity wears a crown of human skulls and has tiger skin around her waist. The hair is disheveled. Mahasahasra Pramardani has eight arms. Her four right hands exhibit Varada Mudra, a sword, an arrow and a goad while her left hands hold a lotus, noose, bow and axe. Mahasahasra Pramardani is seated in *Lalitasana*. Mahasahasra Pramardani also wears a garland of severed human heads. Mahasahasra Pramardani tramples upon a human corpse and is seated on a lotus throne. In Nispannayogavali she is described as having ten arms.

Mahamayuri has three heads. Mahamayuri is green in color and her three faces are green, white and blue in color. Mahamayuri is eight armed. One of her four right hands displays Varada Mudra while the other three hands hold a sword, Vajra and jewel. In her four left hands she holds Pindapatra, a jar showering jewels, a bell and a flower. Mahamayuri is seated on a lotus throne. Mahamayuri wears all the ornaments and celestial garments peculiar to a Bodhisattva.

According to Sadhanamala *Mahasitavati* is six armed and has three faces. Mahasitavati is green in color. In her right hands, she holds a lotus with the gesture of fearlessness, the arrow, the sword and in her left hands, she holds a jewel banner, a bow and a lasso or a noose. Mahasitavati is seated in the Ardhaparyanka posture and wears a crown. Mahasitavati wears all the ornaments of a Bodhisattva and sits on a lotus throne.

Mahamantranusarini has three heads. She is red in color. Her heads are successively white, green and red. She has twelve arms. With her two right hands she displays the varadamudra and abhayamudra. The other hands hold an arrow and a vajra. Two principal hands disply the vitarkamudra and the other two hands hold an alms bowl. In her left hands she holds a bow, a jewel, a vase and a lasso. She wears a crown and is seated on a lotus throne. She wears all the bodhisattva ornaments and garments of a Sambhogakaya.

DOCTRINE AND OTHERS

The recitation and Sadhana of this protectress deity confer great benefit and protection. One such example befitting to this context is described in the first chapter of the Pancharaksha sutra. It is said that one who holds the Dharani of Mahapratisara will be protected from all forms of illness, eliminate the past non-virtuous karma, protect from all sorts of dangers. They take rebirth in higher realms. Their body becomes a vajra body not affected by fire, weapons and others.

In Bhadrakalpavadana it is said that Buddha Shakyamuni renounced his palace life before the birth of his son Rahula. He touched his wife Yasodhara's navel with his thumb finger of right foot and made a great vow that she be protected from great dangers which were to come to her in the future. After his great renunciation Yashodhara bore his child for six years inside her womb. Before the delivery of the child Rahula she was put to many hazardous trials and tribulations by his cousin Devadutta. But in all cases Yashodhara came out unhurt due to the miraculous power of Mahapratisara Devi. Nepalese Buddhists thus wear amulets for their protection against various sorts of unseen dangers. These amulets contain the Dharani of Mahapratisara Devi.

In the Pratisara Sutra, the Buddha delivers his sermon from a beautiful and delightful place. A vast audience of gods, demons, and spirits had gathered there to listen. The Lord Buddha spoke to all present, but mostly addressed 'O Brahman'. Buddha told of the power of the Mahapratisara dharani, which has an incredible amount of power. Chanting the dharani of Mahapratisara or wearing an amulet derived from it can destroy the causes of stress, prevent harm by demons, reconcile enemies, bestow immunity from fire, poison, weapons, etc, and basically keep one free from all dangers. It is extraordinary to imagine that a verse or amulet has such enormous power. The Buddha says that the dharani of Mahapratisara should be learned and memorized. There is a remarkable story. By hanging an amulet around the neck of the dead body of remorseful monk, the entire Avici hell was freed from pain and torment. The transgressors suffered no injury, felt no pain and could not even be harmed. Her mantra is as follow :

Mantra : *Om amrtavara vara vara pravara visuddhe hum hum phat phat svaha.*

MAITREYA BUDDHA

Photo no 56 : *Maitreya Buddha*

INTRODUCTION

Maitreya Bodhisattva (Tib: *Jampa*) is the future Buddha of this world, who will eventually appear on this earth, achieve complete enlightenment, and teach the pure Dharma. Maitreya Bodhisattva will be the successor of the historic Úâkyamuni Buddha. He is predicted to be a "world-ruler", uniting those over whom he rules.

The prophecy of the arrival of Maitreya is found in the canonical literature of all Buddhist sects (Theravâda, Mahâyâna and Vajrayâna) and is accepted by most Buddhists as a statement about an actual event that will take place in the distant future.

ICONOGRAPHY

Maitreya is typically pictured seated, with both feet on the ground, indicating that he has not yet completed ascending his throne. He is dressed in the clothes of a Bhiksu. As a Bodhisattva, he would usually be standing and dressed in jewels. Usually, he wears a small stupa in his headdress and could be holding a chakra wheel resting on a lotus. A scarf is always tied around his waist. He is flanked by his two acolytes—Asanga and his brother, Vasubandhu.

DOCTRINE AND OTHERS

Maitreya resides in the Tucita Heaven said to be reachable through meditation. Úâkyamuni Buddha also lived here before he was born into the world. Some Bodhisattvas live in the Tucita Heaven before they descend to the human realm to become Buddhas.

In Mahayana schools, Maitreya is traditionally said to have revealed the Five Treatises of Maitreya through Asanga. These important texts are the basis of the Yogachara tradition and constitute the majority of the Third Turning of the Wheel of Dharma.

Maitreya's coming will occur after the teachings of the current Buddha Gautama, the Dharma, are no longer taught and are completely forgotten. Maitreya is predicted to attain Bodhi in seven days (which is the minimum period), by virtue of his many lives of preparation for Buddha-hood (similar to those reported in the Jataka stories of Shakyamuni Buddha).

Maitreya's coming is characterized by a number of physical events. The oceans are predicted to decrease in size, allowing Maitreya to traverse them freely. The event will also allow the unveiling of the "true" dharma to the people, in turn allowing the construction of a new world. The coming also signifies the end of the middle time in which humans currently reside (characterized as a low point of human existence between the Gautama Buddha and Maitreya).

Some of the events foretold at the coming of the 5th Buddha (29th Buddha according to Theravada) include an end to death, warfare, famine, and disease, as well as the ushering in of a new society of tolerance and love.

The name Maitreya or Metteyya is derived from the word maitrî (Sanskrit) or mettâ (Pâli) meaning "loving-kindness", which is in turn derived from the noun mitra (Pâli: mitta) in the sense of "friend".

Photo no 57 : *Laughing Buddha (Hotei)*

In the Greco-Buddhist art of Gandhara, in the first centuries CE in northern India, Maitreya was the most popular figure to be represented, together with the Buddha Úâkyamuni. In China, the cult of Maitreya seems to have developed around the same time of that of Amitâbha, as early as the 3rd century AD.

The Chinese monk Budai (Hotei) has been popularly regarded as an incarnation of the bodhisattva Maitreya. His depiction as the Laughing Buddha continues to be very popular in East Asian culture.

While a number of persons have proclaimed themselves to be Maitreya over the years following the Buddha's nirvana, none have been officially recognized by the sangha and Buddhists. A particular difficulty faced by any would-be claimant to Maitreya's title is the fact that the Buddha is considered to have made a number of fairly specific predictions regarding the circumstances that would occur prior to Maitreya's coming—such as that the teachings of the Buddha would be completely forgotten, and all of the remaining relics of Sakyamuni Buddha would be gathered in Bodh Gaya and cremated.

MANDARAVA

Photo no 58 : *Mandarava*

INTRODUCTION

Mandarava (Tib: *lha lcam dkar mo*), was a princess of Zahor also known simply as the White Princess. Mandarava was one of the five consorts who practiced and studied with Padmasambhava. In terms of historical time, Mandarava was actually the first of these five, chosen and initiated when she was 16 years old in India. (Other consorts of Guru Padmasambhava were Kalasiddhi, Sakyadevi, Yeshe Tsogyal and Mangala).

In due course and by diligent practice, Mandarava attained a degree of mastery equal to that of her consort, a fact given expression in her honorary title of Machig Drupa Gyalmo (ma gcig grub pa'i rgyal mo), Singular Queen Mother of Attainment. Compassionate and loving by nature, she also saved the life of young Kalasiddhi - and helped her grow up - who later became another of Padmasambhava's favorite ladies.

Her full name, Mandarava Flower (Tib: *man da ra ba me tog*), refers to one of the five mythical trees said to grow in Sukhavati.

BRIEF HISTORY

Mandarava was born of Vihardhara, King of Zahor and Queen Mohauki. Her birth was said to be accompanied by miraculous signs and her renunciation and spiritual inclination was marked from a young age. She was beautiful and there were many marriage suitors. Although she was not born a Buddhist, she was interested only in solitary retreat, away from the samsaric obstacles of marriage and other activities. She became a nun on reaching adulthood. Her father, who was worried about the possibility of his daughter disrobing which would affect the kingdom's reputation, sent five hundred ordained nuns to live with her, to practice with her and to guard her from male suitors.

When Guru Padsambhava journeyed from the Swat Valley (located in present-day Pakistan) to Tibet, he stopped at Mandi and discovered Princess Mandarava to be a suitable spiritual companion.

The princess and her entourage became disciples of Guru Rinpoche. A local shepherd discovered them and news of the princess living with a man finally reached the ears of the king. He was so outraged that he commanded that his daughter be stripped and wrapped in thorns, and locked in the dungeon near the river. At the same time, he demanded that Guru Rinpoche be burned in the charnel grounds high in the mountains, while he watched the smoke from the Royal Park.

Photo no 59 : *Standing Mandarava*

Guru Rinpoche turned the fire into a lake and re-appeared on a lotus (the lake became known as Tso Pema, or the Lotus Lake, later). The sight of this converted all the witnesses into following Buddha dharma, and when the king knew about it, he too became the Guru's follower. Immediately, he ordered that the princess be released from the dungeon.

Mandarava became Guru Padmasambhava's first consort. She accompanied him to practice and spread the dharma. Both Mandarava and Padmasambhava achieved the unified vajra body on the vidyadhara level of mastery and realised some of the practices of long life or longevity that were concealed in the Maratika Cave (this cave which is later called Maratika Monastery, is located in Khotang District of Nepal, circa 185 kilometres south west of Mount Everest). Later, while Padmasambhava continued spreading teachings throughout the Himalaya, Mandarava remained in India. Mandarava attained the vajra rainbow body (jalus).

SPECIFIC MASTERYS AND CONTRIBUTIONS

Mandarava is said to have manifested her sambhogakaya form at the great Dharma Wheel of Tramdruk, where she engaged in a dialogue of mantra and mudra with Padmasambhava. Extensive details of this are rendered in the Padma Kathang.

Mandarava is considered a wisdom, knowledge or awareness dakini among whose different names and manifestations are: the yogini Mirukyi Gyenchen at the time of Marpa; Risulkyi Naljorma during the time of Nyen Lotsawa; and Drubpey Gyalmo during the time of Rechungpa. Chushingi Nyemachen, the spiritual consort Maitripa, is considered to be none other than Mandarava. The dakini Niguma is also considered to be Mandarava.

Through practice and diligence, Mandarava realised a degree of spiritual mastery equal to that of Padmasambhava her consort, evidenced in her honorific Machig Drupa Gyalmo (ma gcig grub pa'i rgyal mo), "Singular Queen Mother of Attainment".

Mandarava was famed for her compassionate and loving nature.

MANJUSHREE

Photo no 60 : *A fully gold plated statue of Manjushree*

INTRODUCTION

Manjushree (Tib: Jampelyang), is viewed both as a historical bodhisattva, and as an emanation of Vairochana Buddha. He manifests as a bodhisattva to provoke investigation into such topics as Emptiness, free will, and the nature of the self. He is one of the most popular Bodhisattvas following Avalokitesvara

Within Tibetan Buddhism, Manjushree is a tantric meditational deity or Yidam, and considered a fully enlightened Buddha. He sometimes is depicted in a trinity with Avalokiteshvara and Vajrapani.

Manjushree is mentioned in many Mahayana sutras, particularly the Prajnaparamita Sutras. The Lotus Sutra assigns him a paradise called Vimala, which according to the Avatamsaka Sutra is located in the east. Another epithet is Vakishvara (Lord of Speech) and it is this aspect of Manjushree that associates him with a great historical teacher known as Manjughosha.

Manjushree is known as the God of Divine Wisdom, and is considered the founder of Nepalese civilization and the creator of the Kathmandu Valley. Devotees believe that he confers wisdom, memory and intelligence.

ICONOGRAPHY

Manjushree is depicted wielding a flaming sword in his right hand, representing his realization of wisdom which cuts through ignorance and wrong views. The scripture supported by the flower held in his left hand is the Prajnaparamita, representing his attainment of ultimate realization and Enlightenment. Manjushri's sword of discriminating wisdom is tipped with flames to show that it severs all notions of duality. It can cut away delusion, aversion and longing, to reveal understanding, equanimity and compassion

Sometimes, in the case of Vakishvara, he is depicted with his hands making the gesture of teaching at the level of his heart. Often, we see him with a double set of arms, which combines internal and external qualities.

Manjushree is either seated on a lion throne or on an elephant. Both animals are associated a fully enlightened Buddha. However, as a bodhisattva, he is depicted as a sixteen-year old youth. This is a confirmation of the fact that wisdom is not merely associated with maturity and age; it but is a direct consequence of anyone's logical inquiry into the true nature of reality.

Variations upon his traditional form as Manjushree include Guhya- Manjushree, Guhya-Manjuvajra, and Manjuswari, most of which are Tantric forms associated with Tibetan Buddhism. The two former appearances are generally accompanied by a Shakti deity embracing the main figure, symbolising union of form and spirit, matter and energy.

DOCTRINE AND OTHERS

When the primordial Buddha Vairochana vowed to emanate throughout the universe as the princely and ever-youthful, bodhisattva of Wisdom, his purpose was to lead beings in an inquiry whereby they could discover the true nature of reality. For that reason, he is usually depicted displaying the two tools essential to that investigation: in his right hand, he wields the double-edged sword of logic or analytic discrimination and in his left, the Prajnaparamita Sutra, the text of the teaching on Emptiness. This teaching is fundamental to all forms of Buddhism and for that

Photo no 61 : *A fully gold plated statue of Maha-Manjushree.*

reason, it is often called "Mother of All Buddhas." It is cushioned on the lotus of Compassion.

In Nepal, he is regarded as creator of Kathmandu valley. His intuition told him of the blue flame (symbolizing *Adibuddha* or *Swayambhu*) on a lotus in Kalihrada, a lake in Nepal. He went to the place together with his two wives for worshipping. To reach the flame in the water, he cut away with his sword a part on the south wall of the hill. The water rushed out, and the Bagmati River drained the valley, that became Kathmandu Valley. Swayambhunath Stupa was built on the spot where the flame came out of the lotus. In sculptures, he holds the flaming sword in his right hand to symbolize cutting of the root of the delusion, which is the cause of suffering, ignorance and the self grasping. He holds the scriptural text entitled "Perfection of Wisdom" which cuts off all delusions. While the left hand is in teaching pose (Jnan Mudra). He is sits in the Vajraparyanka attitude.

Manjushree is regarded as God of Agriculture or celestial architect. He is also God of Science. People believe that worship of Manjushree can confer upon them wisdom, memory, intelligence etc. He is invoked especially for increasing intelligence by reciting his mantra *"Om A Ra Pa Ca Na Dhih"* many times.

On the same day, when Saraswati Puja is observed, which is on the 13th of February, the worshipping of Manjushree is also done in the form of Vakishvara.

Chanting the Manjushree Mantra *"Om Ah Ra Pa Tsa Na Dhih"* is believed to enhance wisdom and improve one's skills in debating, memory, writing, explaining etc. "Dhih" is the seed syllable of the mantra and is chanted with greater emphasis.

OTHER FORMS/EMANATIONS OF MANJUSHREE

Namasangiti is the title of the tantric Praises to Manjushree and is also used to refer to this deity as well. Here, he is depicted as yellow having one face and four hands. He holds in the first right a blue sword of wisdom licked with flame and in the left at his heart, he holds a pink utpala flower; the blossom at ear-level supports the Prajnaparamita, as above. In the lower pair of hands are a bow and arrow. On a multi-coloured lotus seat, he emanates pale yellow rays of light and also a green aura framed in dark green leaves and lotuses.

As Yamantaka, Manjushree assumes a fierce blue-black bull-headed form to defeat Yama, god of death.

MARICHI

Photo no 62 : *Marichi (a partly gold plated statue).*

INTRODUCTION

Marichi (Marici, Tib: *Öser Chenma*) is a Goddess associated with the sun and with the dawn. Although, there may be slight differences in description, this deity is invariably depicted as Buddhist personification of the Sun, the Dawn, & the Sun's Rays in different countries.

She rides across the sky in a chariot drawn by seven white boars, as seen here at the right, boars drawing her throne, weapons in her six arms. While she rarely appears in Chinese Buddhist pantheon, this deity often appears in that of Japan and Tibet. Marichi is called Marishiten, Queen of Heaven, in Japan and is worshipped as a protection against fire, wealth giver and as the protector of warriors. She is sometimes included as one of the twelve Yaksha Generals associated with Yakushi (*Bhaisajyaguru*), the Buddha of Medicine.

Marichi is even considered the emanation of Vairochana Buddha and his Shakti.

Marichi is also considered as the Shakti of Hayagriva as the left head of this deity is that of a pig.

Although, Marichi is worshipped for different reasons by people in many countries, primarily, she is a goddess, independent and sovereign, protectress against all violence and peril.

ICONOGRAPHY

Marichi assumes a variety of forms and may have one, three, five or six faces and two, six, eight, ten or twelve arms; in her many-faced manifestations one of her faces is that of a sow, and she rides either a sow or a chariot drawn by seven pigs.

One of the popular form of Marichi has an orange-colored body (the color of the sun at dawn), and three faces, eight arms and two legs. Of the three faces, the first (central) is orange and smiling, her right face is red, and her left is the face of a white boar: each has three eyes. Her first right hand holds a vajra at the heart in the mudra of teaching, the second holds a vajra axe, the third holds an arrow, and the fourth, in the mudra of generosity, holds a (sewing) needle. Her first left hand, in the mudra of teaching, holds the stem of a plant.

Her second left hand holds a noose, the third holds a bow, and the fourth holds a hook. Marichi's left leg is extended, while the right is tucked in. She is dressed in the royal robes of a bodhisattva: five-pointed crown surmounting each face, jewels, silks and so forth. Marichi rides a throne/chariot drawn along by seven white boars.

She is also depicted as the "Goddess of the Dawn" riding her chariot, drawn by seven boars, which carries the sun. As she is seated in front of the sun, she is, therefore, invisible. Her right hand is in the gesture of granting wishes, while her left hand holds a branch of the Asoka tree–a plant with medicinal properties. Marichi oversees thirty-six celestial deities and seventy-two earthly deities. These one hundred and eight deities are in charge of bestowing blessings and punishment depending on the karmas from people's previous lives and their current lives.

DOCTRINE AND OTHERS

Although Marichi is diversely represented, she is mostly linked with the sun, or the light as Marichi means "light" or "mirage". Marichi was regarded as a deification of mirages and being, thus, invisible or difficult to see was invoked in order to escape the notice of one's enemies.

Marichi's origin lies in early Indian scriptures such as *The Laws of Manu* (Skt.: *Manava Dharma Shastra*) and the Puranas, where Marichi is one of 10 Prajapatis or primal parents /chief of the Maruts produced from the mind of Brahma. In this male aspect, Marichi is father of Surya, the sun and (with his wife Sambhuti) and also of Kashyapa 'Old Tortoise Man' one of the seven primordial sages. Thus, Marichi, the beam of divine light that initiates creation of the physical world is not only illumination in a physical but also in the spiritual sense.

This 'illuminating' aspect of Marichi is emphasized in an 18th century thangka of the Karma Kagyu at Tibet Art where she is crowned by a stupa, and instead of driving, she is seated on a great sow with its piglets. The accompanying Sakya verse emphasizes her ability to dispel the fears of the night.

Photo no 63 : *Another statue of Marichi, fully gold plated riding on a bore.*

Legend has also it that one of these abbesses in Semding Monastery had a growth behind her ear which resembled a sow's head. When the Mongol warrior, Dzungar came to attack the monastery, he called out for her to come out and to show her sow's head. When he and his army destroyed the walls of the monastery, all they found were a group of sows and pigs inside led by a sow larger than the rest of the group. Dzungar was so amazed that he stopped the pillage, at which the sows and pigs transformed into monks and nuns; the largest sow transformed into the abbess. Dzungar was doubly amazed at the miracle and he converted himself and later even enriched the monastery.

The *Nispannayogavali* also describes a mandala centred on Marichi.

The embodiment of the first rays of dawn, Marichi is invoked by travelers for protection from robbers and other hazards of the road. The mantra is: *Om Marichi svaha.*

MARPA LOTSAWA

Photo no 64 : *A statue of Marpa.*

INTRODUCTION

Marpa Lotsawa (1012-1097), or Marpa the translator was a Tibetan Buddhist teacher credited with the transmission of many Buddhist teachings to Tibet from India, including the teachings and lineages of Vajrayana and Mahamudra.

Other introduction of Marpa is that he was the principle disciple of Naropa and he was the teacher of Milarepa.

He is portrayed as a fearsome, aggressive and powerful looking person.

SHORT BIOGRAPHY

Marpa was born in a village called Lhodrak, in the southern part of Tibet. His father's name was Wangchuk Oser and his mother's name was Gyamo Sa Dode. He was one of four sons. As a child Marpa was very energetic. His natural magnetic power was so great that even his own parents, if they looked directly into his eyes, were unable to bear the feeling of strength coming from him. When he was young, he was sent to a teacher named Lugyepa to study. Again, Marpa's understanding and wisdom was so profound that whatever the teacher taught him on one day, he would know that by heart. In a way, he surpassed his own teacher.

Not only did Marpa look fearsome, he was also quite aggressive. All the people in the village got so frightened by his natural look of power and strength that he was not welcome in many homes. In fact, the only people Marpa could visit in his village were his teacher and his one friend. All the rest developed a fear of the magnetic power that Marpa displayed, and they would not welcome him. For these reasons, his father felt it best to send him to a different area to be educated. He was sent to far off a place, to a teacher known as Drokmi Lotsawa, who was a Translator. From him, Marpa was to learn Tibetan writing and reading, poetry, drama, and so forth. Marpa studied under Drokmi for fifteen years, and became a master not only in the Tibetan language but also in the Sanskrit language as well. Having mastered those languages, Marpa returned to his home village, but he was not to stay long. He decided to go to Nepal for further study, even though the journey from Tibet to Nepal was very long, hard, and dangerous. To help him get there, he collected all the possessions he could get from his friend and from relatives, and made the journey.

Marpa journeyed first to Nepal. He met Paindapa and Chitherpa who were famous students of Naropa. He studied with them at Swoyambhunath in Kathmandu. Later, Paindapa accompanied Marpa to Pullahari, near Nalanda University, where Naropa used to teach. Marpa spent twelve years receiving abhishekas, instructions, and studying with Naropa and other great Indian gurus to whom Naropa sent him to study or receive instructions. At the end of twelve years, Marpa offered a ganachakra and sang his first song of realization to his guru, Naropa. Shortly after, he set forth on his journey back to Tibet, where he taught and continued his dharma activities.

Subsequently, Marpa traveled to India two more times and studied with Naropa and other great mahasiddhas of India. Of these, his main gurus were Naropa and Maitripa. In total, he traveled three times to India and four times to Nepal. On his third visit, Marpa went through an adventure in finding Naropa, because Naropa, having already entered into the tantric conduct, was nowhere to be found. However, with determination, trust, and devotion, Marpa managed to find Naropa and receive the final teachings and instructions from him. At that time, Naropa prophesied that a family lineage would not continue for Marpa, but that his lineage would be carried on by disciples—especially one with the appearance of a monk and the inner realization of Mahayana. This prophecy foretold of the arrival of Lord Gampopa.

Marpa now had received the full transmissions, so Naropa formally declared Marpa to be his dharma successor. Having received such a blessing and empowerment, Marpa offered a great feast. With the precious teaching from Naropa, Marpa returned to Tibet. He had brought the teachings and lineages of vajrayana and mahamudra back to Tibet.

On his return, Marpa gave many teachings. He was especially trying to spread the teaching of ejection of consciousness, of which he had had a very special transmission. With the accomplishment of this practice one can enter into the physical body of any dead being, and then become that being.

But Marpa was not too successful during his lifetime at accumulating students. He remained a short-tempered and aggressive teacher, and not many students liked him, and not many believed in his realization and his accomplishment.

But when Marpa was passing away, he performed many miracles. And after he passed into parinirvana, his transmissions became very widely cultivated and spread around Tibet. Only then did the people in his village and other villages realize what a highly realized and important person Marpa really was; only then did they start to develop profound feelings for him.

After his passing, there were four students who continued to spread Marpa's teachings, or the transmission of Marpa. There were three students who emphasized the learning of the skills that Marpa taught, and only one student, Milarepa, who emphasized meditation, the practice, and the experience of Marpa's teaching. (The four most outstanding students of Marpa were known as the "Four Pillars:" viz. 1) Ngok Chöku Dorje, who became the principal student to receive the transmissions and master the explanations of the Tantras, 2) Tsurtön Wanggi Dorje, who became the main student to receive the transmissions and master the practice of Phowa (transference of conciousness), 3) Meytön Chenpo, who became the primary student to receive the transmissions and master the practice of Ösal [luminosity], and 4) Milarepa, who became the principal student to receive the full transmissions and master the view, meditation, and conduct.

SPECIFIC SKILLS AND CONTRIBUTIONS

Upon his return to Tibet, Marpa spent many years translating Buddhist scriptures and contributed to the effort to bring the complete Buddha dharma to Tibet. Many of his translations are part of the Kagyur and Tangyur.

Marpa continued to practice and give teachings, abhishekas, and transmissions to many students in Tibet. After his third visit to India, Milarepa became his disciple, who inherited his lineage in full.

MEDICINE BUDDHA
(BHAISAJYAGURU)

Photo no 65 : *A partly gold plated statue of Medicine Buddha.*

INTRODUCTION

Bhaisajyaguru or Medicine Buddha (Tib: *Sangye Menla*), more formally Bhaisajyaguruvaidûryaprabha is known as the Master of Healing. In Mahayana Buddhism, Bhaisajyaguru represents the healing aspect of the historical Buddha Sakyamuni.

Bhaisajyaguru is described in the Bhaisajyaguru-sûtra as bodhisattva who made and fulfilled 12 vows, two of them related to healing. On achieving Buddhahood, he became the Buddha of the realm of Vaidûryanirbhâsa.

Medicine Buddha is often considered the Buddha of the Eastern Pure land (as red Amitabha is considered the Buddha of the Western Pure Land). Also, according to Sakya "Wish-fulfilling Gem" tradition, there are eight images of medicine buddha and they are as following :

1. Buddha Suparikirti'tanama'shri, (meaning- excellent name), depicted in golden.
2. Buddha Svaraghosha, (meaning- king of melody), depicted in yellow.
3. Buddha Suparna'bhadra (meaning- appearance of stainless fine gold), depicted in golden.
4. Buddha Ashok'attama'shri, (meaning- glorious supreme one, free of misery), depicted in pink.
5. Buddha Dharmakirti'sagaraghosha, (meaning- resounding dharma melody), depicted in white with reddish glow
6. Buddha Abhijna'raja, (meaning- king of direct knowledge), depicted in red as coral.
7. Buddha Bhaisajya'guru vaidurya'prabharaja, depicted in dark blue as lapis lazuli.
8. Buddha Shrijing Shakyamuni, (meaning- king of the Shakyas ('historical' Buddha) golden. As Supreme Physician or "Supreme Healer" there is a practice in which he alone is the Medicine Buddha.

ICONOGRAPHY

Medicine Buddha is depicted in deep blue color as that of gemstone lapis lazuli. He is typically shown in meditation mudra, wearing the three robes of a Buddhist monk. He holds a lapis-colored jar filled with medicine nectar or emerald in his left hand. His right hand rests on his right knee, holding the stem of the myrobalan plant between thumb and first finger.

DOCTRINE AND OTHERS

About the third century A.D., the Medicine Buddha was recorded in Buddhist texts as an emanation of the historical Buddha, who was considered the preeminent healing deity in the Mahayana Buddhist tradition.

The practice of Medicine Buddha, the Supreme Healer) is not only a very powerful method for healing and increasing healing powers both for oneself and others, but also for overcoming the inner sickness of attachment, hatred, and ignorance, thus to meditate on the Medicine Buddha can help decrease physical and mental illness and suffering.

Tibetan Buddhists consider the Medicine Buddha Empowerment to be the most powerful blessing for healing, dispelling sickness and for awakening the innate healing wisdom that lies within every individual

The practice of veneration of the Medicine Buddha is also popular in China, as he is depicted as one of the trinity of Buddhas, the others being the Gautama Buddha and Amitabha of the Pure Land sect. Like Tibetan Buddhists, Chinese Buddhists recite the mantra of the Medicine Buddha to overcome sickness.

A short version of the Medicine Buddha Mantra, which is known as the Medicine Budddha Heart Mantra is (tadyathâ) Om Bhaisajye Bhaisajye Mahâbhaisajye Bhaisajye Râjaya Samudgate Svâhâ.

Since the practice of Medicine Buddha is considered a Sutrayana practice (i.e., based mainly on scripture) no empowerment is necessary, but it is good to attend one or to ask for one when you have an opportunity.

MILAREPA

Photo no 66 : *A fully gold plated statue of Milarepa.*

INTRODUCTION

Jetsun Milarepa (1052-1135 CE) is generally considered one of Tibet's most famous yogis and poets, a student of Marpa Lotsawa, and a major figure in the history of the Kagyu school of Tibetan Buddhism.

SHORT BIOGRAPHY

Milarepa, whose childhood name was Mila Thopaga, was born to wealthy parents, Sherab Gyaltsen and Nyangtsa Kargyen, in a village called Kya Ngatsa in the western Tibet. His father passed away when he was seven years old. As stated in the will, his uncle was to take care of their property and riches until Milarepa came of a marriageable age. But, Mila, his sister and his mother were soon treated as servants by their greedy relatives. At fifteen years old, his mother requested that the land be returned because Milarepa was to marry. However, this was refused. So, his mother sent Milarepa to learn black magic with a motive to take revenge. After the completion of Milarepa's studies as a sorcerer, he caused the house of his evil relatives to collapse during a celebration, killing over thirty-five of them. The villagers were also angry and set off to look for Milarepa, but his mother got word to him, and he sent a hailstorm to destroy their crops. Although Mila's mother was content, Mila was disappointed and depressed. He thought the result of black magic would only be a negative rebirth. Also, Mila's own teacher of black magic said that at the time of death only the dharma, not magic, would help. Mila was comfortable to learn that his teacher of black magic also thought that such evil practices were not proper. His teacher told him to go to the Dzogchen teacher Rongton Lhaga. The Dzogchen Lama was unable to bring Mila to realization because Milarepa possessed a lot of negative karma and obstacles. So, he suggested Mila to go to Marpa Lotsawa. Great devotion arose in Milarepa, and he went to study under Marpa. When Marpa still refused to teach Milarepa he went to Marpa's wife, who took pity on him. She forged a letter of introduction to another teacher, Lama Ngogdun Chudor, under whose tutelage, he began to practice meditation. However, when he was making no progress, he confessed the forgery and Ngogdun Chudor said that it was vain to hope for spiritual growth without the guru's approval. Milarepa returned to Marpa, Marpa put Milarepa under several trials and hardships before teaching him the dharma. First, Mila was ordered to construct different sorts of oddly shaped houses and each one of them was then told to break down after completion. His hands often would be sore and his body worn after doing this many times. During that time, Marpa would give him the teachings of the common dharma. Once, Mila was ordered to build a nine story tower. Even after its completion, Milarepa did not receive any Vajrayana teachings from Marpa as he was expecting. Mila became increasingly depressed. He thought that dying would be the only solution to his suffering. On the other hand, Marpa thought Milarepa had been purified of his obscurations and non-virtues. It was the proper time then for him to bestow the Vajrayana transmissions. Subsequently, an empowerment of Chakrasamvara was held for Milarepa by Marpa Lotsawa. Milarepa began receiving transmissions and practice. In another ceremony, Marpa bestowed the Hevajra transmission to Milarepa by opening his chest and he showed the entire mandala of the deity there.

During most of his life, Mila meditated alone in the mountains and caves in the region of Tibet and Nepal, often unyielding to threats by demons and scarcity of food and water. For a considerable time, he merely sustained himself upon pine-like nettles. His body turned green due the same reason. There was a cave called by the name of Drakar Taso – which was later named after him as 'Milarepa's Cave'. After practicing very diligently for twelve years Milarepa attained the state of *Vajradhara* (complete enlightenment). Milarepa was consecrated in a Gompa called Pelgye Ling which was built near that cave. It was destroyed but has now been rebuilt and decorated by Nepali artisans.

Milarepa became renowned for his spontaneous poetic songs of realization which could tame the mind of even the most non-virtuous people. Milarepa often had to prove himself to many individuals, and had great powers of clairvoyance. He reached the summit of Mount Kailash, the abode of Chakrasamvara, in seconds, stunning everybody there. Other miracles of Milarepa included his ability to hold an entire region in his palm, and the ability to fit inside a yak horn.

Milarepa's main disciples were Rechungpa and Gampopa. Milarepa's teachings were capable to destroy dualistic views of persons. For example, Rechungpa's stubborn attitude was gradually overcome by Milarepa. Rechungpa would always desire to wander off and even travel to holy sites throughout India and Tibet, but Milarepa reminded him that with a realized guru the need for such places isn't necessary. Also, Milarepa cut through Gampopa's attachment as well.

SPECIFIC SKILLS AND CONTRIBUTIONS

Milarepa is famous for many of his songs and poems, in which he expresses the profundity of his realization of the dharma with extraordinary clarity and beauty. In Tibet, recordings of many of these songs and poems, which are known as *dohas* are available. Also the accounts of numerous wondrous acts of Milarepa which were performed in turning the minds of others towards the dharma are also documented.

He also had many disciples. Rechung Dorje Drakpa and Gampopa were two prominent ones. Gampopa became his spiritual successor who continued his lineage and became one of the main lineage masters in Milarepa's tradition.

Milarepa is said to be the first to achieve the state of Vajradhara within one lifetime.

A movie has been made about the life of Milarepa in 2006.

NAGARJUNA

Photo no 67 : *Nagarjuna.*

INTRODUCTION

Acharya Nâgârjuna (Tib: *Klu Sgrub*) (c. 150 - 250 CE) was an Indian philosopher, the founder of the *Madhyamaka* (Middle Path) school of Mahâyâna Buddhism, and arguably the most influential Buddhist thinker after Gautama Buddha himself.

His writings were the basis for the formation of the Madhyamaka (Middle Way) school, which was transmitted to China under the name of the Three Treatise (Sanlun) School.

He is credited with developing the philosophy of the Prajnaparamita sutras, and was closely associated with the Buddhist University of Nalanda.

In the Jodo Shinshu branch of Buddhism, he is considered the First Patriarch.

BRIEF BIOGRAPHY

(Nagarjuna was predicted by the Buddha Shakyamuni in the *Lankavatara sutra*: *"In Vedaili, in the southern part, a monk most illustrious and distinguished will be born; his name is Nagahvaya. He is the destroyer of one-sided views based on being and non-being. He will declare my vehicle, the unsurpassed Mahayana, to the world; attaining the stage of Joy, live for over six hundred years and he will go to the Land of Bliss."*)

Nagarjuna was born at a village called Vidarbha of South India to a Brahmin family in mid of the second century. It was predicted that the child would live for only seven days. It was also told that his life span would be extended by another seven days if alms were given to a hundred people, by a further seven months if offerings were made to a hundred brahmins, or by a further seven years if offerings were made to a hundred monks. The prophet knew of no method to extend his life beyond that. Accordingly, his parents made offerings to a hundred monks and he lived well for seven years. As the child's seventh birthday drew near, the parents sent him on a pilgrimage with several of their servants, for they could not bear to witness his death. It is said that the boy experienced a vision of Khasarpana Lokeshvara while traveling. The party reached Nalanda monastery. While they were standing near the dwelling of one Brahmin called Saraha, the boy uttered some verses of poetry. The Brahmin heard the lines, invited the party inside and enquired about their journey. He came to know about the plight of the boy. Brahmin Saraha replied that if the boy was to take a vow of renunciation, he would live. The boy agreed to do so. He gave the child an empowerment into the long-life practice of Buddha Amitayus, and told him to practice that yoga extensively. On the eve of his eighth birthday the child recited the mantra of Amitayus without interruption and, as a result, averted untimely death. The following day, he was ordained as a monk and his new name was Bhiksu Shrimanta.

At Nalanda, Nagarjuna studied sutra and tantra with Ratnamati, who was said to be an emanation of Manjushree and, with Saraha, especially *Guhyasamaja Tantra*. In addition, he learned alchemy from a Brahmin, and gained the ability to transmute iron into gold. Using this ability, he was able to feed the Nalanda monks during famine. Eventually, Nagarjuna became the abbot of Nalanda. He strictly observed the vinaya monastic rules and in the process, he expelled some eight thousand monks who did not do so.

During the time when Acharya was teaching the dharma of Tripitaka, two youths, who were emanations of the sons of the naga king called Taksaka, had also come. They smelt fragrance of sandalwood. Nagarjuna came to know about their reality and he asked for some sandalwood for a statue of Tara and also nagas' help in constructing temples. They returned to the naga realm and asked their father, who said he could help only if Nagarjuna came to their realm beneath the sea to teach them. Nagarjuna accepted this offer and went to their place and taught the nagas with some offerings as well. Nagarjuna had known that the nagas had *One Hundred Thousand Verse Prajnaparamita Sutra* (Skt. *Shatasahasrika-prajnaparamita Sutra*) and requested for that. When Buddha Sakyamuni had taught Prajnaparamita, (the perfection of wisdom), the nagas had taken one version of it back to their realm for safekeeping, while the gods kept another version, and the yaksha kept yet another version. Nagarjuna brought with him this one hundred thousand verse version. But the nagas had kept the last two chapters to ensure that Nagarjuna would return and teach them later. It is said that those missing last two chapters were later made up from the same of The *Eight Thousand Verse Prajnaparamita Sutra* (Skt. *Ashtasahasrika-prajnaparamita Sutra*). For that reason, the last two chapters of these two retentions are the same. Nagarjuna also brought back naga clay and built many temples and stupas with it. After securing the *Prajnaparamita Sutras* Acharya greatly advanced the influence of the Mahayana tradition. When he preached the Dharma in the monastery park, the nagas performed acts of reverence such as six of the serpents forming a parasol to shade him from the sun.

Later, Nagarjuna traveled to the northern continent of Kurava to teach. On the way, he met some children playing on the road. While reading palms, he prophesied that one of them, named Jetaka, would become a king. When Nagarjuna returned after completing his visit to Northern Island, the boy had in fact become the king of a large kingdom in South India. Nagarjuna stayed with him for three years, teaching him, and then spent his last years elsewhere in his kingdom, at Shri Parvata, the holy mountain overlooking modern-day Nagarjunakonda. Nagarjuna wrote for the King *A Precious Garland* (Skt. *Ratnavali*). This was the same king to whom Nagarjuna wrote *A Letter to a Friend* (Skt. *Suhrllekha*), namely King Udayibhadra. It is believed that King Udayibhadra was the same King Gautamiputra Shatakarni (ruled 106 – 130 C.E.) of the Shatavahana Dynasty. The Shatavahanas were patrons of the stupa in Amaravati, where Buddha had first taught *The Kalachakra Tantra* and which was close to Shri Parvata.

King Udayibhadra had a son, Kumara Shaktiman, who wanted to become king. His mother told him that he could never become a king until Nagarjuna died, because the King would not die as long as Nagarjuna lived. His mother said to request Nagarjuna for his head as he would not deny being a compassionate person. In fact, Nagarjuna did agree to Kumara for such a request. But Kumara could not cut his head off with a sword. Nagarjuna said that in one of his previous lives, he had killed an insect while cutting grass and as a karmic result, his head could only be cut off with a blade of *kusha* grass. Kumara did so and Nagarjuna died. The blood from the severed head turned into milk and the head said, "Now I will go to Sukhavati Pure Land, but I will enter this body again." Wicked Kumara took the head far away from the body, but it is said that the head and the body are coming closer together each year. When they join, Nagarjuna will return and teach again. All in all, it is said that Nagarjuna lived six hundred years.

SPECIFIC SKILLS AND CONTRIBUTIONS

Nagarjuna and his teachings are the forefront of Mahayana Buddhism. He is considered a patriarch in all the Mahayana schools. He commentated on the *Prajnaparamita Sutras*, and elucidated the *Middle Way* rejecting all opposites and dualistic views. He is credited with rediscovering the hidden treasures of the Buddha, which included the *Prajna Paramita and Avatsamsaka Sutras*. These sutras were under the protection of the *nagas*, serpent like dragons.

Nagarjuna also had many extraordinary abilities, such as changing ordinary phenomena into gold. He perfected longevity practice, thereby living for many centuries in India.

Among the many texts on sutra topics that Nagarjuna wrote are his *Collections of Reasoning, Collections of Praises* and *Collections of Didactic Explanations*

The *Six Collections of Reasoning* are:
- *Root Verses on Madhyamaka, called "Discriminating Awareness" (Skt. Prajna-nama- mulamadhyamaka-karika),*
- *Precious Garland* (Skt. *Ratnavali*),
- *Refutation of Objections* (Skt. *Vigrahavyavarti*).
- *Seventy Verses on Voidness* (Skt. *Shunyatasaptati*),

- *Sutra Called "Finely Woven"* (Skt. *Vaidalya-sutra-nama*),
- *Sixty Verses of Reasoning* (Skt. *Yuktishashtika*),

Included among his *Collections of Praise* are:

- *Praise to the Sphere of Reality* (Skt. *Dharmadhatu-stava*),
- *Praise to the Deepest Truth* (Skt. *Paramartha-stava*),
- *Praise to the Supramundane (Buddha)* (Skt. *Lokatita-stava*).

Included among Nagarjuna's *Collections of Didactic Explanations* are:

- *A Commentary on (the Two) Bodhichittas* (Skt. *Bodhichittavivarana*),
- *Anthology of Sutras* (Skt. *Sutrasamuccaya*),
- *Letter to a Friend* (Skt. *Suhrllekha*).

Also attributed to Nagarjuna are several two commentaries to *The Guhyasamaja Tantra*, including:

- *Abbreviated Means for Actualization* (Skt. *Pindikrta-sadhana*),
- *Method for Meditating on the Generation Stage of the Mahayoga Tantra Guhyasamaja Mixed with Its Textual (Sources)* (Skt. *Shri-guhyasamaja-mahayogatantra-utpattikrama-sadhana-sutra-melapaka*).
- *The Five Stage (Complete Stage)* (Skt. *Pancakrama*).

Nagarjuna's most famous disciple was Aryadeva, the author of *Four Hundred Verse Treatise on the Actions of a Bodhisattva's Yoga* (Skt. *Bodhisattvayogacarya-catu: shatakashastra-karika*) and several commentaries on *The Guhyasamaja Tantra*.

NAIRATMA

Photo no. 68 : *A statue of Nairatma.*

INTRODUCTION

Nairatma (translated as *"Lady of Emptiness"* or "She Who Has Realized Selflessness." Tib. Dagmena) is the egoless yogini and a fully enlightened female Buddha.

She is the source of all creation, the formless infinite reality form which all visible forms arise. She is enlightened spontaneity in female form,

Nairatma is another name for sunyata, or emptiness and selflessness. Her blue body signifies the emptiness of the sky.

ICONOGRAPHY

Photo no 69 : *Sacred dance ritual performance of Hevajra and Nairatmya.*

Her body is blue, the color of infinite space, reflecting the limitless expanse of her awareness. Like the element of space, she flows through the universe without impediment, for she has transcended ego-centered existence. Her eyes blaze with the wisdom of one who understands

160

the mysteries and depths of life. She raises her curved knife (kartika) skyward, poised to sever negative mind states wherever they arise. In her skull cup (kapala), she pulverizes illusions and returns them to their original state—a mere play of light, a rainbow of energy, shimmering in empty space.

DOCTRINE AND OTHERS

Photo no 70 : *Nairatma in Hevajra Statue*

The underlying methodology of the Hevajra teaching is the overcoming of ego and the attainment of non-self (Nairatma) that leads to enlightenment. Hevajra, dances, embracing his prajna, Nairatma. In his eight right hands he holds skull cups containing animals, while in his eight left hands he holds skull cups containing humans. Each of these cups is a specific offering made to Hevajra by the meditators as Nairatma and her emanations.

In Hevajra tantra, Nairatma is described thus :

A supremely blissful divine yogini.
She is the mansion of enlightened awareness,
Possessor of the five Buddha-wisdoms
She is pure, universal awareness,
The sovereign of the mandala.
She is Nairatmya Yogini,
The essence of ultimate reality.

NAMGYALMA
(USHNISHAVIJAYA)

Photo no 71 : *A partly gold plated statue of Namgyalma (Usnisha-vijaya)*

INTRODUCTION

Namgyalma or Ushnishavijaya (Tib: *Tsug Tor Nam Par Gyelma* or shortened to Namgyalma) is a Buddha Mother who arises from the Buddha's Crown. The eight-armed goddess Namgyalma is one of three deities associated with longevity and the fulfillment of earthly desires (other two being White Tara and Amitayus).

Namgyalma also represents the Mother of all Buddhas. Like all Buddhist deities, she is essentially a manifestation of Emptiness acting as a bodhisattva. She is able to bestow longevity.

She is a purification deity as well, invoked in the presence of the dead, and she is also invoked as a means of settling disputes.

ICONOGRAPHY

Ushnisha-vijaya is a peaceful white deity and an emanation of Vairochana Buddha. She has three faces and eight hands. Each face has one eye at the forehead. There is also an eye in the palm of one hand. Her three right hands hold a small Buddha image, a vishva-vajra (double dorje) and an arrow respectively and the fourth right hand is held in giving posture rested at the knee. Her first hand is kept facing away and an eye is shown in the palm. Other left three hands hold a lasso, a bow, and a vase with the nectar of immortality.

Her middle face and eight arms are white, symbolizing the elimination of disasters. The yellow face on the left side symbolizes prosperity and longevity while the blue face on the right side symbolizes the defeat of devils.

DOCTRINE AND OTHERS

There is a story about a deva called Paripu Denpa from the time when Shakyamuni Buddha was on earth. As a result of karma, when devas start experiencing the signs of death, they spontaneously remember their previous lives and see their future lives. They perceive that they are about to be reborn in the lower realms and so forth. As their realm has unbelievable enjoyment which is thousand times better than those of the richest on earth and when they realize that they are about to leave a life of such pleasure and be reborn where there is an unbearable suffering, then their minds suffer greatly.

Thus, as he was going to die, the deva Denpa saw that he was about to be reborn as seven types of animal viz. a pig, a dog, a fox, a monkey, a snake, an eagle and a hawk. He was very worried and asked King Indra what can be done. King Indra suggested that he should see the Buddha, which he did. Buddha manifested as the deity Namgyalma and gave him the mantra. Denpa recited it six times daily and in seven days completely changed his karma so that he did not have to be reborn as those seven types of animals.

The kind, compassionate Shakyamuni Buddha taught the benefits of reciting the Namgyalma mantra to the Four Guardian Kings also

The long mantra of Namgyalma is a practice which is very powerful not only for granting long life but also for purification. For example, if it is written on a piece of cloth or a piece of paper and placed on a mountain top or roof where the wind can blow it, whoever is touched by the wind receives blessings and their negative karma is purified. Circumambulating a stupa that contains the mantra purifies all the karma to be reborn in the hot hells. It is said that if one engraves or pastes Namgyalma's mantra on a bell, when anyone hears the clear resonating sounds of the bell, one's troubles are dispelled in a moment. It also helps wisdom to grow and develop. It also has the profound effect of inducing the thought of repentance among beings suffering in the unfortunate realms. Even if any other beings, say animals, etc hear it, they will never again be reborn in the lower realms.

A short mantra of Namgyalma is like this:

Mantra : *Om drum soha, Om amrita ahyur daday soha om ah hung tam hri/ang ah rakya rakya mam sarwa satam tsa soha!*

NAMSANGITI MANJUSHREE

Photo no 72 : *Namsangiti Manjushree.*

INTRODUCTION

Namasangiti is one of the important manifestations of Manjushree, the embodiment of wisdom of all the Buddhas. It is said that Namasangiti Manjushree was already enlightened countless aeons ago.

Countless Buddhas of ten directions have been his disciples. Therefore he was called Adi-Buddha Manjushree. Namasangiti text has more than eight hundred words of deep spiritual significance describing this deity.

During Shakyamuni's time, he appeared himself as one of his eight chief bodhisattva disciples.

ICONOGRAPHY

In the usual form, Namasangiti Manjushree has one head and twelve arms. He is seated with dhyanamudra. He wears all the bodhisattva ornaments typical of Sambhogakaya aspects. He has Ushnisa in his head and wears a crown. His uppermost pair of arms forms the *uttarabodhi mudra* (prostration position) above his head. His other pair of hands at the chest level forms in a dharma chakra mudra. Another pair of hands forms a *tarpana mudra* i.e about to offer water from the alms bowl. Other pair of hands holds an alms bowl kept in the lap. Two right hands hold a sword and an arrow respectively. Similarly, two left hands hold a scripture on a lotus and an arrow respectively. This form of Namasangiti is very popular in Kathmandu valley and one fully gold plated statue can be seen at Golden Temple, Patan, Nepal.

DOCTRINE AND OTHERS

The mentions of Manjushree are found as early as 3rd century in Aryamanjushrimulakalpa and Guhyasamajtantra. In Namsangiti he is referred to as Adi Buddha. The depiction of twelve armed Manjushree as Namsangiti Manjushree may be perhaps the birat rupa almighty emanation of Manjushree. As such, there are several other forms of Manjushree with different attributes and essence as well. Both tantric and non-tantric depictions of Manjushree have resulted in multitude of his representations. Saddharmapundarik, Manjushree is described as being closely related to Shakyamuni Buddha. In Svayambhupurana, Manjushree is described as the founder of Nepalese civilisation and culture. Some people believe that, as a Buddhist monk, Manjushree spread Buddhism in Nepal. He is also regarded as the god of agriculture, architect of the spiritual world and the god of science. In Nepal, the first day of the year is dedicated to Manjusri and is celebrated in grand style.

In Mahayana Buddhism, perhaps, the popularity of Manjushree comes next to the Avalokiteshvara. Since 4th century, Manjushree occupied a very important position among Buddhists as the god of metaphysical knowledge. Mahayana Buddhists believe that Manjushree is one of the leading Bodhisattvas and that those who worship him obtain knowledge, superior memory, intelligence, ready wit and oratorical powers.

NAROPA

Photo no 73 : *Naropa*

INTRODUCTION

Nâropa (956-1050) was an Indian Buddhist mystic and monk, the disciple of Tilopa.

Another introduction of him is that Nâropa was the main teacher of Marpa.

Nâropa was a part of the 'Golden Garland', meaning a lineage holder of the Tibetan Buddhist Kagyu lineage, and was considered an accomplished scholar. A great meditator, he is best known for having enumerated and developed the six yogas of Nâropa. These practices were designed to help achieve a more rapid attainment of enlightenment.

ICONOGRAPHY

Naropa is generally dressed in white lower garments of a yogi. His body is of ash color like that of a wandering mendicant. His right hand holds a skull cup filled with nectar and his left hand holds fish which is an auspicious symbol.

BRIEF BIOGRAPHY

Naropa was born in the small kingdom of Bengal. His father was a royal chieftain of an area named Shantivarman and his mother was called Srimati. His yearning for spiritual development was so strong that, when he was eight years old, he journeyed to Kashmir (one of the main seats for Buddhist studies in historical times) in order to study with the master Gaganakirti. It was from Gaganakirti that he received his lay ordination.

Naropa remained in Kashmir for three years, learning Buddhist teachings and philosophies from many great masters. By the end of his stay there he was an erudite scholar and, upon returning home, already had a number of students following him as their master.

Three years after his return from Kashmir, Naropa was forced by his parents to marry a lovely Brahmin girl, Vimaladipi (also known by her caste name, Niguma). Although, they were happily married, Naropa's ardent wish to live a full spiritual life in a monastic environment became increasingly strong and Niguma also began to take spiritual practice seriously. After eight years of marriage, the couple decided to divorce and take ordination orders. Later, Niguma became one of Naropa's most advanced disciples and a devoted spiritual companion; she served Naropa when he lived in Pullahari, Kashmir.

After the divorce, Naropa went to the hermitage of Anandarama, where he was ordained as a novice by Abbot Buddhasarana and the guru Jnanaprabha, with whom, he stayed for three years, mastering various Mahayana and Tantrayana philosophies. He then stayed in Pullahari for six years and wrote several commentaries on Guhyasamajatantra, Abhidharma-uttaratantra, Samvara-udbhava and Hevajratantra and composed many other works based on the Buddha's teachings. Pullahari, later became an important pilgrimage site in the Tibetan Buddhist tradition, because it was one of the places where Marpa received instructions from Naropa.

After his stay in Pullahari, Naropa went to Nalanda University at the age of 28. He studied Sutra and Tantra there. His wisdom, oratory skills and spiritual understanding earned him the chancellorship of the university. He gained the reputation as a great scholar and faultless debater, essential at that time as the tradition of debate was such that the loser automatically became a student of the winner. He eventually become Gatekeeper of the North; engaged in many debates, taught and won many students. Throughout his eight years' residence at Nalanda, he was constantly faced with difficult debates with the Tirthikas, but was regularly victorious in these. At this time, he was known as Mahapandita Ahbaya Kirti (Tib. *Jigme Dragpa*).

Naropa's years at Nalanda were mostly engaged in intellectual activities until an old and ugly woman – who was in fact a manifestation of Vajra Yogini – appeared before him and made him realize that he was not managing to break through his spiritual misconceptions and misunderstandings. She pointed out that he should look for his destined guru Tilopa, if he wished to attain Ultimate Liberation. As a result of this meeting, Naropa left Nalanda, searching earnestly for Tilopa – a great master who could lead him to realize the ultimate nature of his own mind.

Traveling eastward, Naropa finally met his destined root guru, who instantly put him through difficult tests. Naropa experienced twelve major and twelve lesser hardships in order to purify his karma and emotion-induced obscurations. Through receiving great blessings from Tilopa and accomplishing his own purification, Naropa realized the clarity and harmony of mind – truly experiencing the state of Vajradhara.

After attaining this magnificent realization, Naropa taught in many places and had numerous disciples, especially in Kashmir and Zanskar where he established many monasteries.

Naropa spent twelve years serving his guru Tilopa until the latter's death. He is remembered for his trust and devotion to his teacher, which enabled him to attain enlightenment in one lifetime.

Naropa himself was said to live until AD1050 or 1100 (according to the other source) and then resurrected into light, leaving no physical remains.

Amongst Naropa's accomplished disciples was Marpa, the translator, who succeeded Naropa in the lineage and brought the teachings and transmissions in their entirety to Tibet.

SPECIFIC SKILLS AND CONTRIBUTIONS

Naropa is recognized as one of the eighty-four great mahasiddhas in the history of Buddhism.

The six yogic practices put forward by Naropa had been carried through many subsequent Kagyus Karmapas and passed on through an unbroken lineage to the present day.

Naropa University was named in his honour.

PADMAPANI LOKESHVARA

Photo no 74 : *Padmapani Lokeshvara*

INTRODUCTION

Padmapani Lokeshvara is one of the several forms of Avalokiteshvara, the Bodhisattva of Compassion, the most popular deity in the Buddhist pantheon.

Among the many forms of Avalokiteshvara, this two-armed, single-faced form called Padmapani is probably the oldest. He is shown standing at the right side of Amitabha Buddha in Sukhavati heaven.

ICONOGRAPHY

Padmapani Lokeshvara has one face and two arms. His right hand is in *varada-mudra*. His left hand holds *a* lotus flower. He is depicted in red color. Amitabha Buddha is placed in the crown of Padmapani Lokeshvara.

DOCTRINE AND OTHERS

During the Buddha Sakyamuni's life, he manifested as one of the Buddha's major bodhisattva disciples and played an important role in many of the Buddha's discourses, including the Heart Sutra, in which he explains how a bodhisattva gains direct insight into the ultimate nature of reality.

There is a popular legend relating to the name of Padmapani. Once, an elephant was just coming out of a pond after picking up a lotus flower, but he got swamped and could not come out. Then he prayed Narayan for help. During that time, Arya Avalokiteshvara was in that area and he heard the prayer. He immediately took the form of Narayan and rescued the elephant from drowning into the pond. The elephant offered the lotus flower out of gratitude to Arya Avalokiteshvara, who offered the same to Buddha Sakyamuni, who was residing in the nearby Jetavana grove. Buddha Sakyamuni in turn, requested him to offer the lotus flower to Amitabha Buddha on his behalf. When Arya Avalokiteshvara offered the lotus flower to

Amitabha Buddha, Amitabha Buddha told him to keep that lotus flower to himself after appreciating his benevolent act of rescuing the elephant and keep continuing such acts of benefiting all sentient beings. That form of Avalokiteshvara was thus named Padmapani Lokeshvara.

There are several images of Padmapani Lokeshvara especially in Kathmandu valley of Nepal.

PADMASAMBHAVA

Photo no 75 : *Padmasambhava*

INTRODUCTION

Padmasambhava (also Padmakara or Tib: *Pema Jungne*), in Sanskrit meaning "lotus-born", is said to have brought Tantric Buddhism to Tibet in the 8th century.

In Bhutan and Tibet he is better known as Guru Rinpoche ("Precious Master") where followers of the Nyingma School regard him as the second Buddha.

SHORT BIOGRAPHY

The history of the *Oral Transmission of Kilaya* and most Indian sources state that Padmasambhava was born as the son of a royal heir, Prince Mahusita of Dhankosha in Uddiyana (732 AD) and his name was Dhanaraksita. But the terma treasures of most part narrate that he was incarnated as an eight-year-old child appearing in a lotus blossom floating in Lake Dhanakosha, in the kingdom of Uddiyana. Moreover, in some texts, he is said to have appeared from a bolt of lightning at the summit of Mount Malaya.

Padmasambhava had his childhood times at the care of the King Indrabuti of Uddiyana. He was named Padmakara then. His ability to memorize and comprehend esoteric texts in a single hearing established his reputation. About five years of his stay in palace, in one incident, a wife and a son of a minister were killed by letting fall a scepter and a trident from the roof. As a result, Padmasambhava was punished and exiled in a charnel ground. Instead of being discouraged, he quit the princely dress and engaged in the conduct of yogic disciplines. During this time, he received empowerment and blessings from the two dakinis.

Later, political turmoil griped Uddiyana and many things underwent changes there. Padmasambhava moved in the direction of Kashmir. He journeyed through the northern mountains bordering Tibet. He passed his time wandering with yogis and saddhus, in exile from his homeland. Also, it was during this period that he acquired worldly knowledge and skill in various crafts. However, in Kashmir he earned the name Sthiramati, the Youthful Genius.

On pilgrimage to Bodh Gaya this Yogi-Prince became a disciple of Bhikshu Prabhahasti. With the Kashmiri pandit Ananda acting as the master (acarya) and Prabhahasti acting as the preceptor (upadhaya), Padmasambhava received the full ordination of a Buddhist monk. He then received the ordination name of Bhikshu Sakyasimha, the Lion of the Sakyas. Living in the Bodh Gaya area, he disciplined himself in the path of virtue and contemplation, while receiving instruction in the Vinaya Discipline from Ananda and instruction in philosophy, logic and metaphysics from Prabhahasti. Then, he was told to go to the Sitavana cremation ground and study the traditions of the Vidyadharas living there. In the Sitavana cremation ground near Bodh Gaya, he received empowerment and instruction from Vajra Humkara in the practice of Vajrasattva. Then, when he was a little matured, he received special transmission into the wrathful aspects of the great Bodhisattvas from the eight great Insight-holders, or Vidyadhara. Each of these Vidyadharas, taught him a unique sadhana, or spiritual practice, based on their own realization and on the practice by which they had attained Enlightenment. Thus he acquired eight sadhana practices. These practices pertain to what is known as the Mahayoga tantra.

Photo no 76 : *One form of Padmasambhava (Shakya Senge)*

Of the eight Vidyadharas whom Lord Padmasambhava studied under in the Sitavana grove, the chief guru was Vajra Humkara, who was also the guru of his teacher and abbot Prabhahasti. Vajra Humkara told Padmasambhava to go and study at the feet of his own beloved guruji, Sri Simha. Going to the Cina Valley, Padmasambhava found Sri Simha living as a yogi in a cremation ground. He requested the guru Sri Simha to teach him. From Sri Simha, Padmasambhava received the mystical tantric empowerments and teachings. Then in various cremation grounds, inhabited by yogis and yoginis in Cina, and in the famous Eight Sacred Cremation grounds of India, the diligent practitioner Padmasambhava struggled to attain realization. Living like an ascetic hermit, he was known as *Suryabhasa Yogi*, the Sun-ray Mystic.

Photo no 77 : *Two form of Padmasambhava (Padmasambhava)*

Then, Padmasambhava went to the Kathmandu Valley of Nepal. At that time, the main Buddhist center of Nepal happened to be the town of Patan where four stupas were built by the Emperor Ashoka in the third century B.C. The Yogi stayed there for some time, but chose to move to to Pharphing, which lies in the hills to the southwest of Kathmandu (which happened to be the place where his guru Humkara had gained the final Great Seal of Buddhahood and beheld the Divine Being (Vajrasattva) face to face after practicing for six months with his yogini-wife in the nearby cave called *Lang-le-sho*). In this cave, Padmasambhava and his consort Sakyadevi jointly practiced the sadhana of Vajrasattva as Sri Samyak Vajra Heruka (Tib: *Yangdag Heruka*). They practiced for about twelve months initially. Some obstacles arose and they did not succeed in acquiring true union, or mahamudra, with Divinity. Obstacles also manifested on the external plane. Disease and famine caused by drought spread throughout the Kathmandu Valley. Then, upon the suggestion of Sakyadevi, Padmasambhava wrote a missive to Vidyadhara Prabhahasti, beseeching his guidance. Bound by compassion for his beloved disciple and heir, the guru sent two mule-loads of Vajrakilaya-practice texts. Immediately all the obstacles afflicting the course of progress was eradicated and Padmasambhava began to meditate with renewed ease.

It is said that as soon as the mule-load arrived on the outskirts of Katmandu with sacred texts, it began to rain thus, ending the drought. It is said that when Padmasambhava performed the powerful Vajrakilaya rites, he made it rain by subduing three kinds of elemental spirits. These spirits, or forces, are referred to as Nagas or serpentine spirits of water, Yakshas or giant spirits of the earth, and Kumbhandas or sylph-like spirits of air. He mastered these primitive spiritual forces through mastery of the Garuda or phoenix-like spirit of fire. Meditating on Supreme Vajrasattva Heruka as the translucent image of compassionate wrathful (energized) activity, they together acquired the mahamudra of Divinity and attained complete Great Enlightenment. In an exulted state of mind, upon emerging from the cave where their meditations had taken place, Padmasambhava placed his hand against the rock face of the mountain, leaving impressed for ever in stone a miraculous handprint. His handprint can be seen even now outside the entrance of Lang-le-sho cave, where he and his consort Sakyadevi attained simultaneous Enlightenment.

180

Photo no 78 : *Third form of Padmasambhava (Pema Gyalpo)*

Later, Padmasambhava was asked to come to Nalanda University to debate against a number of proud Hindu intellectuals, who were drawing many away from the practice of the Dharma by means of their brilliant scholastic arguments. Consequently, he left Nepal and once more ventured down into the hot plains of India. Having vanquished the Hindu scholars through means of impeccable logic, the five hundred chief professors of Nalanda University conferred on him the honorary title of *Maha-pandita*, or great Pandit, and he was given the name of Vadisimha, fierce Lion of Debate.

A group of Hindu religious who had been defeated by the Lord in the great debate at Nalanda University became so enraged that they determined to attempt assassination. Seizing Lord Padmasambhava, while he was out walking one day near the Ganges River, they dragged him to the bank of the river and threw him down into the fast rushing waters. Then, they began to stone him. Yet miraculously, Padmasambhava merely floated, unharmed, in a meditative pose, on the surface of the river, while each stone, as it struck his body, turned instantly into a delicate flower. In a very short time, his luminous bodily form was surrounded by flower petals, dancing on the sparking waves, and the mob, which had only moments earlier felt such enmity towards him, was completely awed by what they saw.

Photo no 79 : *Fourth form of Padmasambhava (Senge Dradrok)*

Then, the precious Lord thought it was time he propagated the Dharma in different parts of the world, beginning with the Himalayan kingdom of Zahor. The sovereign of Zahor was King Arshadhara, a powerful ruler of a small state closely aligned with the Tibetan Empire. The brother of the King of Zahor was a renowned Buddhist monk and scholar known as *Upadhyaya Santaraksita*. The king also had a daughter called Mandarava. It was in Zahor, that the great Master was first addressed as Lord Padmasambhava, the Lotus-born Guru, and was praised as a second Buddha. Princess Mandarava had many suitors, but not wishing to be married to any of them, she had abandoned worldly life and had become a Buddhist nun. She lived in a royal convent of nuns in Zahor. Lord Padmasambhava became Mandarava's teacher and soon they became tantric lovers. When King Arshadhara heard that his daughter was involved with a man, and not understanding the situation, he ordered that the culprits should be punished. The King's officers, therefore, had the princess dragged from her convent and thrown into a pit. They seized Lord Padmasambhava, flogged him, and bound him to a stake, to be burnt. They then set fire to the stake.

Photo no 80 : *Fifth form of Padmasambhava (Nyima Ozer)*

Unbelievable, as it might seem, the Lord's transfigured body was invincible to the elements. Fire could not touch him. Although, he looked and appeared physical, his body was so highly developed into what is called a "rainbow-body" that it behaved more like a light-image or like a type of energy, rather than an ordinary material body. When the King's men burnt him at the stake, he miraculously escaped injury. Then, rain is said to have extinguished the flames. The rain caused floods to pour into the valley, where he was bound. When the storm cleared and the smoke from the pyre was gone, instead of a charred corpse, what the witnesses saw was an image of the yogi and yogini together on a lotus, in the midst of a small lake, in the holy form of the eternal Vajrasattva. That sacred lake near the town of Mandi, still exits today.

Afterwards, Lord Padmasambhava married Princess Manadarava and together they departed for the Maratika Cave in the Himalayas to perform the sadhana of Amitayus, the Bodhisattva of Vitality and Longevity. The mystic couple continued to live in Nepal for many years after that.

183

Padmasambhava's visit to Tibet: - When King Trisong Deutsen was twenty years of age, he developed a strong aspiration to spread the sacred teachings of the Dharma. He invited Khenpo Bodhisattva from India who taught about dependent origination and the ten virtuous actions. A year later, the foundation was laid for a huge temple but the spirits of Tibet created obstacles and prevented the building. In accordance with the Khenpo's prediction, the king sent five runners to invite the great master Padmakara to come. In 786, Padmasambhava made a visit to Tibet from Nepal.

Photo no 81 : *Sixth form of Padmasambhava (Dorje Drollo)*

Fresh enthusiasm flourished to initiate the plans for founding a major Buddhist establishment in the heart of Tibetan territory. After exorcising the negative demonic forces and consecrating of the site by Guru Rinpoche, Samye Monastery, Tibet's first sizeable Buddhist academy was brought under construction in 787 A.D.

Guru Rinpoche then came back to Nepal. Construction of Samye continued for the next four years. Samye Monastery was completed in 791 A.D. After the completion of Samye, four lamas were sent to Vrikramasila University in India. They brought back with them twelve monks of the Sarvastivada Order. Then, the first candidates for monastic life were selected. And first ordination ceremony took place that year. This marked the founding of the Nyingma School in Tibet.

It was not until seven years after his first visit that our Lotus Master came once again to the auspicious realm of Tibet. By that time, Samye Monastery had been erected. This time, the Emperor begged for tantric teachings. Consequently, Lord Padmasambhava conferred the sacred Empowerments of the sadhanas of the Eight Mandalas of Mahayoga Tantra upon his chief Disciples.

Photo no 82 : *7th form of Padmasambhava (Loden Chokse)*

It is customary for the disciple to offer a mandala of the whole material world to his or her guru in exchange for instruction. Such a mandala is a symbolic renunciation of the worldly condition. Trisong Detsan went to extreme lengths in making his mandala offering. He actually gifted his entire empire into the guru's hands. Seating Lord Padmasambhava on a jewel-encrusted throne, he offered the four districts of Central Tibet along with Tsang as the center of the mandala; eastern Kham province and his territories in China and Jang as the eastern realm; Jar, Kongpo and Bhutan as the southern realm; the kingdoms of Hor, Central Asia and Changthang as the northern realm; Kailash, Zang-zung, Baltistan and Hunza as the western realm. He arranged pieces of gold and silver to represent the sun, moon and stars, and as an offering of sensual delight he bestowed Yeshe Tsogyal, princess of Karchen, one of the ladies of his harem. This was no mere symbolic gesture. The Emperor legally bestowed his possessions in this manner on Padmasambhava.

Lesser spiritual leaders might readily have been enticed by the power, wealth and vast lands placed in his hands. But, Guru Padmasambhava, was unmoved by material desire. He thanked the humble Emperor, but returned the gifts. The princess Yeshe Tsogyal alone he accepted, taking her only on 100 Suvama Sampradaya condition that she freely become his disciple, which she did. With his deep insight, he had seen in her the potential to become his successor and spiritual heir. He therefore was glad to retain her in his company.

In similar ways, the Guru gradually tamed the Emperor's heart and made him a disciple worthy to receive the light of understanding. He taught Tri-song Detsan, imbued with the spirit of warfare, to lay down his weapons of fear and embrace the gentle Buddhist law of love and compassion. He taught him how to become a devotee of the spirit of Truth.

When the time was right, Lord Padmasambhava bestowed on the imperial disciple the mystical Empowerment and Oral Transmissions for Mahayoga practice. He gave the blessings of the lineage of Masters and bestowed on Tri-song Detsan an ocean of grace to plant within him the seeds of Enlightenment. Through the power of the Lord's blessing, the intellect of the Sage-Emperor acquired the wished for treasure of treasures: an unobstructed vision of his own true nature. The Sage-Emperor abdicated the throne in 797 in favour of his son Mu-ne Tsanpo and went into Meditation Retreat, where he practiced meditation until his death in 803 A.D.

Having taught her the innermost Heart Point doctrine of Dzogchen, he empowered Yeshe Tsogyal, the princess of Kharchen, as his spiritual heir. She fully practiced his instruction and attained enlightenment in her lifetime. Then she too accepted disciples and passed on the precious teachings. The succession of Dzogchen Masters that descends from her is known as the Khadro Nying-t'ig lineage.

In Tibet, Padmasambhava had a great number of other disciples. The predominant members of his following consisted of: the Twenty-five Imperial Disciples; the Eighty Disciples of Yerpa, all of whom attained rainbow-body; the 108 Great Contemplatives of Chu-wo Mountain; the 30 Great Ngakpas (tantric masters) of Yang-dzong, in the Drak Valley; the Twenty-five sainted female Dakinis; the fifty-five Realized Ones of Shel-drak, in the Yarlung Valley; and the seven precious Yoginis.

Guru Rinpoche had visited in person the 20 Snow Mountains of Ngari, the 21 places of practice in Central Tibet and Tsang, the 25 sacred places of Dokham, the three hidden valleys, and numerous other places each of which he blessed to be a sacred place of practice. Knowing that a descendant of the king would later try to destroy Buddhism in Tibet, he gave many predictions for the future. Conferring with the king and the close disciples, Padmakara concealed countless terma teachings headed by the eight personal treasures of the king, the five great mind treasures, and the 25 profound treasures.

Photo no 83 : *8th form of Padmasambhava (Tsokye Dorje)*

The reasons for hiding these termas were to prevent the teachings of Secret Mantra from destroying, to avoid corrupting or modifying the Vajrayana scriptures by so-called intellectuals, to preserve the blessings and to benefit future disciples. For each of these hidden treasures, Padmakara predicted the time of the disclosure, the person who would reveal them, and the destined recipients who would hold the teachings. He manifested in the terrifying wrathful form of crazy wisdom in the thirteen places named Tiger's Nest binding all the mundane spirits under oath to serve the Dharma and entrusted them to guard the terma treasures. At that time he was named Dorje Drollo.

To inspire faith in future generations, he left an imprint of his body at Bumtang, hand prints at Namtso Chugmo, Pharping, Nepal and footprints at Paro Drakar, as well as in innumerable other places of practice.

Guru Rinpoche remained in Tibet for 55 years and six months; 48 years while the king was alive and seven years and six months afterwards. He arrived when the king was 21. The king passed away at the age of 69. Padmakara stayed for a few years after that before leaving for the land of the rakshas.

After the death of King Trisong Deutsen, Padmakara placed Mutig Tsenpo on the throne. He performed a drubchen at Tramdruk where he entrusted the profound teachings to Gyalsey Lhaje, the second prince, and prophesized that he would benefit beings by becoming a revealer of the hidden treasures in thirteen future lives.

It is impossible to count exactly how many students in Tibet received empowerment from Padmakara in person, but the most renowned are the original twenty-five disciples, the intermediate 25 disciples and the later 17 and 21 disciples. There were 80 of his students who attained rainbow body at Yerpa and also the 108 meditators at Chuwori, the 30 tantrikas at Yangdzong, the 55 realized ones at Sheldrag. Of female disciples there were the 25 dakini students and seven yoginis. Many of these close had blood lines that have continued until the present day.

When about to leave for the land of rakshas to the southwest, the king, the ministers and all the disciples tried to dissuade Padmakara from parting but to no avail. He gave each of them extensive advice and teachings and departed from the pass of Gungtang, riding on a horse or a lion, accompanied by numerous divine beings making offerings. At the summit of the Glorious Copper-colored Mountain on the Chamara continent he liberated Raksha Totreng, the king of the rakshas, and assumed his form. After that, he miraculously created the palace of Lotus Light endowed with inconceivable decorations and also emanated a replica of himself on each of the surrounding eight islands where they reside as kings who teach the eight heruka sadhanas.

When in 804 A.D, it came time for the Lord to depart from the great land of Tibet; he was escorted by the young Emperor Mu-ne Tsan-po, by the powerful nobility, the people, and especially by his favoured disciples, to the Mang-yul Pass. He went, it is said, towards the southwest, to the Sacred Red Mountain of Lankapuri, where he took possession of the Palace and ruled as a king of righteousness. It is said eventually, he entered the pure Buddha-field of Akanishta where he abides in spirit to this day. There are other fascinating stories about him describing his final days in the world. According to one, it is said that at the Mang-yul Pass he climbed onto a celestial *Changshe-Ta* and flew away like a shooting star, passing out of sight into the depths of the shining sky. Yet one another account declares that it was a Ta-chok or sacred white horse that carried him into the heavens. Still other stories state that he rode a sky-faring tiger. When he arrived at Lankapuri, he tamed a presiding ruler who was an ogre named *Rosary of Skulls* while others stated that he incarnated and took possession of the body of this evil king called Kapalamala. Then he spread the gentle ways of true Dharma in the kingdom and he came also to be known as Vajra Kapalamala.

People believe that, at present, he dwells on the vidyadhara level of spontaneous presence in the form of the regent of Vajradhara. Full of compassion he sends out emanations to benefit beings. In the future, when Buddha Maitreya appears in this world, Padmakara will emanate as Drowa Kundul and spread the teachings of Secret Mantra to all worthy people.

Specific Masterys and Contributions:

It is said that even the great bodhisattvas are incapable of fully explaining his life example. Padmakara's activity for bringing people to the path of liberation by means of appearing in various places, in various forms, speaking various languages is indeed beyond measure. Padmasambhava is said to have taken eight forms or manifestations (Tib. Guru Tsen Gye) representing different aspects of his being - wrath, pacification, etc.:1. Guru Orgyen Dorje Chang 2. Guru Shakya Senge 3. Guru Pema Gyalpo 4. Guru Padmasambhava 5. Guru Loden Chokse 6. Guru Nyima Ozer 7. Guru Dorje Drolo and 8. Guru Senge Dradog

He had hidden a number of religious treasures (*termas*) in temples, lakes, caves, fields and forests of the Himalayan region to be found and interpreted by future *tertöns* or spiritual treasure-finders. Tertons have been revealing those termas as predicted. It is almost impossible to access how much benefits such activities of Guru Rinpoche this world would be getting out of all this. According to Tibetan tradition, the Bardo Thodol (commonly referred to as the Tibetan Book of the Dead) was among these hidden treasures, subsequently discovered by a Tibetan terton, Karma Lingpa.

He is truly the archetypal Sage and Saint, and the mystical Prince of the kings of this earth. For the Dzogchen adept he is the supreme example of the perfect, accomplished yogi-master. For Tibetan Buddhism as a whole he is the living embodiment of compassionate Buddhahood.

Mantra : *Om Ah Hum Vajra Guru Pema Siddhi Hum*

PALDEN LHAMO

Photo no 84 : *Palden Lhamo*

INTRODUCTION

Palden Lhamo (Skt: *Sri Devi*) is considered the chief guardian-goddess of the Tibetan pantheon, and is the only female among the eight *Dharmapala*, the Guardians of the Dharma. She appears as an acolyte or protector figure in the galaxy of most Tibetan Buddhist sects. But in the Gelugpa, she is given particular prominence, as a protectress of the Dalai and Panchen Lamas, and the principal guardian goddess of Lhasa. She is also greatly venerated by followers of the Gelugpa in Mongolia and China. She is named *Okkin Tungri* there.

Palden Lhamo is also one of the most important Dharmapalas or Dharma protectors in the Sakya tradition, second only to the Mahakala Parjanatha. She is considered to be the consort of Mahakala, and the wrathful manifestation of *Saraswati*.

Palden Lhamo is a powerful protector against obstacles in practice, and is the special protector of H.H. Dagchen Rinpoche and his family.

Remati is also a name of the very wrathful form of Palden Lhamo.

This deity is called *chhasakamani* in local language in Nepal and worshipped to drive away evil incidents.

ICONOGRAPHY

As, Remati she is depicted as dark blue, with 3 eyes, she is shown wielding a sickle or a sandalwood club, and holding a blood-filled skull while seated on her mule. Some depictions show her with four arms.

The iconographic representation of Palden Lhamo is rather unique. The following description would elaborate the point -

- Palden Lhamo is depicted riding a white, wild, mule crossing a sea (of blood).
- Palden Lhamo's main distinctive mark is the peacock plumage in her hair. The peacock is known to be able to consume a great deal of poison without coming to harm, therefore it symbolizes the eradication of sin, the 'spiritual poisons'.

- The flayed skin of her son (an enemy of Buddhism) serves s saddle blanket.

- The single eye on the rump of the mule was formed when Lhamo removed the arrow that her husband, the cannibal king of Sri Lanka and an enemy of the Buddhist doctrine, shot at her as she escaped him.

- The trappings of the mule are made of snakes and from them hang many of Palden Lhamo's tools: a pair of dice for divination, a stack of red tablets, a ball of magic thread, and a skin bag full of diseases with which she destroys enemies of the faith.

- In her right hand, she brandishes a club topped with a half-dorje (*vajra* in Sanskrit), which is used to crush those who have broken their promises.

- In her left hand, is a *kapala* filled with blood;

- Many of her other paraphernalia, such as the moon disc in her hair and the sun disc at her navel, are gifts from the gods. Her myriad destructive powers aid Lhamo in her quest to conquer the destructive forces of egotism.

- The goddess holds a skull cup and a flaming sword, its hilt made of a scorpion.

- From her right earring, a lion emerges; from the left, a snake. She cradles, under her left arm, a sack made from the skin of a mongoose, spilling jewels, but also described in the literature as containing diseases.

- She wears a crown of five skulls, adorned by a crescent moon and a peacock feather finial, earrings, bracelets, and anklets. Her other fierce accoutrements include flaming hair, human skin, snake and skull ornaments. Flames and smoke spring forth from her robes, creating a fearsome aura.

- Her mule, which she rides side-saddle is led through the flames by Makaravaktra, the makara-headed dakini, with lion-head dakini Simhavaktra following behind.

- Palden Lhamo was armed by the gods themselves. Hevajra is the one who gave her the dice to determine men's lives. Her peacock feather fan is the gift of Brahma. Kubera gave her a lion which protects and decorates her right ear. The naga king gave her a serpent for her left ear. Vajrapani gave her a hammer to use as a weapon. Her mule is the gift of the other gods.

- In many monasteries, her image is kept in a corner and is always kept covered.

DOCTRINE AND OTHERS

Photo no 85 : *A statue of fully gold plated Palden Lhamo*

Remati (earlier name of Palden Lhamo) was married to Shinje, the king of the *dudpo*s, who at the time of their marriage was the king of Lanka. She had vowed, then, that she would pursue him to be gentle and make him follow the Buddha dharma, or else she would put an end to that whole dynasty. Despite her hard efforts for many years, she could not induce any improvement in his evil ways. So she determined to kill their son who was being raised to be the one to finally destroy Buddhism in that kingdom. During the king's absence,

Remati accomplished the dreadful deed of killing her son. She then left the palace on one of the finest steed of the king. On his return, seeing what had happened, the king chased her and seized his bow and with a fierce and terrible curse shot off a poisoned arrow. But the arrow only pierced the horse's rump. The queen easily neutralized the king's assault, and removing the deadly bow from the horse's rump, she said: "May the wound of my horse become an eye large enough to watch over the twenty-four regions, and may I myself be the one to terminate the lineage of the malignant kings of Lanka!" Then Palden Lhamo continued northwards, easily traversing India, Tibet, Mongolia, and part of China, and finally settled, on the mountain Oikhan, in the Olgon district of Eastern Siberia. This mountain is said to be surrounded by large, uninhabited deserts, and by the ocean Muliding.

While she served as a protector of the Buddhist faith (as a *dharmapala* - the only female deity to do so) she was also associated with ancient pre-Buddhist deities, including those connected with the creation and suppression of disease. She herself also has a number of important forms and emanations, as well as an extensive retinue of minor goddesses and gods.

She is frequently shown in the entourage of wrathful deities, especially Yama, Dharmaraja, and Mahakala. Once incorporated into the pantheon of Buddhist protectors, Palden Lhamo replaced these earlier pre-Buddhist goddesses, though a particular set of twelve such deities remained in her mandala, which is extremely complex as a result of her composite nature.

Her sect is said to have been introduced to Tibet by Urgyen Sangwa Sherab around 10th century. But little is known about the history of her veneration thereafter. When the Sakya and then, the Gelukpa order worshiped from the sixteenth century onward, this goddess became associated with the protection of Lhasa and of the Dalai Lama.

Palden Lhamo is the only female dharma protector common to all four schools of Tibetan Buddhism. Palden Lhamo is pictured as a wild and energetic force that defeats the harmful force of egotism.

PRAJNAPARAMITA

Photo no 86 : *Prajnaparamita*

INTRODUCTION

Prajnaparamita (meaning, Perfection of Wisdom, Tib: *Yum Chenmo*) embodies the bliss/emptiness that gives rise to all phenomena – hence, her title as Mother of all the Buddhas. Prajnaparamita is one of the most important female bodhisattvas in Mahayana Buddhism. As an actual creator of the universe she attained the state of enlightenment and dedicated herself to guiding all mankind to the true path of Buddha that leads to nirvana. She is the personification of wisdom and is regarded as the mystic mother of all Buddhas.

ICONOGRAPHY

She usually appears as a tranquil seated figure clothed in silks; her body is gold in color, and she has one face and four arms. Her first two arms are held in meditation posture in her lap, while the other right hand holds a vajra (thunderbolt scepter symbolizing compassion/bliss) and the left, the text of the Heart Sutra which is the essential wisdom-text on the emptiness of phenomena.

DOCTRINE AND OTHERS

The Perfection of Wisdom Sutras or *Prajñâpâramitâ Sutras* is a genre of Mahayana Buddhist scriptures dealing with the subject of the Perfection of Wisdom. The term Prajñâpâramitâ alone never refers to a specific text, but always to the class of literature.

The earliest sutra in this class is the Astasâhasrikâ Prajñâpâramitâ Sûtra or "Perfection of Wisdom in 8,000 Lines", which was probably put in writing about 100 BC, and is one of the earliest Mahayana sutras. More material was gradually compiled over the next two centuries. As well as the sutra itself, there is a summary in verse, the RatnaguGasaAcaya Gâthâ, which some believe to be slightly older because it is not written in standard literary Sanskrit.

Between the years 100 and 300 this text was expanded into large versions in 10,000, 18,000, 25,000 and 100,000 lines, collectively known at the "Large Perfection of Wisdom". These differ mainly in the extent to which the many lists are either abbreviated or written out in full; the rest of the text is mostly unchanged between the different versions. Since, the large versions proved to be unwieldy; they were later summarized into shorter versions, produced from 300 to 500. The shorter versions include the Heart Sutra (Prajñâpâramitâ Hrdaya Sûtra) and the Diamond Sutra (Prajñâpâramitâ Vajracchedikâ Sûtra). These two are widely popular and have had a great influence on the development of Mahayana Buddhism. Tantric versions of the Prajnaparamita literature were produced from 500 on. The Prajnaparamita terma teachings are held to have been conferred upon Nagarjuna by Nagaraja, the King of the nagas, who had been guarding them at the bottom of a lake.

The central idea of *the Perfection of Wisdom* is complete release from the world of existence. The Perfection of Wisdom goes beyond earlier Buddhist teaching that focused on the rise and fall of phenomena to state that there is no such rise and fall — because all phenomena are essentially void. The earlier perception had been that reality is composed of a multiplicity of things. The Perfection of Wisdom states that there is no multiplicity: all is one. Even existence (*samsara*) and *nirvana* are essentially the same, and both are ultimately void. The view of the Perfection of Wisdom is that words and analysis have a practical application in that they are necessary for us to function in this world but, ultimately, nothing can be predicated about anything.

Within this context of voidness, the Perfection of Wisdom offers a way to enlightenment. It represents the formal introduction to Buddhist thought of a practical ideal — the ideal of a bodhisattva. Unlike an arhat or pratyekabuddha, beings who achieve enlightenment but cannot pass on the means of enlightenment to others, a bodhisattva should and does teach. A bodhisattva must practice the six perfections: giving, morality, patience, vigour, contemplation and wisdom. Wisdom is the most important of these because it dispels the darkness of sensory delusion and allows things to be seen as they really are."

In Tibetan Buddhism, Prajnaparamita is closely associated with

CHD practice. Chöd is one of the four daily offerings of the Bön tradition. The other three are smoke offering (sang chöd), water offering, and burnt food offering (sur chöd). In the chöd practice, we transform into the deity and cut our illusory body and offer it to all the enlightened and sentient beings. Offering our body (Lu Gyin) in this way allows us to cut attachment to ego and cultivate generosity toward others. Through this practice we cut through our misunderstanding of our own real condition and reconnect to our own true nature.

There are many chöd liturgies within the Bön tradition. "Laughter of the Skygoers" was composed by Shardza Tashi Gyaltsen, who achieved the rainbow body in 1934. This is the sadhana currently used at both Bönpo Monasteries of Menri (Himachal Pradesh, India) and Triten Norbutse (Kathmandu, Nepal).

Mantra : *Gate gate paragate parasamgate bodhi svaha*

RAHULA

Photo no 87 : *Rahula*

INTRODUCTION

Rahula (Tib. *kyab jug*): is wrathful protector of the Revealed Treasure Tradition of Nyingma lineages, one of eight highest protector deities and who rules over a class of *gza* demons. He is called the god of planets as well.

ICONOGRAPHY

Rahula is a smoky figure with nine heads, four hands and a thousand blazing eyes. Each face has three large eyes and a gaping mouth with exposed fangs. He holds a makara-headed vajra club, and the bow & arrow with which he seeks out vow-breakers and 'destroys' them with wisdom and compassion. The bow is the compassionate means with which the arrow of perfect insight is released.

He has a snake body. His gaping mouth in his stomach is said to consume all depraved and degraded attempts to manipulate the meaning of the Fourteen Root Vows of Vajrayana.

There are a drawn bow and arrow in the first pair of hands. The second right holds aloft a makara stick and the left a snake lasso. Adorned with crowns of five skulls and gold earrings, he wears a green scarf and various colored lower garments. The lower body is that of a coiled naga serpent, dark blue in color, rising out of a blood filled black triangle enclosure; surrounded by orange flames and black smoke. In a skull cup in front is a large triangular red torma offering with two more offering skull cups arranged at the sides.

His torso and four arms are covered with eyes (one thousands is the number given in texts). His nine stacked horrible heads are crowned with flaming hair and the head of a raven, which guards religious teachings and whose shadows were believed to cause apoplexy. Rahula leans back to draw his bow and shoot an arrow into the heart of anyone who breaks his religious vows.

DOCTRINE AND OTHERS

Rahula is one of many deities who entered the Buddhist pantheon in Tibet and Mongolia via tantric Hinduism and whose nature is wildly paradoxical. As ruler of all the greater and lesser planets, he holds a particularly important place in the pantheon of the Tibetan Nyingmapa and is generally viewed as a protector of the faith in Tibet and Mongolia, but he is also a demonic figure, the beater of illness and the swallower of the sun and moon during eclipses.

Rahula has dominion over the eight classes of demon (these eight demonic classes refer to various types of mundane 'spirits' who can cause either help or harm, but remain invisible to normal human beings: kingkara (ging); mara (bDud); tsen (bTsan); yaksha (gNod sByin); raksha (srin po); matari (ma mo); rahula (gZa gDong); and naga (kLu).) These eight classes are essentially linked with the dualistic manifestation of the eight distorted modes of consciousness.

During the time of the influence of these malevolent beings, one would not normally start new projects. But since Rahula is an emanation of Vajrapani, a companion to Chenrezi, and the bodhisattva who embodies all the power of all the Buddhas, the evil influences are controlled.

Photo no 88 : *A statue of Rahula with colored parwa.*

According to the Chakdor legend, all the Buddhas gather on top of Mount Meru to consider how to obtain the elixir of life, Dutsi. They are seeking an antidote to Hala, the source of human illness that the demons have in their possession. They churn the ocean and procure the Dutsi, which they entrust to the protector, Vajrapani. However, the monster Rahu manages to steal it. He drinks it down, and then urinates it back into the vessel that it had been put into by the Buddhas. Vajrapani realizes what has happened and sets out to kill Rahu. He questions the Sun as to the demon's whereabouts, but the Sun fears retaliation from Rahu. The Moon felt no different, but still was willing to help the cause and reveals where Rahu is hiding. Slain by Vajrapani at last, the rakshasa comes back to life because he had drunk the Dutsi or, in Sanskrit, *Amrita*. Now, Vajrapani has to take his punishment; he is made to drink the urine. He conceives an even greater rage against Rahu and all demons, and slays him over and over again. Wherever the blood of Rahu dripped onto the surface of this earth, it caused to spring up all manner of medicinal plants.

RANGJUNG RIGPE DORJE
(16ᵀᴴ KARMAPA)

Photo no 89 : *Rangjung Rigpe Dorje*

INTRODUCTION

Rangjung Rigpe Dorje (1924-1981) was the Sixteenth Gyalwa Karmapa. He was spiritual leader of the Karma Kagyu lineage of Tibetan Buddhism. The revered Tibetan Buddhist meditation master is known as a living embodiment of boundless compassion.

BRIEF BIOGRAPHY

Rangjung Rigpe Dorje was born at Denkhok in Derge province in east Tibet. His father's name was Tsewang Paijor and his mother was called Kalzang Chosdun. While still in his mother's womb the baby could be heard reciting the "Mani" Mantra.

Jampal Tsultrim, the fifteenth Karmapa's personal attendant, had been entrusted by him with a prediction letter concerning the details of the incarnation of the 16th Karmapa. Certain details were clarified by the 2nd Beru Khyentse Rinpoche, the 11th Tai Situ Rinpoche and the 2nd Jamgon Kongtrul Rinpoche, which helped to successfully locate Rangjung Rigpe Dorje.

He was taken to Palpung Monastery where Situ Pema Wangchok gave him ordination, the Bodhisattva vows and many teachings. Beru Khyentse Lodro Miza Pampa'i Gocha taught him the tantras. Bo Kangkar Rinpoche taught him the sutras. Jamgon Palden Kyentse Oser taught him Mahamudra and the 6 Yogas of Naropa. He regarded Situ Pema Wangchok and Jamgon Palden Kyentse Oser as his main teachers.

In 1931, at the age of seven, he performed his first Black Crown ceremony. Thousands were witness to this amazing event. It was said that a rain of flowers fell and the sky was filled with rainbows. Even while still very young, the great power of the 16th Karmapa became widely known. It was recorded that he took his attendant's sword and tied it in a knot. He received his hair cutting ceremony at age thirteen from Thubten Gyatso, 13th Dalai Lama.

During his education he received all the Kagyu transmissions and was also taught by the Sakya Trizin for many years. In the beginning of the 1940 he went into retreat and in 1947 started a pilgrimage to India together with Tenzin Gyatso, the 14th Dalai Lama. Rangjung continued his education with the 10th Mindrolling Trichen of the Nyingma School and it was concluded with the Kalachakra initiation of the Gelugpa School. Rangjung had therefore received all the major teachings of all the major Tibetan Buddhist schools.

The 16th Karmapa continued his predecessor's activities, traveling and teaching throughout Tibet, Bhutan, Nepal, Sikkim, India and parts of China. His activity also included locating the rebirths of high reincarnate lamas through his meditation.

Political circumstances altered Tibet radically with the 1950 takeover by the Chinese. Karmapa, along with the Dalai Lama, government officials and other high lamas attended talks in Beijing to negotiate a settlement, which succeeded for a while, but in 1959 the Chinese invaded and annexed Tibet.

In February of that year, Karmapa took 160 students from Tsurphu Monastery and proceeded overland to Bhutan, taking the lineage's most sacred treasures and relics with them.

Tashi Namgyal, the King of Sikkim, offered land to the Karmapa near the site where the 14th Karmapa had established a monastery. It was here that his new seat, Rumtek Monastery was built in 1966. The traditional seat of the Karmapa, Tsurphu Monastery, still exists, but the number of monks is restricted.

In the beginning of the 1970s Karmapa made the predication that Tibet would have a hard struggle gaining independence and even if it does, it will not allow the refugees to return. Rumtek would not be a good place either, and Sikkim and Bhutan are still stable, but can deteriorate as well, however the Western world will embrace Buddhism. And after that predication he sent Lama Gendün to Europe.

In 1974, he embarked on his first world tour, traveling to Europe, Canada and the United States, giving several Black Crown ceremonies, and an audience was granted by Pope Paul VI. In 1976-77, he began a more exhaustive tour, giving extensive teachings and empowerments and visiting nearly every major city in Europe.

Photo no 90 : *An actual photo of Sixteenth Karmapa.*

The sixteenth Karmapa helped foster the transmission of Tibetan Buddhism to the West. He established Dharma centers and monasteries in various places around the world in order to protect, preserve, and spread the Buddha's teachings. As part of an initiative by the Tibetan government-in-exile to consolidate the organization of Tibetan Buddhism, Rangjung Rigpe Dorje became the first formal head of the Kagyu school, although the earlier Karmapas had long been considered the most prestigious and authoritative lamas of that school.

In 1980-81, Karmapa began his last world tour, giving teachings, interviews and empowerments in South East Asia, Greece, England and the United States. Rangjung Rigpei Dorjé died on November 5, 1981 in the United States in a hospital in Zion, Illinois. Doctors and nurses at the hospital remarked on his kindness and how he seemed more concerned with their welfare than his own. One doctor was also struck by the Karmapa's refusal of pain medication and the absence of any signs of feeling the profound pain that most patients in his condition report. Upon his death, against hospital procedure but in keeping with Tibetan tradition and with special permission from the State of Illinois, his body was left in the hospital for three days and his heart remained warm during this time. The Chief of staff Radulfo Sanchez had no medical explanation for this.

During the seven weeks between his death and his cremation, Karmapa's body spontaneously shrank to the size of a small child. He was cremated in Rumtek. His two dogs died on the day of his cremation even though they were healthy. During the cremation a triple circular rainbow appeared above the monastery in a clear blue sky. Many photographs exist of this remarkable phenomenon. While his body burnt, an object rolled from the flames to the edge of the stupa to Lopon Chechu Rinpoche. This object was quickly recovered and proved to be the Karmapa's eyes, tongue and heart. This indicates that the body, speech and mind have come together to be saved as relics for the future and is common in only the highest of accomplished Buddhist yogis - the exact same thing occurred during the cremation of Gampopa and the Second Karmapa, Karma Pakshi.

SPECIFIC MASTERY AND CONTRIBUTION

It was said that the simple presence of Karmapa, Rangjung Rigpe Dorje, would create a profound and lasting blessing on all people coming into contact with him. He himself said that a Buddha should be known by his laugh and it was said that when Karmapa laughed, which he did all the time, one would hear him several houses away.

He also demonstrated a complete ability to communicate with animals, e.g., at a course in Europe, a large raven tapped on the window where Karmapa was teaching. When let in, the bird flew directly to Karmapa, after which he instructed two people to go to a certain barn a few miles down the road where two other birds were trapped and starving. Later, the birds were discovered and rescued. Rangjung Rigpe Dorje had a special fondness for birds and he would often make a visit to the local pet shop in several cities in the world.

Rangjung Rigpe Dorje was considered by many to be a living Buddha. Like his predecessors, he was primarily a spiritual figure and therefore not involved in politics. He, instead, made efforts to keep the spiritual traditions of Tibet intact.

Spiritually, he is an inspiration to hundreds of thousands of people across the worlds who meditate on him daily.

RATNASAMBHAVA BUDDHA

Photo no 91 : *Ratnasambhava Buddha*

INTRODUCTION

Ratnasambhava Buddha (Tib: *Rinchen Jung ne*) is one of the Five Wisdom Buddhas or Pancha Buddhas in Vajrayana Buddhism. The other Budddhas are Vairocana Buddha, Akshobhya Buddha, Amitabh Buddha and Amoghasiddhi Buddha.

The literal meaning of the name is a jewel born. Ratnasambhava Buddha is located in south.

He is linked with freeing being from the negative emotions of pride and feeling sensation.

ICONOGRAPHY

Photo no 92 : *Bronze statue of Ratnasambhava*

Ratnasambhava Buddha is depicted showing his right hand in varada mudra. It is a gesture of giving. He is sometimes shown holding his symbol, the ratna (jewel) or chintamani (wish-fulfilling jewel that grants all desires). The ratna is often depicted in a threefold form as the triratna signifying the union of Buddha, Dharma and Sangha. His color is yellow, the color of the sun in its zenith. The animal that upholds Ratnasambhava's throne is the horse, denoting impetus and liberation. He is shown in the south direction. He is yellow. His consort is Mamaki. His vehicle is horse. His symbol is jewel or triratna.

DOCTRINE AND OTHERS

Ratnasambhava Buddha symbolizes equality and equanimity. He is sometimes described as the Buddha of giving to all without any discrimination. Meditating on his wisdom one develops clarity and equanimity. The wisdom of sameness of Buddha Ratnasambhava gives the clarity of mind to perceive the correct perspective including the eight experiences, arranged into four pair viz. gain and loss, fame and disgrace, praise and blame, and pleasure and pain.

Ratnasambhava Buddha is believed to transform the negative trait especially of pride into the wisdom of equality. He rules over the element of earth and embodies the skandha of feeling or sensation. His bija is *Tram*.

His mantra is *Om Ratnasambhava Tram*.

In short, the particulars of RatnasambhavaBuddha are as following:

Particular	*For Ratnasambhava Buddha*
Meaning of the Name	Source of Precious Things or Jewel-Born One
Direction	South
Color	Yellow
Mudra	Varada (Charity)
Vija (Syllable)	Trah
Symbol	Jewel (ratna) or Three Jewels (triratna)
Embodies	Compassion
Type of wisdom	Wisdom of Equality
Cosmic element (skandha)	Vendana (Sensation)
Earthly element	Earth
Antidote to	Desire and Pride
Sense	Smell
Vehicle	Horse
Spiritual son	Ratnapani
Consort	Mamaki
Paradise	-

SAKYA PANDITA

Photo no 93 : *Sakya Pandita*

INTRODUCTION

Sakya Pandita (1182–1251) (Tib: *Kunga Gyeltsen*) was a Tibetan spiritual leader and Buddhist scholar and the fourth of the Five Venerable Supreme Sakya Masters of Tibet. (viz. Sachen Kunga Nyingpo, Loppon Sonam Tsemo, Jetsun Dragpa Gyaltsen, Sakya Pandita and Chogyal Phagpa).

Kunga Gyeltsen is generally known simply as Sakya Pandita, a title given to him in recognition of his scholarly achievements and knowledge of Sanskrit.

He is believed to have been an incarnation of the Bodhisattva Manjushri, the embodiment of the wisdom of all the Buddhas.

He became known as a great scholar in India, China, Mongolia and Tibet and was proficient in the five great sciences of medicine, grammar, dialectics and sacred Sanskrit literature as well as the minor sciences of rhetoric, synonymies, poetry, dancing and astrology.

ICONOGRAPHY

Sakya Pandita is shown in meditative pose. His hands are shown in dharmachakra mudra.

SHORT BIOGRAPHY

He was born at Sakya of the noble family of Jam-yan-gon. His father was Palchen Opo and mother was Macheg Nitri Cham. He was the nephew of Jetsun Dakpa Gyeltsen (1147-1216) and was also his principal disciple

When Sakya Pandita was born, a multitude of Sakya Pandita received the teaching of the Madhyamika Collection of Reasoning from the same master, Tsur Zhonnu Sengge, such as drawing and design; and other subjects. While still a youth, he already was a treasury of wisdom and good qualities. At the young age, he received empowerment from his father and studied the Hevajra sadhana Lotus Born and the Chakrasamvara Tantra. Every day he performed the practices of Arya Achala, Manjushri, Avalokiteshvara, and many others. He thoroughly studied and mastered a number of important tantric, sutras, and medical texts and also gradually received empowerment, blessings, tantric explanations, and pith instructions on the Dharmas of the founders of the Sakyapa and their ancestral masters.

At the age of nineteen, Sakya Pandita received teachings on logic, and the Dharmas of Maitreya from Master Shuhrul at Trang. When he was twenty, he traveled to meet Master Tsur Zhonnu Sengge, at Nyangtod Changdul. From him he received teachings on the Pramana. He also received the teaching of the Madhyamika Collection of Reasoning. Sakya Pandita started delivering a root text and commentary on the Pramanaviniscaya to the amazement of all.

After that, he returned to Sakya to perform rituals of behalf of his father and spiritual master, who had passed away. Sakya Pandita also received many teachings on logic from the Pandita Danashila, as well as teachings on other vajrayana practices. He studied a cycle of works on the Sanskrit language, and works on logic such as the Pramanavirtika and others from Pandita Sangha Shri from Nepal. He studied the logic text Seven Categories of Pramana as well as from Shakya Shri Badhra. From Shakya Shri Badhra and Bodhisattva Kyewole, he also studied many other teachings on vinaya, sutra, and tantra.

Sakya Pandita also directly perceived many deities such as Arya Manjushri, Arya Achala, Tara, and others. They directly bestowed a multitude of doors of Dharma upon him.

Once night, when he was eighteen, Sakya Pandita dreamed that he received the complete teachings on the Abhidharma Kosha directly from Vasubandi, in front of Achi stupa behind Sakya Monastery. He experienced that night as an entire month, with one teaching session each morning for thirty mornings. The next morning when he awoke, he had both the words and the meaning of the entire Abhidharma Kosa in his memory.

As the fame of Sakya Pandita spread, Godan Khan, the Mongol Emperor of China, invited Sakya Pandita to come to the Mongol court as his spiritual guide. Remembering his uncle's earlier prophecy, Sakya Pandita journeyed to China at the age of sixty-five. In order to determine the extent of the lama's knowledge, Godan Khan devised a test. He had his most clever magician create an illusory temple and asked Sakya Pandita to consecrate it. But when the lama chanted the appropriate prayers and scattered the blessings of water, the temple became completely real one and all could walk in it. That temple is called the Emanation Temple. After this incident, the Emperor had great faith in Sakya Pandita and received many important teachings from him. As a sign of his great reverence, Godan Khan had three exquisite statues of Sakya Pandita cast in gold, silver, and other precious metals. Each was inscribed on the back in Chinese, Tibetan and Mongolian and personally consecrated by Sakya Pandita. One remained in China, one in Mongolia and the third was sent to Tibet.

Shortly before he passed away in the Mongol court, Sakya Pandita named his nephew, Chogyal Phagpa, as his successor. Sakya Pandita died in 1252, at the age of seventy in the city of Gyu-ma. After Sakya Pandita was cremated, many relics were found and numerous Buddhist images appeared on his bones.

SPECIFIC MASTERY AND CONTRIBUTIONS

He is known as a great scholar in India, China, Mongolia and Tibet and was proficient in the five great sciences of medicine, grammar, dialectics and sacred Sanskrit literature as well as the minor sciences of rhetoric, synonymies, poetry, dancing and astrology.

He is considered in Tibet to by the fourth "Great Forefather" and sixth Sakya Trizin, and one of the most important figures among the Sakya lineage.

He is best known for his works such as the *Treasury of Logic on Valid Cognition (Tsod-ma rigs-gter)* and the *Discrimination of the Three Vows (sDom-gsum rab-dbye)*. He also wrote a collection of moral precepts in verse which was translated into Mongolian. He focussed on doctrine and logic basing himself upon the *Pramanavarttika* of Dharmakirti.

SAKYAMUNI GAUTAMA BUDDHA

Photo no 94 : *Sakyamuni Buddha*

INTRODUCTION

Sakyamuni Gautama Buddha (also called Siddhartha Gautama Buddha) was the founder of Buddhism. He is generally recognized by Buddhists as the Supreme Buddha (Sammâsambuddha) of our age.

BRIEF HISTORY

Buddha was born in Lumbini of Kapilvastu district of Nepal some 2500 years ago. His father was King Suddhodana, the chief of the Shakya's class, one of several ancient tribes during that time. His mother was Queen Maha Devi who died seven days after the birth of Siddartha. Siddhartha was brought up by his mother's younger sister, Maha Prajapati. At the age of 16, prince Siddhartha was married to Yasodharâ, a Koliyan princess. Yasodhara gave birth to a son, Rahula. Siddhartha spent 29 years as a Prince in Kapilavastu. At the age of 29, Siddhartha escaped his palace leaving behind this royal life to become a mendicant.

Siddhartha initially went to Rajagaha and began his ascetic life by begging for alms in the street. Having been recognized by the men of King Bimbisara, Bimbisara offered him the throne after hearing of Siddhartha's quest. Siddhartha rejected the offer, but promised to visit his kingdom of Magadha first, upon attaining enlightenment. Siddhartha left Rajagaha and practiced under two hermit teachers. After mastering the teachings of Alara Kalama, Siddhartha was asked by Kalama to succeed him, but he moved on after being unsatisfied with his practices. He then became a student of Udaka Ramaputta, but although he achieved high levels of meditative consciousness and was asked to succeed Ramaputta, he was still not satisfied with his path, and moved on.

Siddhartha and a group of five companions led by Kondanna then set out to take their austerities even further. They tried to seek enlightenment through near total deprivation of worldly goods, including food, practicing self-mortification. After nearly starving himself to death by restricting his food intake to around a leaf or nut per day, he collapsed in a river while bathing and almost drowned. Siddhartha began to reconsider his path.

After asceticism and concentrating on meditation and Anapana-sati (awareness of breathing in and out), Siddhartha discovered what is called the Middle Way—a path of moderation away from the extremes of self-indulgence and self-mortification. Then, sitting under a *Pipal* tree, now known as the Bodhi tree in Bodh Gaya, he vowed never to arise until he had found the Truth. Other companions had abandoned him by that time. After 49 days meditating, he finally attained Enlightenment. He was 35 years at that time. He was known as the Buddha or "Awakened One". At this point, he realized complete awakening and insight into the nature and cause of human suffering. He realized steps necessary to eliminate it. These truths were then categorized into the Four Noble Truths.

Photo no 95 : *A silver statue of Siddhartha Gautama.*

After becoming enlightened, two merchants whom the Buddha met, named Tapussa and Bhallika became the first lay disciples. The Buddha then journeyed to Deer Park near VârâGasî (Benares) in Northern India. He set in motion the Wheel of Dharma by delivering his first sermon to the group of five companions. These teachings, which include the Sutra of the Four Noble Truths and other discourses, are the principal source of the Hinayana, or Lesser Vehicle, of Buddhism. The first *Sangha* was formed. Soon, there were thousands of followers of Buddha.

Upon hearing of the enlightenment, Suddhodana dispatched royal delegations to ask the Buddha to return to Kapilavastu. Nine delegations were sent in all, but the delegates joined the sangha and became *arahants*. The tenth delegation, lead by Kaludayi, a childhood friend, also became an *arahant*. Later, King Suddhodana invited the Sangha to the royal palace for a meal, followed by a dharma talk, after which he became a *sotapanna*. During the visit, many members of the royal family joined the Sangha. His cousins Ananda and Anuruddha were to become two of his five chief disciples. His son Rahula also joined the sangha at the age of seven, and was one of the ten chief disciples. His half-brother Nanda also joined the sangha and became an *arahant*. Another cousin Devadatta also became a monk although he later became an enemy and tried to kill the Buddha on multiple occasions.

Of his disciples, Sariputta, Mahamoggallana, Mahakasyapa, Ananda and Anuruddha comprised the five chief disciples. His ten foremost disciples were completed by the quintet of Upali, Subhoti, Rahula, Mahakaccana and Punna.

When the Buddha was staying at Mahavana near Vesali, the news of the impending death of Suddhodana came, the Buddha went to his father and preached the dharma, and Suddhodana became an *arahant* prior to death. The death and cremation led to the creation of the order of nuns. Buddhist texts record that the Buddha was reluctant to ordain women as nuns. His foster mother Maha Pajapati approached him asking to join the Sangha, but the Buddha refused, and began the journey from Kapilavastu back to Rajagaha. Maha Pajapati was so intent on renouncing the world that she led a group of royal Sakyan and Koliyan ladies, following the Sangha to Rajagaha. The Buddha eventually accepted them five years after the formation of the Sangha on the grounds that their capacity for enlightenment was equal to that of men, but he gave them certain additional rules (*vinaya*) to follow. This occurred after Ananda interceded on their behalf. Yasodhara also became a nun, with both becoming *arahants*.

During his ministry, Devadatta (who was not an *arahant*) frequently tried to undermine the Buddha. At one point, Devadatta asked the Buddha to stand aside to let him lead the sangha. The Buddha declined, and stated that Devadatta's actions did not reflect on the Triple Gem, but on him alone. Devadatta conspired with Prince

Ajatasattu, son of Bimbisara, so that they would kill and usurp the Buddha and Bimbisara respectively. Devadatta attempted three times to kill the Buddha. The first attempt involved the hiring of a group of archers, whom upon meeting the Buddha became disciples. A second attempt followed when Devadatta attempted to roll a large boulder down a hill. It hit another rock and splintered, only grazing the Buddha in the foot. A final attempt by plying an elephant with alcohol and setting it loose again failed. Failing this, Devadatta attempted to cause a schism in the Sangha, by proposing extra restrictions on the *vinaya*. When the Buddha declined, Devadatta started a breakaway order, criticizing the Buddha's laxity. At first, he managed to convert some of the *bhikkhus*, but Sariputta and Mahamoggallana expounded the dharma to them and succeeded in winning them back.

When the Buddha reached the age of 55, he made Ananda his chief attendant. The Buddha taught the second and third Wheels of Dharma, which include the Perfection of Wisdom Sutras and the Sutra Discriminating the Intention, respectively. These teachings are the source of the Mahayana, or Great Vehicle, of Buddhism.

Photo no 96 : *Buddha Statue with pedal and parwa.*

For the remaining 45 years of his life, the Buddha traveled several places in the Gangetic Plain, currently Uttar Pradesh, Bihar and southern Nepal, teaching his doctrine and discipline to an extremely diverse range of people. The Buddha founded the community of Buddhist monks and nuns (the Sangha) to continue the dispensation after his *nirvana*. His religion was open to all races and classes.

There is difference of opinions about the time of Buddha's passing. However, many agree that to be 544 or 543 BCE. At his death, the Buddha told his disciples to follow no leader, but to follow his teachings (dharma).

Three months after Buddha passed away, his followers called for the first meeting in order to preserve his teachings. Mahakasyapa was chosen the leader. One of his disciples, Ananda, famous for having a good memory, was also chosen as one of the members amongst the 500 *Arahants* to recite all the Buddha's sermons. Ananda was bestowed the responsibility of Sutra collections. Upali recited all the guidelines, rules etc to form Vinayapitaka, and Purna answered questions about Buddha's teaching then gather together to form Abhidhamma.

Two other Buddhist Councils were later held after 100 and 236 years respectively from the first one.

Buddha's teaching. Buddha's first teaching is summarized in the Four Noble Truths. The second wave of teachings called the second turning of the wheel of dharma is the teachings on emptiness and on the Prajnaparamita teachings. These are teachings of the Mahayana. Finally, the third wave of teachings was the bridge between the sutras and the tantras. These were the teachings in which the Buddha taught that absolutely everyone has Buddha-nature or Buddha-essence.

There are 84,000 different ways to cultivate enlightenment and Buddha's teaching is about helping others, doing good deeds, to love and respect all sentient beings, perfecting ourselves, understanding, abstaining from "greed, hatred, and to learn in order to overcome ignorance" etc.

His teachings later spread northward into Tibet, China, Korea and Japan, southward to Thailand, Cambodia, Sri Lanka, and Vietnam; and in 19th century to Europe, Australia and the USA.

SAMANTABHADRA

Photo no 97 : *Samantabhadra/Samantabhadri.*

INTRODUCTION

Samantabhadra (same as Vajradhara and Vicevabhadra, Tib: *Kuntu zangpo*) is the Primordial Buddha or Adi-Buddha associated with originary wisdom and compassion. He is the antecedant of all and the expanse of reality.

(Samantabhadra is also a bodhisattva at the time of Sakyamuni Buddha according to the *Avatamsaka Sutra*, who made the ten great vows which are the basis of a bodhisattva. Usually this bodhisattva is shown riding a white elephant).

ICONOGRAPHY

Samantabhadra as the Primordial Buddha is always represented naked, with a dark blue body, in union with his consort Samantabhadri who is in white color. The blue color symbolizes the emptiness essence of the mind while white color symbolizes clear knowing aspect of mind. The unity of emptiness and cognizant aspect is thus depicted in male and female from of Adi-Buddha. Samantabhadra/Samantabhdri are depicted without any ornaments in order to denote that the nature of mind is free from conception or thought constructs – a dharmakaya state.

DOCTRINE AND OTHERS

It is said that Adi Buddha or primordial Buddha had manifested in a form of a flame or a clear light (Skt. *Prabhashvara*) which is explained as self-cognizant and unfabricated original wakefulness and which is also present in all sentient beings. It is also called Buddha nature or Tathagata-garbha. Since, it is a dharmakaya aspect, it cannot be represented in any image or form. However, for people to have something to resort to, it is depicted in a form of a stupa or a chaitya. But, tractic Buddhism has led to depict this Adi-Buddha in the form such as Samantabhadra or Vajradhara. So, it should be understood that although the basic understanding and concept is the same, there has been difference only in depiction as per convenience of different sects of Buddhism.

224

Photo no 98 : *A copper statue of Samantabhadra with antique finish.*

From the primordial Samantabhadra (Vajradhara) were manifested the Five Wisdom Buddhas.

SIMHAMUKHA

Photo no 99 : *Simhamukha*

INTRODUCTION

Simhamukha (Tib. *Seng-gdong-ma* or *Seng-dong-chen*) is a wrathful dancing dark-blue figure similar to Vajravarahi in appearance and ornaments, holding a curved knife in her right hand and a skullcup in her left, except that she also has the face of a lion — hence her name in Tibetan and Sanskrit (meaning "lion-face").

Her practice was founded by a woman, Jetsun[ma] Lochen. Simhamukha's practice is found in the Sarma (New Translation) schools is associated with the Chakrasamvara Tantra.

The Simhamukha, is a deity from the Sakya, Kagyu, and Gelug traditions and resides in the "Lotus Family" of deities, but in the Nyingma tradition it is held that she is one of many Padmasambhava manifestations. Here she is in the form of a Red Simhamukha (Tibetan: seng ge dong ma chen mar mo) — with the face of a lion, is fierce by nature, possessing three piercing eyes, the bite of an angry lioness, and wild red fur — she tramples a corpse of ignorance.

Simhamukha is a Jnana Dakini or wisdom According to Jigmed Lingpa (1726-1798), the famous Nyingmapa master and discoverer of hidden treasure texts or Termas, Simhamukha represents a Nirmanakaya manifestation, appearing in time and history, whereas her Sambhogakaya aspect is Vajravarahi and her Dharmakaya aspect is Samantabhadri, the Primordial Wisdom herself.goddess.

ICONOGRAPHY

Snarling and roaring with a gaping large mouth on a white lion face, she stands fierce and menacing with two hands, dark blue in color, with protruding fangs, curled tongue, two large round eyes and dark green flowing hair. The right hand holds aloft a curved flaying knife with a gold vajra handle. The left clutches to the heart a white skull cup filled with blood. Adorned with a crown of five skulls, bone necklace and gold ornaments she wears a green silk scarf and a barely discernable tiger skin skirt. In a dancing posture with the left leg extended and the right drawn up she stands atop a red corpse seat, sun disc and a pink lotus surrounded by a circle of flame and smoke.

DOCTRINE AND OTHERS

The "Padma" (or Lotus) Family" resides in the Western "Pure Land." Simhamukha and the other Lotus family members (with the primary figures being Amitabha, Avalokiteshvara, Amitayus and in certain schools, the Red Tara). She is in the color associated with this Padma family, having the element of fire, and a mental symbolism that contends with such matters as desire and lust.

When fully appreciating the benefits of this wrathful wisdom deity (according to the Nyingmapa tradition), it is important to understand that, regardless of her exceedingly wrathful appearance and ferocious animal head, she is not a guardian spirit rather, she is the principal Dakini teacher of Padmasambhava.

In a homage Nyingma text to Simhamukha it is written "Arising from the state of the dharmadhatu, Mother of all conquerors, Queen of all the numberless dakinis; With magic powers smashing to dust hindrances and enemies".

In the Sarma (new) Schools the dakini Simhamukha is a tutelary deity arising out of the Cakrasamvara cycle of Tantras and belongs to the anuttarayoga 'wisdom' classification. The Sarma tradition Simhamukha is unrelated to the deity of the same name and appearance in the Nyingma 'Terma' (treasure) traditions. In that tradition, of the many forms of Padmasambhava, she is regarded as the secret form of Guru Rinpoche

In terms of these Higher Tantras, a meditation deity (yi-dam lha) who is both wrathful and female is the Jnana Dakini Simhamukha. It is important to understand that, despite her exceedingly wrathful appearance and animal head, she is not a guardian spirit (srung-ma), subdued by magic, converted to the Dharma, and bound by oaths of service by some powerful Mahasiddha in the past. Rather, she is a wrathful manifestation of Guhyajnana Dakini, who, according to the

Nyingmapa tradition, was the principal Dakini teacher of Padmasambhava in the country of Uddiyana.

Therefore, although Simhamukha is a Dakini in her aspect, she functions as a Yidam or meditation deity and her special functions are averting and repulsing (bzlog-pa) psychic attacks that may assault the practitioner and the subduing of negative female energy as personified by the Matrikas or Mamos.

SHABDRUNG NGAWANG NAMGYAL

Photo no 100 : *Shabdrung Ngawang Namgyal.*

INTRODUCTION

Shabdrung Ngawang Namgyal (1594-1651) was a Tibetan lama who was enthroned as the 18th Abbott of Ralung monastery, the first monastery to be established in Tibet as Gyalwang Drukpa, the traditional leader of the Drukpa Kagyu school of Tibetan Buddhism.

However, later he went Bhutan and he became a very famous and powerful religious leader as well as unifier of Bhutan as a nation.

He is believed to have been reborn successively, and each of his successors is known as the Shabdrung.

ICONOGRAPHY

Shabdrung Ngawang Namgyal is shown in meditative pose wearing a heavy robe. He wears a round and big cap. He is depicted with long beard.

BRIEF BIOGRAPHY

Shabdrung Ngawang Namgyal was considered the reincarnation of the 4th Drukchen, the Omniscient Pema Karpo. His father was Drukpa Mipham Tenpai Nyima, the son of Drukpa Mipham Chögyal, and his mother Sonam Pelkyi Butri, daughter of the ruler of skyid shod.

Ngawang Namgyal was enthroned as the 18th Abbot of Ralung monastery as Gyalwang Drukpa, the traditional leader of the Drukpa Kagyu school of Tibetan Buddhism. However, the same claim was raised by the crown prince of Tsang, Pagsam Wangpo (1593-1641). In this connection, there was dispute and Ngawang Namgyal was attacked time Ngawang Namgyal and some of his men were killed. He realized that his life at Ralung was not safe. So, in 1616, at the age of 23, he traveled to Bhutan with his men. There, he received high respect and honor. He had carried a number of artifacts with him from Ralung at that time. He was warmly received by Hoptso

Lam, a Bhutanese leader, who wanted to strengthen the Drukpa Kagyu locally.

In 1617, the Tibetan rulers, who were very jealous over the increasing popularity of Ngawang Namgyal in Bhutan, launched an invasion to Bhutan. However, the unity of people in Bhutan managed to repulse that invasion and the commander of the Tibetan force was killed during time. Having repulsed the first invasion successfully, Ngawang Namgyal had subsequently sought the friendship with Nepal. He recognized the might of strong, simple and dedicated Gorkhalis. He obtained warring materials from other countries as well. In fact, at that time, Bhutan was fragmented into petty principalities and numerous clans ruled in different valleys. They engaged in quarrels among themselves and with Tibet. Ngawang Namgyal unified the country under his central leadership and established himself as the country's supreme leader.

Tibetan rulers invaded seven times in Bhutan between 1634 and 1649. In 1644, a combined force of Mongol and Tibet attacked Bhutan. The militias of Gushri Khan was led by the Vth Dalai Lama, who was nominated as the spiritual and temporal head of the Tibet and proclaimed the Gelukpa or the followers of Yellow Hat Sect to be the national religion of the land of Tibet. This combined force was also repulsed by the Bhutanese force. In that battle, Ngawang Namgyal was said to have used his miracles to defeat his opponents.

After being successful in repelling such multiple invasions of Tibetan rulers, he became a powerful spiritual leader. He took the title of the Shabdrung (literally "at whose feet one submits"). He was credited with unifying Bhutan. He also established Drukpa Kagyu as the state religion, which continues to this day.

He ruled over Bhutan for thirty-five years until his retirement in 1651 A.D. During his reign of 35 years, he built several dzongs (fortress), monasteries, and religious institutions. He had brought artisans and craftmen from Kathmandu, Nepal for that purpose. (It was from that time the tradition of lighting thousand lamps in

Swayambhunath temple in Kathmandu by the Bhutanese lamas had started).

He was also credited for introducing a unique ruling system in Bhutan. His reign was marked by the introduction of the unique dual system of governance called the *Chhoesid*. This new system was characterized by the sharing of power between the *Deb Raja* or the *Desi* who was the head of secular affairs and the *Dharma Raja* or the *spiritual head*, called as *Je Khempo*. He also codified laws for the country which were based on medieval theocratic principles called the *Tsa-Yig*.

So important was the Shabdrung Ngawang Namgyal to the stability of Bhutan during this period that his death was kept secret. In 1651, his closest aids announced that Shabdrung had entered into a strict retreat. And they continued to maintain this status that he was "in retreat" for more than 50 years by issuing various statements in his name until 1705.

Principal Dzongs & monasteries founded by Shabdrung Ngawang Namgyal were Cheri Monastery [1619], Semtoka Dzong [1629], Punakha Dzong, Wangdue Dzong, Rinpung Dzong [1644], Drugyel Dzong and Darkar Tashi Yangtse Dzong.

In course of time, the Dharma Rajas preferring religious matters withdrew themselves into seclusion while the Deb Rajas consolidated their authority exercising sole responsibility over the state affairs. The successive 'Dharma Rajas' were the incarnations of the Shabdrung whereas the post of the Deb Raja was like that of the administrative ruler.

The dual form of governance continued until the birth of the Wangchuk dynasty and establishment of hereditary Monarchy in 1907. Ugyen Wangchuck was elected as the first hereditary monarch of Bhutan on December 17, 1907. The present King Jigme Singye Wangchuck is the fourth hereditary king. The seventh and eighth Shabdrung reincarnates died in 1931 and 1953.

SPECIFIC MASTERY AND CONTRIBUTION

Shabdrung Ngawang Namgyal is regarded as second most popular
spiritual leader after Padmasambhava in Bhutan. He is credited to be
the uniting force behind present day Bhutan. He had constructed
several dzongs (fortress), monasteries, and religious institutions in
Bhutan. He is considered the founder of Drukpa Kagyu of Mahayana
Buddhism in Bhutan.

THOUSAND-ARMED AVALOKITESHVARA (SAHASTRABHUJA LOKESHVARA)

Photo no 101 : *Thousand-armed Avalokiteshvara.*

INTRODUCTION

Thousand-armed Avalokiteshvara (*Sahastrabhuja Lokeshvara*) is one of many manifestations of the Avalokiteshvara.

ICONOGRAPHY

The image of Avalokiteshvara, depicted with a thousand arms and eleven heads has the following meanings: The head on top portrays the Buddha Amitabha, symbolizing the Dharmakaya nature of Avalokiteshvara. The second head from the top represents Vajrapani, the wrathful aspect of Avalokiteshvara, who helps practitioners in fighting against negative forces and overcoming obstacles on their path. There are three rows of three faces which are in the color of white (*sambhogakaya*), green (*nirmanakaya*), and red (*dharmakaya*). This represents the three principle aspects of buddhahood. The thousand arms with one eye in each of the palms exhibit Avalokiteshvara's pervasiveness. In this thousand armed Sambhogakaya form, the Bodhisattva as a shining wish-fulfilling gem represents the supreme Bodhicitta and the awakened mind, the enlightened thought wishing to benefit all sentient beings. In this form, Avalokiteshvara has eight main hands. The two central hands are held in a cupped gesture symbolizing an attitude of homage (In some depiction, these two hands holds a wish fulfilling jewel). Another main hand is held in an open-palm gesture symbolizing generosity. The other main hands hold five objects: a bow and arrow, lotus, vase, rosary, and eight-spoked wheel. The bow and arrow represents bodhisattva's ability to aim at the heart of all beings. The vase contains the nectar of immortality. The lotus blossom represents enlightenment. The eight-spoked wheel represents the Buddha's teaching. The aura around the painting represents his one thousand hands and symbolizing his inexhaustible compassion. In each of his hand, there is an eye (wisdom) in the center of the palm (skills) which symbolizes the union of wisdoms and skills.

DOCTRINE AND OTHERS

One prominent Buddhist story tells of Avalokiteshvara or Chenresiz vowing never to rest until he had freed all sentient beings from samsara. Despite strenuous effort, he realized that still many unhappy beings were yet to be saved. After struggling to comprehend the needs of so many, his head splits into eleven pieces. Seeing such plight, Amitabha Buddha gave him eleven heads so as to enable him to attend to cries of the more suffering beings. While trying to attend to such cries from increased number of suffering beings, Avalokiteœvara once again found his two arms shattering into pieces. Once again, Amitabha Buddha came to his rescue and conferred thousand arms and thousand eyes to go ahead with his effort.

TILOPA

Photo no 102 : *A fully gold plated statue of Tilopa.*

INTRODUCTION

Tilopa (988-1069) was one of the most authoritative and renowned Indian mahasiddhas and masters of mahamudra and tantra.

He was the proponent of the principle of the Kagyu lineage of Tibetan Buddhism. He was the teacher of Naropa who founded Kagyu lineage.

He had developed the Mahamudra method, a set of spiritual practices that greatly accelerated the process of attaining bodhi (enlightenment).

It is said that Tilopa had received the full mahamudra and vajrayana transmissions directly from Vajradhara.

He is one of the eighty-four mahasiddhas of India.

ICONOGRAPHY

Tilopa is shown in a sitting posture with his right leg crosslegged over the left leg. He holds a fish in his right and his left is kept in holding position at the level of the chest.

However, there are other postures of Tilopa.

SHORT BIOGRAPHY

Tilopa, whose childhood name was Prajnabhadra, was born in the town of Chativavo (Chittagong, which is now in Banladesh), in a Brahmin royal family. (His birthplace is also recorded to be Jagora in eastern Bengal, India). His father was Pranyasha and mother, Kashi. When he grew up he learned all the doctrinal treatises of Brahminism. Later, he entered the monastic life and learnt the Tripitaka. During this period, he had a vision of a dakini who gave him an explicit tantric initiation that connected him directly with the Void. She enjoined him to throw away his monk's robes, to act spontaneously and to practice in secret. He started practicing tantric lessons. He was later expelled from the monastry as he was found practicing trantic with ksetra yogini. He looked for suitable masters in other places in

India. He met Nagarjuna, who suggested him to stay as the ruler as he was a brave man thus benefiting his countrymen.

When Tilopa returned to his kingdom to look after his people he found his country in a state of crisis and engaged in a war with another powerful state in India. Because Tilopa was a weak king, his people feared that they would be unable to defeat their enemy. But Tilopa made a public pronouncement in which he told his people that they need not fear; he knew of a way the enemy could be defeated without bloodshed.

Tilopa went out to defend his country. The army marching against his kingdom was big in number. Alone, Tilopa approached the forest where the army was encamped. When the soldiers saw him approach, they prepared to charge; Tilopa instantly transformed all the trees in the forest into soldiers ready to follow his command. When Tilopa ordered, "Look at the enemy!" all the trees that were transformed into soldiers gazed at the enemy. When Tilopa ordered, "Charge!" they all ran toward the enemy. Since there were uncountable trees, the trees were transformed into uncountable soldiers whose numbers were so frightening that the enemy fled the battle. In this way, Tilopa's prediction to his people, that he could defeat the enemy without bloodshed, really happened.

Later, Tilopa went to the northern part of the country to practice the Dharma. There he obtained teachings from the dakinis and went to meditate in a cave. After making a commitment to meditate there for twelve years, he chained both his legs together so he would not be able to come out of the cave. In this way he meditated for twelve years.

After passing twelve years, the chains that were tied around his legs broke off. He had achieved some realization as a result of his diligent meditation but had not yet accomplished the ultimate realization of Vajradhara. He wished to go out and wander and lead the simple life of a siddha. However, the dakinis were hesitant to let Tilopa leave out of the cave. As it was not proper for him to disobey, he thought he would try to influence them by demonstrating his realization. He picked up a fish in his hand and transferred its consciousness out of its body. The dakinis were thus convinced that he had become a highly realized being and hence, gave permission to wander as a simple siddha just as he wished. Tilopa's goal was to travel to the eastern part of Bengal and find Nagarjuna.

When Tilopa was abiding in a certain cave, Nagarjuna sent the dakini Matongha to give him teachings. When Matongha appeared, Tilopa inquired about Nagarjuna and was told that Nagarjuna was not in the human realm at that time but was giving teachings in the god realm. Matongha also told Tilopa that Nagarjuna knew Tilopa would be in this particular cave and had sent her to give him teachings. As wished by Nagarjuna, Tilopa received teachings from Matongha. During this time, Matongha noticed that Tilopa's mind possessed a strong pride that hindered his progress because of his being a king and of royal caste. With the purpose of removing his arrogance, he was given instruction to go to a nearby village and work for a certain lowly woman. That woman happened to have a livelihood of making oil out of sesame seeds during the day. But she was a prostitute by night. As Tilopa was instructed by the dakini, he worked for the woman during the day by pounding sesame seeds, and even helping with the customers in the night. In this way Tilopa worked for that woman for several years.

One day, at a meditation session during the break of his job of pounding sesame seeds, he received a vision of Buddha Vajradhara and, according to legend, the entire mahamudra was directly transmitted to Tilopa. As a sign of his achieving the complete realization, Tilopa was raised above the ground to the height equal to seven royal palm trees while still holding a mortar and pestle in his hands. The news that Tilopa kept floating in the air at the height of seven royal palm trees quickly spread throughout the village.

When the woman who employed Tilopa heard that someone was floating in the sky, she also hastened to see who he was. To her surprise she saw that it was her own employee. She felt ashamed to have given such a work to a highly realized being. With great regret, she thought to beg for an apology and to be a disciple of that great man. Tilopa read her mind and threw a flower down to her from the sky. As the flower hit her head, she instantaneously felt a complete realization and she was also lifted at par to Tilopa. Once again, the news spread out about this latest development, a great number of people gathered there. When the news reached the king, he also came there to witness the wondrous event along with his people. With lots of people assembled below, Tilopa sang a song of the Dharma, using the example of the sesame seed in his teaching. In his song, Tilopa explained that although a sesame seed contains oil, the oil cannot come out by itself and it needs a hard work of grinding the seed. So also is the Buddha nature of all living being. Without hard work of practicing the Dharma, there is no way to realize inherent Buddha nature. As Tilopa sang this song, the king and all his people immediately understood his teaching and they all came to complete realization.

After having received the transmission, Tilopa embarked on a wandering existence and started to teach people. His two most well known students were Naropa and Lalitavajra. He appointed Naropa, his most important student, as his successor. Thus he became renowned as the Siddha Tillipa. After many years of benefiting beings and guiding his disciples for a long time, he departed for the enlightened realms without leaving his physical body.

SPECIFIC MASTERY AND CONTRIBUTIONS

Tilopa had travelled throughout India getting teachings from many gurus. He learnt tummo (inner heat) from Saryapa. Similarly, from Nargajuna he received the radiant light (Sanskrit: *prabhasvara*) and illusory body (Sanskrit: *maya deha*) teachings (refer *Chakrasamvara Tantra*), *Lagusamvara tantra*, or *Heruka Abhidharma*). From Lawapa, he learnt the *dream yoga*. From Sukhasiddhi, he learnt the teachings on life, death, and the *bardo* (between life states, and consciousness transference) (*phowa*). From Indrabhuti, he learnt the insight (*prajna*). From Matangi, he learnt about the resurrection of the dead body.

The famous "six words of advice" given to Naropa by Tilopa was like this :

1. Don't recall (i.e. let go of what has passed
2. Don't imagine (i.e. let go of what may come)
3. Don't think (i.e. let go of what is happening now)
4. Don't examine (i.e. don't try to figure anything out)
5. Don't control (i.e. don't try to make anything happen) and
6. Rest (i.e. relax, right now, and rest).

He had developed the Mahamudra method, a set of spiritual practices that greatly accelerated the process of attaining bodhi (enlightenment).

He is also regarded as the proponent of the Kagyu lineage of Tibetan Buddhism.

He is famous as teacher of Naropa, who became the founder of Kagyu lineage later.

JE TSONGKHAPA

Photo no 103 : *A partly gold plated statue of Tsongkhapa.*

INTRODUCTION

Tsongkhapa (1357 - 1419), was the founder of the Geluk (*Dge-lugs*) school of Tibetan Buddhism. He is also known by his ordained name Lobsang Drakpa or simply as "Je Rinpoche".

His direct source of inspiration was the Kadampa tradition, the legacy of Atiœa. Based on Tsongkhapa's teaching, the two distinguishing characteristics of the Gelug tradition are: the union of Sutra and Tantra, and the emphasis on Vinaya (the moral code of discipline).

ICONOGRAPHY

Tsongkhapa is shown in generally in a meditative position with hands in *dharmachakra-mudra* (gesture of teaching). He wears a long pointed yellow cap. A sword is shown in the right hand side above the lotus while in the left, a scripture is shown kept above the lotus.

Usually, he is flanked by two of his prime disciples viz. Gyaltse and Khejse.

SHORT BIOGRAPHY

Born in Amdo province of Tibet during 1357, Tsongkhapa received the layman ordination at the age of three from the 4th Karmapa, Rolpe Dorje and was entitled "Kunga Nyingpo". At the age of seven he took the novice ordination from Choje Dhondup Rinchen and was entitled "Lobsang Drakpa" It was to his credit then, that at such an early age, he was able to receive the empowerments of Heruka Chakrasamvara, Hevajra, and Yamantaka, three of the most prominent wrathful deities of Tibetan Buddhism, as well as being able to recite a great many sutras, not the least of which was Manjushri-namasamgiti. Additionally, he would go on to be a great student of the Buddhist Vinaya, the doctrine of behaviour, and even later the Six Yogas of Naropa, the Kalachakra Tantra, and the acclaimed practice of

Mahamudra. At the age of 24 Tsongkhapa received the ordination of a full monk

Tsongkhapa traveled extensively in search of knowledge and studied with more than 100 teachers of all the existing traditions all topics of the doctrine, including Dzogchen. In addition to his studies, he engaged in extensive meditation retreats. He is reputed to have performed millions of prostrations, mandala offerings and other forms of purification practice. Tsongkhapa had often visions of meditational deities and especially of Manjushri, with whom he could communicate directly to clarify difficult points of the scriptures.

As such an accomplished scholar and practitioner, he was therefore quite effective as a teacher in Tibetan Buddhism, and became a leading figure amongst his peers as well as his students. Most of his teachers became also his students, like Rendawa, Umapa, the Nyingma Lama Lhodrak and they taught and revered each other. Out of his strong influence, compassion, and wisdom he is referred to as a second Buddha.

Photo no 104 : *Tsongkhapa with Gyaltse and Khejse disciples.*

Tsongkhapa founded the Geluk order, built on the foundations of the Kadampa tradition, with an emphasis on the Vinaya and scholarly pursuits. He had studied at Sakya, Kadam and Drikung Kagyu monasteries, built up his knowledge, received many empowerments, and was one of the foremost authorities of Tibetan Buddhism at the time. Further, it is said that the Buddha Sakyamuni spoke of his coming as an emanation of the Bodhisattva Manjusri in one of the verses in the Root Tantra of Manjushri.

Although Tsongkhapa finally passed away in 1419 at the age of sixty, he left to the world 18 volumes of collected teachings, with the largest amount being on Guhyasamâja tantra. These 18 volumes contain hundred of titles relating to all aspects of Buddhist teachings and clarify some of the most difficult topics of sutrayana and vajrayana teachings.

SPECIFIC MASTERY AND CONTRIBUTIONS

Major works of Tsongkhapa can listed as following:
- The Great Exposition of the Stages of the Path (Lam-rim chen-mo),
- The Great Exposition of Tantras (sNgag-rim chenmo),
- The Essence of Eloquence on the Interpretive and Definitive Teachings (Drang-nges legs-bshad snying-po),
- The Praise of Relativity (rTen-'brel bstodpa),
- The Clear Exposition of the Five Stages of Guhyasamaja (gSang-'dus rim-lnga gsal-sgron) and
- The Golden Rosary (gSer-phreng).

These scriptures are the prime source for the studies of the Gelugpa tradition and these and other teachings of Tsongkhapa endured into the modern age and are seen as a protection against misconceptions in Mahayana and Vajrayana Buddhism.

The 14th Dalai Lama has highlighted the fidelity of Tsongkhapa's work to the meaning found in Buddhapalita's work. Tsongkhapa's work is praised as being profound and true to tradition, essentially a clarification and condensation of the transmitted teachings, which after all, are intended to encapsulate unchanging truth.

Tsongkhapa founded the monastery of Ganden in 1409, and it became his main seat. He had many students, among whom Gyaltsab Dharma Rinchen (1364-1431), Khedrup Gelek Pelzang (1385-1438), Togden Jampal Gyatso, Jamyang Choje, Jamchenpa Sherap Senge and Gyalwa Gendün Drup, the first Dalai Lama (1391-1474) were the most outstanding. After Tsongkhapa's passing, his teachings were held and kept by Gyaltsab Dharma Rinchen and Khedrub Gelek Pälsang. From then on, his lineage has been held by the Ganden Tripas, the throne-holders of Ganden Monastery, among whom the present one is Khensur Lungri Namgyal, the 101st Ganden Tripa.

After the founding of Ganden Monastery by Tsongkhapa, Drepung Monastery was founded by Jamyang Choje, Sera Monastery was founded by Chöje Shakya Yeshe and the Gyalwa Gendün Drup founded Tashi Lhunpo Monastery. Many Gelug monasteries were built throughout Tibet and also in China and Mongolia.

Among the many lineage holders of the Yellow Hat Tradition (Gelugpas) there are successive incarnations of the Gyalwa Rinpoche (commonly known as the Dalai Lama), and the succession of the Panchen Lama as well as the Chagkya Dorje Chang, Ngachen Könchok Gyaltsen, Kyishö Tulku Tenzin Thrinly, Jamyang Shepa, Phurchok Jampa Rinpoche, Jamyang Dewe Dorje, Takphu Rinpoche, Khachen Yeshe Gyaltsen and many others.

The annual Tibetan prayer festival called "Monlam Prayer Festival" was the legacy of Tsongkhapa where he had offered service to ten thousand monks. The establishment of this Great Prayer Festival is seen as one of his Four Great Deeds. It celebrates the miraculous deeds of Buddha Shakyamuni.

TWENTY-ONE TARAS

Photo no 105 : *Statues of Twenty one Taras.*

INTRODUCTION

From the tantra known as the *'Twenty-One Praises of Tara'* spoken by
the Samantabhadra Bodhisattva arises a system of practice of Tara
with 21 emanations. These 21 emanations were depicted with each
form of Tara having a specific color, an attribute and a special activity.
There have been minor differences in such depictions across different
lineages. This teaching of the 21 Taras appears to have been introduced
into Tibet by Atisha. In Nyingmapa, there are three main lineages of
Tara and the 21 Taras. There is a lineage which is associated with the
Khyentse tradition, and there is the Long-Chen Nyin-Thig lineage.

However the most famous lineage of Tara, which is found in all schools, is from the *Terton* Chogyur Lingpa. But, these should not be taken as confusing issue as combination of different ritual from different lineages in Tibetan Buddhism is customary.

The twenty-one Taras are distinguished by the colour of their bodies, attributes and postures. They protect people from eight kinds of fears. The eight fears are 1) lions and pride 2) wild elephants and delusions 3) forest fires and hatred 4) snakes and envy 5) robbers and fanatical views 6) prisons and avarice 7) floods and lust 8) demons and doubt

According to another lineage there are sixteen fears that are removed through practising of Tara mantra. They are the fear of earthquakes, floods, wind, fire and lightening, fear of tyrannical authority/state injustice, war/riot/struggle, robbers/thieves, ghosts/spirits, animals, poisons, conflicts/bad dreams, sickness, misfortune, untimely death, and poverty.

Tara has 21 primary emanations which perform different activities such as pacification, increase and so forth. As classified by Ven. Kirti Tsenshab Rinpoche, the numerous enlightened activities of Tara can be grouped into four types viz. pacifying, increasing, overpowering and wrathful. They are characterized by four different colors as following:

- White represents the enlightened activity of pacifying, for example overcoming sickness, causes of untimely death and obstacles to success in one's life or one's practice.
- Yellow represents the enlightened activity of increasing the positive qualities conducive to a long life, peace, happiness and success in one's Dharma practice.
- Red represents the enlightened activity of power, or overpowering external forces that cannot be tamed through the first two activities, for example, removing obstacles to sickness, untimely death, etc., and forcefully accumulating conducive conditions for one's Dharma practice.

- Black represents the enlightened activity of wrath, which involves using forceful methods for accomplishing activities

Sanskrit	Tibetan	English	Statue	Attributes
1. Pravire	Nyurma Palmo	Swift Lady of Glory-The Swift Heroic, who destroys hindering demons and injuries		Red
2. Candrakanti	Shiwa Chenmo	Lady of Supreme Peace - The Tara white as the autumn moon, who defeats diseases and evil spirits		White
3. Kanakavarna	Serdog Chen	Lady of Golden Yellow color - The Tara who increases life and enjoyment		Yellow with a slightly bluish-hue
4. Ushnisha	Tsugtor Nampar Gyalma	Lady of Complete Victory, Embodying All Positive Qualities—The Tara victorious, who grants the highest life		White

Sanskrit	Tibetan	English	Statue	Attributes
5. Humkar-nadini	Hung Dradrogma	She, who Proclaims the Sound of HUM—The Tara crying the sound of HUM who subjugates and summons with the gesture of wisdom.		Red/yellos
6. Trailokya-vijaya	Jugten Sumle nampar gyalma	She, who is Completely Victorious over the Three Worlds - The Tara victorious over the triple world, who tames gosts		Black with ting with Red
7. Aparijita	Shen Jomma	She, who conquers others - The Tara defeating othes, who averts the magic mantras of others		Black
8. Mar-mardaneswori	Du Dra Jomma	She, who Conquers Maras and Enemies - The Tara who defeats mara demons and enemies		Red/Black

Sanskrit	Tibetan	English	Statue	Attributes
9. Shoka-	Jigpa Kunkyob ma	She Who Protects from All Fears– The Tara whose gesture symbolizes the Three Jewels, who protects from all terrors.		White
10. Jagadvashi	Dudang Jigten Wangdu Dema	She Who Brings Maras and the World under Her Power - The Tara who tames all maras and obstructions		Red
11. Paricayaka	Pongpa Selma	She, who Eradicates Poverty - The Tara dispelling the suffering of poverty, who grants the magical attainments		Red/Yellow
12. Mangala-Loka	Trashi Tamche Jinma	She, who Grants All That is Auspicious - The Tara who grants all good fortune		Red/Yellow

Sanskrit	Tibetan	English	Statue	Attributes
13. Janguli	Metar Barma	She, Who Blazes Like Fire - The Tara who who defeats hindering demons and obstacles.		Red
14. Kruddha	Tronyer Chen	She, who is Frowning Wrathfully		Red/Black
15. Maha-shanta	Shiwa Chenma	She, of Supreme Peacefulness - The Tara great and calm who cleanses sins and obscurations.		White
16. Raga-nishudana	Rigpa Hungle Drolma	Tara, Who Arises from the Hung of Intrinsic Awareness - The Tara victorious over the contentious of others, who increases one's intelligence.		Red
17 Sukhada Sumyowa	Drolma Jigten	She, Who Causes the Three Realms to Tremble - The Tara pacifying mara demons and obscurations who shakes the triple worlds.		Red/Yellow

Sanskrit	Tibetan	English	Statue	Attributes	
18. Sit-vijaya	Dug Selma	She, Who Neutralizes Poison - The Tara pacifying the poison of the nags, who dispels it.		White	
19. Dukha-dahana	Dug NGal Tamche Selwei Drolma	She, Who Alleviates All Suffering– The Tara who dispels bad dreams and suffering		White	
20. Siddhisa-mbhava	Rimne Selwei Drolma	She, Who Removes Pestilence — The Tara who dispels all fevers		Red/Yellow	
21. Pari-nispanna	Trinle Tamche Yongsu Dzogpar	She, Who Completely Perfects All Enlightened Activitie—The Tara who fulfills all active functions		White	

for enlightened purposes that cannot be accomplished through other means.

ICONOGRAPHY AND DOCTRINE

According to the tradition of Lord Atisha, the following are the list of the 21 Taras, their names, activities and attributes with respective color of representation.

USHNISHA-SITATAPATRA

Photo no 106 : *Ushnisha Sitatapatra*

INTRODUCTION

Ushnisha-Sitatapatra (also called Sitapatra, White Parasol, Tib: *Dukar*) is a protector described in the *Shurangama Sutra*.

She is regarded as a female counterpart to Avalokiteshvara, the Bodhisattva of Compassion.

Her parasol indicates her ability to protect sentient beings from natural catastrophes, diseases, and so forth. She is white in color, because the principal means by which she accomplishes this function is the enlightenment energy of pacification.

Sitatapatra, one of the most complex Vajrayana goddesses manifests in many elaborate forms: having a thousand faces, arms and legs, or simply as a feminine deity of great beauty. Known foremost for her "White Parasol" she is most frequently attributed with the "Golden Wheel" as well.

ICONOGRAPHY

Sitatapatra is depicted in various forms such as one face, two arms; three faces, six arms; four faces, eight arms; eleven faces, twelve arms; a thousand faces, a thousand arms; etc. The main face and body color of thousand-armed Sitatapatra is white. Other faces are shown in different colors. Each of the depicted heads has three eyes, and there is one in each palm and sole. The deity stands with her feet treading on the living six destinies. She is also shown in a seated posture. Her right hands hold dharma wheels and her left hold arrows, except for the one holding the parasol representing the protection she offers. In some variations, she holds a lotus and puts a small white umbrella on it. The other attributes are sword, ax, dharma wheel, bow, arrow, book, lasso, bell, vajra, rosary, vase, etc. Her image is often mistaken for that of 1,000-armed Chenrezi.

Surrounded by flames and radiating indomitable energy, the great protectress Usnisa-Sitãtapatrã stands on a blue lotus. Below her feet are representations of jealousy, greed, and other forces that bind one to suffering, all suppressed by her boundless energy and compassion.

DOCTRINE AND OTHERS

According to *Mahavairocana sutra* the first one of Five Buddhas on top of Tathagata is the white parasol which would mean that Sitatapatra is the forerunner of the Five Buddhas. According the doctrine of Tantric Buddhism, the Buddha's cranium has a topknot on the forehead (called *usnisha*) and Sitatapatra was originated from there. There is also a legend regarding the appearance of Sitatapatra, according to which, once Sakra-devanam-Indra was pursued by a bad deity *Asura* and he requested for help from the Buddha. The Buddha emanated Sitatapatra from his usnisha. Sitatapatra took a big umbrella and read her mantra. Following which the Asura was forced to leave and thus freed Sakra-devanam-Indra from danger. Because of this, the people believe deeply in the power of the Sitatapatra tantra.

There are mention of four Sitatapatra dharanis (magic spells) in the Tibetan *Kanjur*. People believe that their recitation can drive away disasters and release the beings. It was very popular during Yuan Dynasty in China and a festival was held annually called the "Welcome Sitatapatra to visit." Worshipping of Sitatapatra is more prevalent in Tibet, China and Mongolia even today. People practice sadhana of Sitatapatra for dispelling illness, interferences, spirit harms, etc. In order to practice such sadhana in full, there is a need of *Kriya tantra* empowerment. However, practice can be done without such an empowerment with permission from a qualified master.

A Prayer to the White Umbrella Deity runs thus :

I prostrate to the feet of the one renowned as Ushnisha Sitatapatra:
The stainless white wisdom umbrella,
Undefeatable by others, the most sublime goddess,
Who took excellent birth from the ushnisha,
The supreme mark of all the buddhas.
Please destroy all interferences and bestow all happiness and supreme
attainments.

Mantra : *om sarva tathagata unika sita'tapatre hum phat hum mama hum ni svaha!*

VAIROCANA

Photo no 107 : *Vairochana Buddha.*

INTRODUCTION

Buddha Vairocana (Tib: *rNam-par-snang mdzad)* is one of the Five Wisdom Buddhas or Pancha Buddhas in Vajrayana Buddhism. The other Budddhas are Akshobhya Buddha, Ratnasambava Buddha, Amitabh Buddha and Amoghasiddhi Buddha.

The name Vairochana means "He Who is Like the Sun". Vairochana represents either the integration of or the origin of the all five wisdom Buddhas. His wisdom is the Wisdom of the Dharmadhatu which is the Realm of Truth, in which all things exist as they really are.

Vairocana is said to be the sum of all the Wisdom Buddhas and combines all their qualities. He is therefore, pure white. Vairochana's wisdom is also referred to as the All-Pervading Wisdom of the Dharmakaya. The Dharmakaya is the Body of the Law, or the absolute Buddha nature.

Vairochana's transcendent wisdom reveals the realm of highest reality and overcomes the poison of ignorance, or delusion. His wisdom is considered to be the origin of or the total of all the wisdoms of the Dhyani Buddhas.

Vairocana is an idealization of this central function of the Buddha as a teacher, without which there would have been no Buddhism, and no path to enlightenment. While Amitabha Buddha is seen as a personification of Compassion (balanced by Wisdom), Vairocana is often seen as a personification of Wisdom.

ICONOGRAPHY

Vairochana is usually located in the center of mandalas of the Dhyani Buddhas. According to some texts, he is positioned in the east. Vairochana's mudra is the dharmachakra mudra, the gesture of turning the wheel of the Teaching. His color is white (or blue), symbolizing a pure consciousness. He rules over the element of ether and embodies the skandha of consciousness. His symbol is the dharmachakra, the wheel of the Teaching, or the wheel of the Law. It denotes the teaching of the Buddha. Its eight spokes represent the Noble Eightfold Path, which Gautama revealed in his first sermon after his enlightenment. Vairochana's lotus throne is supported by the lion, symbol of courage, boldness and an eager, advancing spirit.

Because he embodies the wisdom of all Buddhas, Vairochana's bija is the universal sound Om.

DOCTRINE AND OTHERS

The doctrine of Vairocana Buddha is based largely on the teachings of the Mahavairocana Sutra and to a lesser degree the Vajrasekhara Sutra. Vairocana features prominently in the Chinese school of Hua-Yen Buddhism, and also later schools including Japanese Kegon Buddhism, and Japanese Shingon Buddhism. In the case of Shingon Buddhism, Vairocana is the central figure

In the Buddhist Mahavairocana Sutra, Vairocana teaches the Dharma to Vajrasattva. Vairocana provides esoteric techniques and rituals to help conceptualize the Dharma beyond verbal form.

Vairocana is specifically believed to transform the delusion of ignorance into the wisdom preached by the Dharma. When Gautama Buddha turned the Wheel of the Dharma, it illuminated the hearts of men and women darkened by ignorance.

Mantra : Om *Vairochana Om.*

In short, the particulars of Vairocana Buddha are as following :

Particular	For Vairocana Buddha
Meaning of the Name	· Buddha Supreme and Eternal; The Radiant One
Direction	Center
Color	white
Mudra	dharmachakra (wheel-turning)
Vija (Syllable)	Om

Particular	For Vairocana Buddha
Symbol	wheel
Embodies	sovereignty
Type of wisdom	integration of the wisdom of all the Buddhas
Cosmic element (skandha)	rupa (form)
Earthly element	ether
Antidote to	ignorance and delusion
Sense	sight
Vehicle	lion
Spiritual son	Manjushree
Consort	White Tara
Paradise	

VAJRADHARA

Photo no 108 : *Vajradhara.*

INTRODUCTION

Vajradhara (Tib. *Dorje Chang*) is the ultimate Primordial Buddha, or Adi Buddha, according to Tibetan Buddhism. Vajradhara is the primordial Buddha, the dharmakaya Buddha. Vajradhara represents the essence of the historical Buddha's realization of enlightenment. Achieving the 'state of vajradhara' is synonymous with complete realization.

Names of Vajradhara and Samantabhadra are often used interchangeably.

Five Wisdom Buddhas (*Dhyani Buddhas*) were manifested from Vajradhara/Samantabhadra. Vajradhara and the Widsom Buddhas are often subjects of mandala.

ICONOGRAPHY

Vajradhara and/or Samantabhadra are cognate deities with different names, attributes, appearances and iconography. Both are Dharmakaya Buddhas, that is primordial Buddhas, where Samantabhadra is unadorned, that is depicted without any attributes. Conversely, Vajradhara is often adorned and bears attributes, which is generally the iconographic representation of a Sambhogakaya Buddha. Both Vajradhara and Samantabhadra are generally depicted in yab-yum unity embodying void and ultimate emptiness.

Vajradhara is depicted seated cross-legged in a *vajraparyanka* pose, on a moon disk and lotus, two-armed, hands crossed over his heart in the *vajrahunkara* or union gesture. His left, hand is holding a bell and his right hand is holding a *vajra*. He is blue. If in union, Vajradhara's consort is red Vajrayoginî (Vajravârâhî), embodiment of *prajñâpâramitâ* (the "perfection of wisdom"), skull in left hand and flaying knife in right. Although *dharmakâya*, and therefore not individual, he wears the regal finery of a s*ambhogakâya*—eight jewel ornaments and five silks. In paintings he is frequently surrounded by the eighty-four *mahâsiddhas*, Tantric Buddhist saints.

Photo no 109 : *Vajradhara in yab-yum.*

Vajradhara (*Dorje Chang*) is depicted with heavenly ornaments and garments to symbolize his capacity to ceaselessly benefit and fulfill the needs of all living beings through the means of sambhogakaya and nirmanakaya emanations.

DOCTRINE AND OTHERS

Historically, Prince Siddhartha attained enlightenment under the bodhi tree in Bodhgaya over 2500 years ago and then manifested as the Buddha.. Prince Siddhartha's achievement of enlightenment, the realization itself, is called the dharmakaya, the body of truth. When he expresses that realization through subtle symbols, his realization is then called the sambhogakaya, the body of enjoyment. When such realization manifested in more accessible or physical form for all sentient beings as the historical Shakyamuni Buddha, it was then Nirmankaya. In other words, Vajradhara is the founder of Vajrayana Buddhism, or Tantra. He is the same mental continuum as Buddha Shakyamuni but displays a different aspect. He appeared as Buddha

Shakyamuni to reveal the stages of the path of Sutra, and as Conqueror Vajradhara to reveal the stages of the path of Tantra. Also, it is relevant here to add that Vajrasattva is the sambhogakaya form of Vajradhara.

The activity of Vajradhara is to benefit all beings without discrimination or judgment. It is not only in the Buddha nature of the Vajradhara aspect of ultimate enlightenment to benefit sentient beings; Buddha nature is also inherent in all living beings like us as well.

Photo no 110 : *Turquoise studded statue of Vajradara.*

Although the state of Vajradhara is beyond words and conception, it is something within ourselves which through our diligence and practice we are able to experience. Vajradhara is not anything separate or different from us.

Despite the fact that there is no physical form to Vajradhara, a dark blue human being who wears ornaments and silks and holds a bell and vajra is depicted as a symbolic gesture to understand the enlightened aspect. The dark blue color, bell, and vajra symbolize the indestructibility of Vajradhara. The dark blue also connotes his ceaseless activity to benefit beings, and his ornaments symbolize the preciousness of benefiting all living beings.

Tilopa (c. 988–1069), is said to have received mahamudra teaching directly from Vajradhara. Then he founded Kagyu lineage thereafter. Later Tilopa instructed the Bengali Nâropa (1016–1100), who taught the Tibetan seeker Marpa, (1002/12–1097), who then carried the lineage back to Tibet and passed it on to Milarepa, (1028/40–1111/23). In the Kagyu traditions, Vajradhara receives special worship as both the revealer of mysteries and the mystery itself.

VAJRAKILA

Photo no 111 : *Vajrakila*

INTRODUCTION

Vajrakila (also, Benzarkila or Vajrakilaya, Tib. *Dorje Purba*) is a winged dark blue wrathful deity or heruka whose characteristic implement is the phurba, the 3-sided 'spirit nail.' He is said to have appeared as an aspect of Padmasambhava to subdue the opposing and chaotic forces which tried to prevent all activities motivated by compassion and generosity from penetrating Tibetan culture.

When Vajrakila works through the activity of the purifier, Vajrasattva, he is called Vajrakumara (Tib. *Dorje Shönnu*) or Indomitable Prince.

Vajrakila is also considered the wrathful embodiment of bodhisattva, Vajrapani, as he acts to subdue, purify and transform the actions of those whether gods, *raksha*s or people, who seek accomplishment or power for selfish or irresponsible reasons.

ICONOGRAPHY

Vajrakila, Heruka (Tibetan: dor je phur ba, thrag thung, English: Vajra Peg, Blood Drinker). The Activity Deity from the set of Eight Herukas (Tib. *ka gye*) of the Mahayoga Tantras of the Nyingmapa School according to the Ancient Khon Tradition of Sakya.

Fearsome and wrathful, blue in colour with three faces, six hands and four legs, the right face is white and left red, each has three eyes, a gaping mouth and yellow hair flowing upward. The first pair of hands holds a kila (three sided peg) at the heart. The right hands hold a five and nine pointed vajra, and the left hands hold a trident and a mass of flame. Unfurled behind are two large wings decorated with vajras. Adorned with a crown of five skulls, earrings, bracelets and a necklace of fifty heads, he wears an elephant hide across the back and a tiger skin as a lower garment. The consort Diptacakra (Flaming Wheel) is black in colour with one face and two hands holding a skullcup in the left and a gold wheel upraised in the right. Adorned with jewels, gold and a garland of fifty dry skulls she wears a leopard skin skirt and the left leg rose to embrace the male consort. Atop the splayed bodies of Maheshvara and Uma, a sun disc and multi-coloured lotus the terrific deities stand surrounded by the orange-red flames of pristine awareness.

Vajrakila or Guru Drag-dmar is a Tantric manifestation of Padmasambhava. The main characteristic of this divinity is a lower body in the form of a magic dagger. The cult of the magic dagger with the Vajra handle and the associated rites for overcoming demons were originally introduced into Tibet by Padmasambhava.

The wrathful red Guru Drag-dmar appears in a halo of blazing flames, his ocher-yellow halo of hair is topped by a crown of five heads and Ratna symbols. The skin of an elephant is slung over his back and his body is adorned with bone bead chains and a garland of snakes. A garland of human heads hangs around his neck

Photo no 112 : *Fully gold coated another form of Vajrakila.*

As attributes, Guru Drag-dmar holds a golden vajra in his right hand and a scorpion in his left. The scorpion is a Tantric representation of Vajrapani, who was initiated into the secret teachings in a cemetery by Padmasambhava.

The lower part of the body of Guru Drag-dmar consists of a three-sided dagger [kila] which is held by the mouth of a Makara, lord of the water element. The Makara has dominion over the Nagas, or snake-demons, who inhabit rivers and lakes.

DOCTRINE AND OTHERS

The practice of Vajrakilaya blazes at the heart of the ancient Vajrayana traditions of Tibet. The wrathful heruka Vajrakilaya is the yidam deity who embodies the enlightened activity of all the Buddhas, manifesting in an intensely wrathful yet compassionate form in order to subjugate the delusion and negativity that can arise as obstacles to the practice of Dharma. In fact, the practice of Vajrakilaya is famous in the Tibetan Buddhist world as the most powerful for removing obstacles, destroying the forces hostile to compassion, and purifying the spiritual pollution so prevalent in this age.

Photo no 113 : *A statue of Maha-vajrakila.*

Vajrakila surrounded by major deities of his field of enlightenment (Buddha field), can be easily recognized by holding a magical dagger (phurba) in his hands, which enforces him to ban all kind of hindrances, caused by lower demons, angry nagas or ghosts. He can be invoked as a protector as well as a deity for self-identification.

This dark-blue Vajrakila is a wrathful emanation of the water element (Akshobhya Buddha). The seed-syllable is *hung*. The Vajrakilaya tantra has a special importance in the Nyinmapa, Sakyapa and Kagyu traditions of Tibetan Buddhism. The tantras of Vajrakila are contained in the sadhana class of Mahayoga, and preserved in the *collected tantras of the Nyingmapa*. Only one small fragment, translated by Sakya Pandita, is to be found in the *Kangyur*. A version of longer *Vajrakila Tantras* is also found in Chinese translations from the Sanskrit.

Vajrakilaya Puja has long unbroken lineage within the Sakyapa. Vajrakilaya Puja was received by Khön Nagendra Rakshita and his younger sibling Vajra Ratna from Padmasambhava. Since then it has been transmitted in the Khön lineage and has been enacted every year until the present. Even in the challenging times of 1959 His Holiness the Sakya Trizin maintained the tradition.

His most common mantra is *'Om Vajrakila Kilaya Sarva Benganin Bam Hung Phet'*.

VAJRAPANI

Photo no 114 : *Vajrapani.*

INTRODUCTION

Vajrapani (also called Dharmevajra, Vajra Garba, Tib: *Chana Dorje*} is one of the earliest bodhisattvas of Mahayana Buddhism. He is the protector and guide of the Buddha. He symbolizes the power of the Buddha.

He was used extensively in Buddhist iconography as one of the three protective deities surrounding the Buddha. Each of them symbolizes one of the Buddha's virtues: Manjusri (the manifestation of all the Buddhas' wisdom), Avalokitesvara (the manifestation of all the Buddhas' compassion) and Vajrapani (the manifestation of all the Buddhas' power). Vajrapani is this tantric aspect of the enlightened mind, transforming the energy of negative emotion into active wisdom and magical perfection. He symbolizes the indestructible vajra mind of a Buddha.

Vajrapani is considered the second Boddhisattva emanated from Buddha Akshyobhya.

Vajrapani Boddhisattva was with Buddha Sakyamuni when Tathagata subdued the gigantic snake in Uddiyana. When the *Nagas* {serpent gods} appeared before the Buddha to listen to the teachings, Vajrapani was bestowed the responsibility by the Tathagata to guard them from the attacks of their mortal enemies, the garudas. In order to deceive and combat the garudas, Vajrapani assumed a form with head, wings and claws like that of garudas themselves.

The Nagas are believed to control the rain-clouds, hence Vajrapani, as their protector, is looked upon as the Rain God, and it is to him the Mahayana Buddhists appeal when rain is needed, or is excessive.

ICONOGRAPHY

Usually Vajrapani is depicted in an active *pratayalidha* (warrior pose). His outstretched right hand brandishes a vajra and his left hand deftly holds a lasso - with which he binds demons. He wears a skull crown with his hair standing on end. His expression is wrathful and he has a third eye. Around his neck is a serpent necklace and his loin cloth is made up of the tiger skin, whose head can be seen on his right knee.

Vajrapani is often depicted in dark blue color. He is shown with Avalokitesvara and Manjushri Boddhisattva of infinite compassion and infinite wisdom/knowledge respectively. His symbol is a vajra. His emblem is an *utpala* (blue lotus) and Shakti (consort) is Sujata.

DOCTRINE AND OTHERS

Photo no 115 : *Vajrapani with consort Sujata.*

Various scriptures put on Vajrapani to start with a lowly yaksh, who incourse of time was promoted to 'great General of the Yaksas'. He goes on to become one of the bodily forms of the Bodhisattva Avalokitesvara and later emerges as a Bodhisattva in his own right. In different scriptures he is also referred to as a fully enlightened Buddha. Besides, the association with Power, Vajrapani like Vajrasattva is connected with Purity. But while Vajrasattva is Purity achieved or the essense of Purity Vajrapani is 'the process of becoming pure'.

Photo no 116 : *A metal statue of Vajrapani in color.*

Vajrapani, the Bodhisattva with many benevolent characteristics, is the impeccable enemy of the demons. His virtuous characters are mentioned in a form of the legend. Once there was an assembly of the Buddhas. All met together on the top of Mount Meru (Sumeru) to deliberate upon the best means of procuring the water of life, nectar (*amrita*) that lied concealed at the bottom of the ocean. The evil demons were in possession of the powerful poison, *Hala-hala*, and using it to bring destruction on humankind. In order to procure the antidote, they decided to churn the ocean with the Mount Meru. When nectar had risen to the surface of the water, they deputed

Vajrapani to guard, until they would decide on the best means of using it. However, Vajrapani left elixir of life a moment unguarded and the monster, Rahu, stole it. It was followed by a fearful struggle for the possession of the amrita. Rahu was defeated in the end, but the water of life had been defiled by him already by adding poison. Thereafter Buddhas, to punish Vajrapani, forced him to drink it whereupon he became dark blue from the poison mixed with amrita.

Vajrapani is the embodiment of the spiritual strength of all the Buddhas. He appears in a wrathful aspect, displaying his power to overcome outer, inner and secret obstacles. Vajrapani is a means of accomplishing fierce determination and symbolizes unrelenting effectiveness in the conquest of negativity. Vajrapani Bodhisattva represents the courage necessary to achieve enlightened spiritual awakening. In order to become ultimately happy and to ultimately help others requires great courage. Vajrapani's activities of courage help beings to destroy delusions and to help overcome the limitations, attitudes, and habits.

Statues of Vajrapani are placed all Buddhist temples to safeguard.

Mantra : *Om Vajrapani hum!*

VAJRASATTVA

Photo no 117 : *Vajrasattva.*

INTRODUCTION

Vajrasattva ((Tib. *dorje sempa)* is regarded as Adi-Buddha in Vajrayana tradition according to the text Vajrasattvakaya.

Vajrasattva is an important figure in *Mahavairocana Sutra* and the *Vajrasekhara Sutra.* In both sutras, Vajrasattva plays the role of the student, who learns the Dharma from Mahavairocana Buddha.

Vajrasattva is sambhogakaya Buddha, the sovereign of all the Buddha families and mandalas.

Vajrasattva is regarded as the priest of five Buddhas too. In some mandala, he changes places with Akshobhya in the East. In Shingon Buddhism it is Vajrasattva that passes on the initiation of Mahâvairocana to Nagarjuna, thereby creating the Vajrayana lineage.

Since, Vajrasattva is the manifestation of the purity of body, speech, and mind of all the Buddhas, Vajrasattva is visualized as an expression of mind's pure essence in the form of the meditational deity.

Vajrasattva is a very popular tutelary deity among Nepalese Vajracharyas and worshipped through *Gurumandala* ritual.

ICONOGRAPHY

Vajrasattva is depicted in white with single face and two hands. Vajrasattva's right hand holds a five pronged vajra at his chest. His left hand holds a bell at his side. He sits in the *vajraparyanka* posture wearing precious silks and ornaments with jewel diadem. Half of his long wavy black hair is gathered on top of his head, the rest curls down his back and around his shoulders. He is seated on a moon disc on a white lotus. His body is adorned with 32 major and 80 minor marks of a Sambhogakaya and emits a clear limitless light. Vajrasattva has father-mother aspect too. His form is however, the same as in the single one but his consort carries a kartika in her right hand and a kapala in her left hand. Generally this form is not exhibited in open. It is shown only to those who are initiated in Highest Yoga Tantra.

DOCTRINE AND OTHERS

Vajrasattva is regarded as the priest of the Five Transcendental Pancha Buddhas. He is not represented in the stupa like other Dhyani Buddhas, but independent shrines are dedicated to his worship. His worship is always performed in secret and is not open to those who are not initiated into the mysteries of the Vajrayana. Vajrasattva's practice is one of purification through the realization that in one's true nature, one is never impure. He is visualized in the foundation meditation practices of Tantra, with the aim of generating Bodhichitta, the cosmic will to enlightenment.

Photo no 118 : *Vajrasattva with shakti.*

Vajrasattva is said to have been originated from seed syllable hum and is generally invoked for removal of obscuration of Kleshavarana and Jneyavarana. Vajrasattva's hundred syllable mantra is very efficacious in purifying the defilements through confession practice. It is said if confession is done with the four opponent powers, then non-virtuous actions or obscurations will be purified. The first opponent power is the force of reliance which means looking upon the visualized image of Vajrasattva as the embodiment of one's refuge. The second opponent power is the sincere regret for the non-virtuous action done by one. The third opponent power is resisting from evil deeds. The fourth opponent power is to apply power of good deeds especially regarding the practicing the meditation and recitation of Vajrasattva without parting from Bodhicitta while remaining in the state of emptiness.

It says that in the past, while on the path of learning, Vajrasattva made the following aspiration:

Photo no 119 : *Vajrasattva statue with colored parwa.*

In future, when I reach complete and perfect buddhahood, may those who have committed the five crimes with immediate retribution, or anyone whose samaya commitments have been impaired, be purified entirely of all their harmful actions and impairments merely by hearing my name, thinking of me, or reciting the hundred syllables, the most majestic of all the secret mantras! Until this is brought about may I remain without awakening! And: May I be present before all those with impairments and breakages of samaya commitments and may I purify all their obscurations!

Due to the strength of these prayers, Vajrasattva's enlightened aspirations are unlike those of other Buddhas. In his nature, he embodies the hundred Buddha families, the five Buddha families and so on. Since he is the all-pervading lord of the hundred Buddha families and the single Buddha family of the great secret, he is unlike any other deity. One might go before each and every buddha dwelling in the ten directions and strive to apply the methods for confession, but it is said that is better still to practice confession by visualizing your own teacher, the one from whom all the mandalas emanate and into whom they are re-absorbed, indivisible from Vajrasattva.

Mantra: A short mantra is *Om vajrasattva hum.*

As mentioned above, a 100 syllable mantra is more popular.

VAJRAVARAHI

Photo no 12 : *Vajravarahi*

INTRODUCTION

Vajravarahi (Tib: *Dorje Phagmo*) is a dakini, a tantric Buddhist yidam. She is the consort of Cakrasamvara. Vajravarahi also is considered an emanation of Vajrayogini.

Vajravarahi is marked by a sow's head protruding above her right ear.

ICONOGRAPHY

She stands in *satyalidha* attitude of a dancing posture. She is shown in a single face with three eyes. She is depicted in red color. Her disheveled hair is marked with six auspicious symbols. She holds a kartika in her right hand at the level of head and holds a *kapala* in her left. She carries a *khattvanga* surmounted by three skulls. She wears a garland of fifty severed heads and various gold ornaments. One of the peculiar features of this deity is that she has an excrescence near the right ear, which resembles the face of a sow hence her name. She tramples an inert body positioned atop an open lotus. Her figure imparts a sense of wild abandonment.

DOCTRINE AND OTHERS

Vahravarahi is considered a form of Vajra Yogini/Dakini. She is associated with Heruka Chakrasambhava. She is the essence of the five kinds knowledge, and is the embodiment of the *Sahaj* pleasure. Vajravarahi is a goddess often invoked by monks newly initiated into tantric meditation practices. The goddess is associated with triumph over ignorance (symbolized by the sow). Early Tibetan translations of Sanskrit texts, such as the *Sadhanamala* (Garland of Means for Spiritual Attainment), the *Nishpannayogavali* (Garland of Perfection Yogas), and the *Hevajra Tantra*, describe Vajravarahi's mandala as unfolding within the heart of a practitioner.

There are ample mentions of the fact that this dakini/deity had played significant role in the lives of the eighty-four mahasiddhas in persuading them in the path of achievement. In Tibet, Vajravarahi is also the patron deity of the Semding nunnery.

Vajravarahi is a popular deity especially among Newar community of Nepal. There are several Caryagita dedicated to her. For the practice of Sadhana of Vajravarahi an initiation (skt. diksha) is required. But, one should not get confused with similar names given to other forms of Asta-matrikas. For example, there are four *varahis* around Kathmandu valley namely, *Vajravarahi,* red in colour, who presides over the west and is believed to protect livestock especially; *Nilavarahi,* blue in colour, who guards the east, *Swetavarahi,* white in color at the southern gate and *Dhumbarahi,* grey in color, who protects the north and defends the valley against cholera. The temple of Vajravarahi (one form of Astamatrika) located in Patan is a very famous one.

VAJRAYOGINI

Photo no 121 : *Vajrayogini.*

INTRODUCTION

Vajrayogini (Tib: *Dorje Naljorma*) is the female sambhogakaya form of Buddha of wisdom and great bliss. She is a meditational deity of the anuttarayoga tantra. She is the consort of Cakrasamvara. She is the Queen of the Dakinis. She is the beloved personal deity to many Kadampa Buddhists.

Vajrayogini is the yidam that a meditator identifies with when practicing *six yogas of Naropa*

Vajrayogini is one of the most famous tutelary deities in Nepalese Buddhism.

ICONOGRAPHY

Photo no 122 : *Vajrayogini in another pose.*

Vajrayogini is visualized as the transparent, deep red form of the young lady with the third eye of wisdom set vertically on her forehead. She is shown standing in satyalidha posture. She holds a khatri in her right hand and holds a kapala filled with blood in her left at a level of the head. She carries a khattvanga staff surmounted by three skulls. She wears a garland of fifty-one severed heads and various gold ornaments. She tramples upon her own emanations Bhairaba and Kalaratri beneath her feet.

Guhyasamayasadhanamala, which has unique collection of sadhanas mentions about various forms of Vajrayogini. Only few forms have been popular in Tantric Buddhism over the successive period.

DOCTRINE AND OTHERS

The two stages of the practice of Vajrayogini were originally taught by Buddha Vajradhara. He manifested in the form of Heruka to expound the *Root Tantra of Heruka*, and it was in this Tantra that he explained the practice of Vajrayogini. The instructions on Vajrayogini in all different lineages can be traced back to this original revelation. Of these lineages, there are three that are most commonly practiced: the *Narokhachö* lineage, which was transmitted from Vajrayogini to Naropa; the *Maitrikhachö* lineage, which was transmitted from Vajrayogini to Maitripa; and the *Indrakhachö* lineage, which was transmitted from Vajrayogini to Indrabodhi.

Photo no 123 : *Differently posed Vajrayogini.*

The instruction of Vajrayogini is the most profound teaching of Highest Yoga Tantra. Yet, it is concise and clearly presented meditations that are relatively easy to practice. The mantra is short and easy to recite, and the visualizations of the mandala, the Deity, and the body mandala are simple compared with those of other Highest Yoga Tantra Deities. Even practitioners with limited abilities and little wisdom can engage in these practices without great difficulty.

Vajrayogini is associated with the Pure Dakini Land which is similar to Tushita and Sukhavati but, the different is that there Heruka and Vajrayogini give teachings on the Highest Yoga Tantra. When through Vajrayogini's guidance those who are very old and infirm reach her Pure Land they will no longer experience the sufferings of old age and sickness. All signs of their old age will disappear and they will be transformed into sixteen-year-olds of great beauty and vitality, enjoying an endless life span.

All the enjoyments they desire will appear spontaneously. They will never be reborn in samsara again, unless they choose to for compassionate reasons. Everyone who reaches this Pure Land will receive teachings on Highest Yoga Tantra directly from Heruka and Vajrayogini and thereby attain enlightenment quickly.

The practice of Vajrayogini quickly brings blessings, especially during this spiritually degenerate age. It is said that as the general level of spirituality decreases, it becomes increasingly difficult for practitioners to receive the blessings of other Deities; but the opposite is the case with Heruka and Vajrayogini – the more times degenerate, the more easily practitioners can receive their blessings.

In the extensive practice of Vajrayogini, there are three aspects: empowerment, approximation, and activity. Upon receiving the four empowerments, a disciple of vajrayogini is granted the permission and transmission of energy from one's guru to engage in Vajrayogini's path of practice. The seeds of the four buddha-bodies are planted in the disciple's mental continuum that will eventually ripen into the actual enlightened bodies of Vajragogini–perhaps even in one lifetime.

Photo no 124 : *Another pose of Vajrayogini.*

Vajrayogini had mainfested herself in an initiatory vision to the great Pandit Mahasiddha Naropa. The image, known as Naro Khachoma, or "Naropa's Space Dancer," represents one of the three main forms of Vajrayogini practiced in Tibet, and the main form of the diety propitiated within the Gelukpa School. The lineage passed from the Indian mahasiddha Naropa to the Pantingpa brothers in the eleventh century, who brought it to Tibet.

VASUDHARA

Photo no 125 : *Vasudhara*

INTRODUCTION

Vasudhara is a name for the Buddhist bodhisattva of abundance and fertility. She is considered to be the consort of Kuvera, the god of wealth.

Vasudhara is popular in Nepal, where she is a common household deity.

ICONOGRAPHY

She is usually represented with six arms. In the lower left hand she usually holds her characteristic symbol, the treasure vase. The hand above holds another distinguishing attribute, the ears of corn. The third left hand holds a book, the Prajnaparamita sutra.

The lower right hand is in the varada mudra of charity; the one above holds three precious wish-fulfilling jewels, while the upper hand makes a mudra of salutation. The right leg is pendent, and the foot is unsupported resting upon a vase.

Seated in lalitasana on a double lotus throne, with her right foot resting on a small lotus flower, Vasudhara wears a saree engraved with a pattern of catfoot prints and double moving engraved lines. She is elaborately adorned with two necklaces, earrings, bracelets, anklets, armlets and ornaments. Her hair is arranged into two buns on either side of an exquisitely rendered three leaved tiara, with a large central diadem. Her lower right hand is in the posture of varada mudra, the gesture of charity. Her upper right hand makes the gesture of adorning the Buddha while her other is holding a sheaf of grain. Her left hands hold the auspicious waterpot (the kalasa, the holy vase containing the amrita, the elixir of immortality), a sheaf of grain and a pustaka, the book which emphasizes her identity with transcendental wisdom. The mudras and attributes signify her role as dispenser of wealth and agent of fecundity.

DOCTRINE AND OTHERS

In the Mahayana Buddhist Pantheon, Vasudhara is the goddess of wealth and prosperity. This popular female Bodhisattva (the actual creators of the universe), achieved the state of enlightenment and dedicated herself to guiding all mankind to the path of Buddha, which in turn leads to Nirvana (the Buddhist heaven). The goddess of fortune is in addition one of the eight Vasus, belonging to the Rig-Veda. Vasudhara is the female partner of Vaisharavana (also known as Kubera or Jambhala).

Mantra : *Om namoratnatrayaya namobhagabate basudhare satjiwam samraksani phalahaste dihyarupam shri basudhare basudde shivamkari shantikari pustimkari bhawanasani sarwadustan bhunja bhunja amrit kuru mama karya siddhikari swaha.*

VIRUDHAKA

Photo no 126 : *Virudhaka*

INTRODUCTION

Virudhaka (Tibetan: *pag pi kye bo*), is one of the four heavenly guardian kings (others being Virudhaka, Virupaksa and Vaisravana). He is the Guardian of the Southern Direction and King of the Kumbhanda.

Virudhaka functions to relieve people of their suffering, signifying one who teaches moderation and gives hope and joy to the people.

ICONOGRAPHY

Regal in stature, blue in colour, he has a full face with black eyebrows, moustache and beard. Large bulbous eyes gaze to the side. The right hand holds at the waist a long sword with the left cradling the blade across the chest. Adorned with an ornate headdress of gold and jewels, earrings and ribbons, he is richly garbed in the brocade raiment of a king, opulent with silks and elaborates design in a variety of colors. Seated on a light brown deerskin mat above a rocky bench, in a relaxed posture and wearing boots, the right foot is extended pressing on the back of a golden turtle. The left foot is held up by a Kumbhanda daemon, green and pink of color, in an acquiescent kneeling posture. The head is encircled by an irregular dark green areola edged with licks of flame in various colors. The background is filled with swirling smoke, dark purple, and the foreground sparse and green.

DOCTRINE AND OTHERS

Four Guardian Kings arose originally with the early Buddhist sutras and became fully developed in the later Mahayana sutras. They are common to all schools of Tibetan Buddhism. All four serve Œakra, the lord of thirty-three gods. On the orders of Œakra, the four kings and their retinues stand guard to protect from another attack by the Asuras, which once threatened to destroy the kingdom of the devas. They are also vowed to protect the Buddha, the Dharma, and the

Buddha's followers from danger. According to Vasubandhu, devas born in the Câturmahârâjika heaven are 1/4 of a kroúa in height (about 750 feet tall). They also have a five-hundred year lifespan, of which each day is equivalent to 50 years in our world; thus their total lifespan amounts to about nine million years (other sources say 90,000 years).

VIRUPAKSHA

Photo no 127 : *Virupaksha.*

INTRODUCTION

Virupaksha is one of the four heavenly guardian kings (others being Virudhaka, Dhritarastra and Vaisravana). He is the Guardian of the West direction.

The function of Virupaksha is to discern evil, and he represents those who can accurately perceive the nature of society and fairly judge good and evil.

ICONOGRAPHY

He is dark red in color with a moustache and goatee. He holds in the right hand a white stupa. and in the left held a writhing snake. Adorned with a crown of gold studded with jewels, earrings and hair ribbons, he wears a rich brocade vest and various colored garments, trousers and boots, all emblazoned with pictures and designs. In a standing posture against dark billowing clouds of blue and pink, he has a ring of orange flame surrounding the head.

DOCTRINE AND OTHERS

Photo no 128 : *Another statue of Virupaksha.*

The stories of the Four Guardian Kings are mentioned in early Buddhist sutras and became fully developed with the later Mahayana. They are common to all schools of Tibetan Buddhism. Each of these guardian kings watches over one cardinal direction of the world. They battle against evils and the Asuras who are ever trying to disrupt the peace and contentment of heaven. Each sits atop a mountain peak that is the highest point of their continent. They are said to guard Buddhist temples. They are also known to have protected the Buddha at the moment of conception in his mother's womb.

These guardians are also regarded as Recorders of the happenings in the Devas' assemblies. On the eighth day of the lunar half-month, they send their councilors out into the world to discover if men cultivate righteousness and virtue; on the fourteenth day they send their sons, on the fifteenth day they themselves appear in the world, all these visits having the same purpose. Then, at the Devas' assembly, they submit their report to the gods of Távatimsa, who rejoice or lament according as to whether men prosper in righteousness or not.

In the Lotus Sutra, these kings vow to "shield and guard those who uphold" it. People receive the protective power from them in direct proportion to their dedication to faith and practice. Such powers include discernment, common sense and listening. In other words full protection comes when one is careful and use own's head.

WHITE TARA
(SAPTALOCANA)

Photo no 129 : *A fully gold plated statue of White Tara*

INTRODUCTION

White Tara (also called Saptalocana Tara, Tib: *Sgrol-dkar*) is one of the principal forms of Arya Tara and is often referred to as the Mother of all the Buddhas. She represents the motherly aspect of compassion.

White Tara is regarded as the consort of Avalokiteshvara, and sometimes that of Vairochana Buddha as well.

Because she has seven eyes - one at forehead, two regular ones, two at two palms and two at palm of the legs, she is called Saptalocana also.

People meditate on White Tara for peace, prosperity, strength, heath and longevity.

ICONOGRAPHY

She is white in color. She is usually depicted in vajra posture. With her right hand she makes the blessing gesture and her left hand, holding the stem of a white lotus flower between her thumb and fourth finger, is in the gesture of providing protection. In her left hand, she holds an elaborate lotus flower that contains three blooms. The first is in seed and represents the past Buddha Kashyapa; the second is in full bloom and symbolizes the present Buddha Shakyamuni; the third is ready to bloom and signifies the future Buddha Maitreya. These three blooms symbolize that Tara is the essence of the three Buddhas.

White Tara is also depicted in standing position. She is adorned with all sorts of ornaments.

DOCTRINE AND OTHERS

According to a sutra, Avalokiteshvara Bodhisattva had been saving and ferrying out enumerable beings from the ocean of suffering. But when he found further countless beings still plunged into this ocean of suffering, his heart ached so much out of compassion and tears dropped from his eyes. It is said that those tears turned into lotus flowers wherein White Tara and Green Tara appeared. They vowed before Avalokiteshvara that they would help in liberating living beings.

Photo no 130 : *A standing White Tara*

.White Tara is regarded as the consort of Avalokiteshvara as well. Usually, the picture of Bodhisattva Avalokiteshvara has White Tara to his right, and the Green Tara to his left. But, White Tara is also regarded as the consort of Vairochana Buddha sometimes.

White Tara is called on for peace, prosperity, strength, health and longevity. White Tara is believed to help beings on long term achievement and spiritual accomplishments. Her white color indicates purity, but also indicates that she is truthful, complete and undifferentiated. Her body is seen by the practitioner as being as dazzling white as a thousand autumn moons. She has a third eye on her forehead, symbolizing her direct vision of the unity of ultimate reality simultaneous with her two eyes seeing the dualistic relative world of beings. Her extra eyes on her palms symbolize her generosity accompanied by perfect wisdom.

In 7th century, the Tibetan King Srongtsen Gambo had married a Nepali princess, Bhrikuti. She had taken the famous Jowo statue of Shakyamuni to Tibet and she led to construct the Jokhang, the great temple in Lhasa and spread dharma in Tibet. She is considered to be the emanation of White Tara.

Photo no 131 : *White Tara well adorned*

Similarly, Guru Padmasambhava's consort Mandarava, who accomplished the *Rainbow Body practice,* is also considered an emanation of White Tara.

Atisha (982-1054), who was one of several Indian pundits who were invited to Tibet to help restore the dharma after the bitter persecutions of the apostate king Langdarma (838-42) and who founded the Kadam order, was a tantric adept and a devotee of Tara. His life was "filled with visions of the goddess Tara," and it was she who encouraged him to make the journey to Tibet. By Atisha's day, Tara was an established goddess in India. Even very early texts, such as the *Manjushrimula-kalpa* and the *Mahavairochana-sutra,* place her near Avalokiteshvara, the bodhisattva of compassion, and the earliest known Indian images of her show her as a celibate consort of Avalokiteshvara, whose active role in compassionate work is described. By the ninth century, however, she had already appeared in the Buddhist cave-temples at Ellora as an independent savioress, who, like Avalokiteshvara, rescued those who prayed to her from both physical and psychological dangers. This role is implied by her name, which means both star and saviour, a reading that derives from the Sanskrit root tar, to "cross over," and, in the Buddhist context, means "to cross over the ocean of rebirths to enlightenment". Her her twenty-one forms, described in the Praise in Twenty-one Homages (*Ekavamstatistotra*), were all well-known to Atisha.

Atisha's visions of Tara were inspired by the tantras, sadhanas and prayers that described her in her green, or active form, but also by the potent, personal revelations of her contemplative white form granted to the Indian Vagishvarakirti, who first conceived of her specialized function of "cheating death" and bestowing long life. Atisha wrote an evocation of Vagishvarakirti's White Tara and another of Green Tara. White Tara, however, was more acceptable to the eleventh-century Tibet, because she was the product of a personal vision, rather than a figure whose authority came through the tantras. During Atisha's brief sojourn in Tibet, it was his own abiding devotion to the goddess more than anything else that sparked the growth of her sect.

Tsongkhapa too was inspired by Atisha's teachings. He reformed Gelugpa and formed "New Kadam," where his teachings recognized Tara as the mother of all Buddhas, past, present, and future; transcendent, yet capable of intercession and compassionate action.

The First Dalai Lama (1391-1475), who was also one of the prime disciples of Tsongkhapa wrote a prayer of praise to White Tara, "*A Gem to Increase Life and Wisdom*" while he was living in retreat. The opening verse of that praise had well inspired Tibetan Buddhists with her compassion and with the hope of long life.

The mantra for White Tara is:

Mantra : Om tare tutare ture. mama ayur punye jnana pushtim kuru, swaha

YAMANTAKA
(VAJRABHAIRAVA,
MEGHSAMVARA)

Photo no 132 : *Yamantaka.*

INTRODUCTION

Yamântaka or Vajrabhairava or Mega-samvara (Tib: *Shinjeshe, also Dorje Jig-je*) is a yidam deity of the Highest Yoga Tantra class in Vajrayana Buddhism. Yamantaka is one of the popular deities of the Nepalese Buddhist Pantheon who presides over the eastern direction. Yamantaka is another name for Vajra (maha) bhairava, who is the highest emanation of Bodhisattva Manjushree. More precisely and also called *Yamari* (Yama's enemy,) Yamantaka is only one aspect of Vajrabhairava (absolutely terrifying) usually depicted as riding or standing on a bull that is trampling Yama.

Manjushree had taken this wrathful form in order to subdue the Lord of death. With great strength but virtuous, he is capable of subduing poisonous serpents and eliminating countless obstacles. Thus Yamantaka symbolizes the victory of wisdom over death, evil and suffering.

It is popular within the Geluk school of Tibetan Buddhism. Vajrabhairava is one of the principal three meditational deities of the Gelug school while others being Chakrasamvara and Guhyasamaja. He is also one of the main yidams in the Sakya School as well where he comes in a variety of appearances (with different mandalas).

In the other schools of Tibetan Buddhism, Yamantaka seems to be mostly revered as a protector deity.

Yamântaka's name literally means "the terminator of death". Within Buddhism, "terminating death" is actually a quality of all Buddhas as they have stopped the cycle of rebirth and dying. In this context, Yamantaka represents the goal of the Mahayana practitioner's journey to enlightenment, or the journey itself: in awakening, one adopts the practice of Yamântaka – the practice of terminating death.

In Newar Buddhism, he is best known as Meghsamvara and practices as Buddhist Guardian God known as *The Great Defender.*

ICONOGRAPHY:

Yamantaka comes in two forms:

(1) As Solitary Hero (Ekavira), and

(2) In union with his consort Vajravetali.

The full form of Vajrabhairava has nine heads, the central one being that of a buffalo, and the top-most being that yellow Manjushri with a slightly wrathful expression. The three right faces are yellow, blue and red and the three left are black, white and smoky. Each face has three large round eyes, bared fangs and frightful expressions; brown hair flows upward like flames. He has thirty-four hands and sixteen legs. The first pair of hands holds a curved knife and skull cup to the heart. The remaining hands hold a multitude of weapons with the second and last set holding in addition the fresh outstretched hide of an elephant. He is adorned with bracelets, necklaces and a girdle all formed of interlaced bone ornaments, a necklace of snakes and a long necklace of fifty human heads. The right legs are bent pressing down on a man, animals and various gods. The left legs are extended straight and press upon eight birds and various gods; standing above a sun disc and multi-colored lotus completely surrounded by the orange flames of pristine awareness.

Photo no 133 : *Yamantaka with single face in a colored statue.*

The central main hands of the deity hold a khatrika and a kapala. The lower main hands hold a phurba and the severed multi-faced head of Brahma the Creator. The upper main hands hold a red right hand holding an arrow and a shield. The other hands hold a vajra, lance, axe, viswo-vajra, dharmachakra, dagger, swirling flames, bell, khatvanga, banner, a red human right foot, a transfixed corpse, various magical knives and stakes, a noose, a skin, and other tantric weapons.

The deity wears snake ornaments such as bracelets, chain, necklace, armbands, an intricate draped girdle, anklets and other Dharmapala ornaments. A garland of human heads is draped around the neck of the deity and descending almost to the ankles. The main legs are in the *alidhasana* posture, the row of right legs bent at the knee and the left legs straight.

The deity stands on the back of a row of birds, animals human together they represent the "four classes of beings" (birds, animals, humans and gods). The three seated figures are the Hindu "trinity" of gods - a multi-headed Brahma holding an elixir-vase, a single-headed Vishnu and a multi-headed Shiva. The large bird is the Garuda, spiritual vehicle of Vishnu.

The basic two-armed form of Vajrabhairava is blue-black in color, with the face of an extremely enraged buffalo; two sharp horns, with the flames coming from their tips. He has three red, blood-shot eyes; his breath swirls from the anger-creased nose in black clouds; his jaws wide agape with the four sharp fangs bared; the tongue flickering like lightning; the orange hair, eyebrows, and moustache bristling upward like the fire. The feet and palms of the hands are red, and the nails are like iron hooks. The two hands hold a curved knife above and a skull-cup below at the heart.

When in union with his consort Vajra-vetali, she has one face and two hands, is blue in color with orange hair pressed against the back, and holds a skull cup in her left hand

The simplest form of Yamantaka has one bull head and two arms. He has a crown of skulls and has a third eye. His right hand holds a khatri while his left hand carries a kapala. He has a belt of heads.

Three main forms of Yamantaka are revered by Tibetans: Vajrabhairava Yamantaka, who is multicolored; Raktayamari, who is red colored (Red Yamantaka); and Krishnayamari, of black color (Black Yamantaka).

DOCTRINE AND OTHERS

Photo no 134 : *A silver statue of Yamantaka.*

The origin of the bull-head is ascribed to the tradition which speaks of a holy man who lived in a cave, practicing meditation. As he was about to achieve his objective and enter nirvana, two thieves with a stolen bull entered the cave and slaughtered it. When they saw the ascetic, a witness to their crime, they beheaded him too. But to their astonishment, the victim lifted the head of the bull and replacing his own severed head with it, became the ferocious form of Yama. He then not only devoured the two thieves, but his insatiable thirst for human blood threatened the whole population. The followers of the Vajrayana, therefore, appealed to Manjusri who, then assuming the fierce bull-headed form of Yamantaka, defeated Yama in a fearful struggle."

According to the *Tangjur*, one of the main Indian gurus of the Yamantaka teachings was Vairochana Rakshita (circa 728-764 C.E), a disciple of Padmasambhava and author of the *Vajrabhairava Mandalavidhi Prakasa*. Other important Vajrabhairava transmissions came from Ratnakara Shanti (circa 978-1030 C.E) author of the *Vajrabhairava Ganachakra* and the *Krishnayamari Sadhana*. There were many other trantric practitioners and siddhas who taught Yamantaka tantra from earlier period as 8th centery.

Yamantaka is especially important for the Gelugpas, because of Tsong Khapa´s special association with Manjushri, the Conqueror of Yama. It is known that Kublai was initiated into the mysteries of Yamantaka.

Anuttara Yoga Tantra is divided into father and mother-tantra. The former emphasizes practices involving the energy-winds for arising in subtle forms known as illusory bodies, which are the immediate causes for achieving a Buddha's body of forms. The latter gives more detail about practices to access clear light mental activity and focus it with blissful awareness on voidness, as the immediate cause for achieving a Buddha's omniscient awareness or dharmakaya. The Vajrabhairava Tantra belongs to the father tantra using negative emotions such as anger and hatred as the path. Vajrabhairava is powerful enough to overcome and subdue even the most powerful negative emotions. Visualizing oneself in this highly energetic form of the yidam is said to help conquer and transform such negative emotions:

All Buddhist textual sources refer to Lalitavajra as the revealer of the Vajrabhairava and Yamari tantras. Lalitavajra, a 10th-century scholar from the Nalanda monastery in Bihar whose main yidam was Manjushri, one day had a vision of the deity telling him to go to the land of Uddiyana and retrieve the tantras of Yamantaka. He went there and encountered the Wisdom-dakini (in the forma of Vajravetali) and other dakinis who eventually revealed the various Yamantaka tantras to him. They refused to let him take the texts with him and he was only allowed to memorize as much as he could in a short time and then to write that down upon his return.

Tsongkhapa, the founder of the Gelug School, emphasized and promoted the practice of Vajrabhairava. Consequently the practice became one of the three principal tantras taught at the tantric colleges and monastic universities. To this very day it is considered one of the most important yidam practices - for monastic and lay practitioners alike.

YESHE TSOGYAL

Photo no 135 : *Yeshe Tsogyal.*

INTRODUCTION

Yeshe Tsogyal (777-837 A.D.) was one of the five consorts of Guru Padmasambhava. (Others being Mandarava, Kalasiddhi, Sakyadevei, and Tashi Kyedren). She is regarded as a direct incarnation of Vajrayogini in the form of a woman. She served Guru Rinpoche as a spiritual consort, engaged in sadhana practice with incredible perseverance, attaining a level equal to Guru Rinpoche himself.

ICONOGRAPHY

She is depicted as a standing woman with all sorts of adornments. She holds kartika in her right hand and she holds a bowl in her left hand.

SHORT BIOGRAPHY

Yeshe Tsogyal was born in the princely Kharchen family. Her father's name was Namkhai Yeshe and her mother was called Ge-wa Bum. (The different versions of her biography give varying details about her place of birth, the names of her parents and so forth).

It is said that as a young girl, she used to pray for the hapiness of all sentient beings. She had a good memory. She was very compassionate and got moved by other peoples' sorrow. Although, there were several suitors, her parents were reluctant to give her away due to her nature. Later, after knowing of all virtues and beauty, the men of King Trisong Deutsen came to take her to the palace. But she ran away from home to a remote place where she took off all her adornments and prayed to Buddhas and bodhisattvas. It is said that once while she was praying there appeared a sixteen year old boy with a mala in his hand and said her not to cry but to go on praying to all the Buddhas and bodhisattvas continuously. He also said he would show her the path to enlightenment. He took her by hand and they instantly came to a place called Tsang. The boy taught her a teaching on life and samsara and told her to go on practicing even after he was gone. She just was thus practicing in that remote place, when the men of the King found her and brought to the palace.

Later, Yeshe Tsogyal was offered to Guru Padmasambhava by King Trisong Deutsen as a customary gift to the guru. Guru Rinpoche saw in advance that she would be his tantric partner and would be his heir as well. She was sixteen years old when she received empowerment (in 794 AD). During that time, her flower fell on the sacred mandala of Vajrakilaya. She practiced the sadhana and rapidly gained accomplishment. Through this practice she became able to tame evil spirits and revive the dead.

She participated in all activities as per practices of Varjayana and as substantiated by Guru Rinpoche, the primary master of Vajrayana. Since Yeshe Tsogyal possessed a phenomenal photographic memory, it was possible for her to memorize vast numbers of texts without the slightest difficulty. For that reason, the entire Khadro Nying-t'ig teachings were handed into her care. Padmasambhava gradually taught Tsoygal all of his spiritual doctrine and rituals. She helped make the temple complex a reality by winning over the kingdom's leading women and by debating with women who spoke for the older religion. When she had achieved spiritual maturity, she began to travel on her own, gathering followers for Vajrayana Buddhism.

Guru Padmasambhava had sent Yeshe Tsogyal to Nepal to meet Acharya Sale in 795 AD. They practiced various tantric sadhanas and traveled to several hermit caves in Nepal, Tibet and Bhutan. It was said that Yeshe Tsogyal had revived a dead person there to obtain gold so that she can repay the parent of Acharya Sale in return for her to take him. After knowing the fame of her, the parents however consented to send their son with her and did not take any gold. Afterwards, at the lonely cave of Paro Taktsang in the highlands of Bhutan, with her consort Acharya Sale, she disciplined herself through vigorous fasts, long meditation, and the spiritual practice known as karmamudra. Yeshe Tsogyal gained the basic stages of Enlightenment there.

Later she traveled all over Tibet with her Precious Guru, the Lord Padmasambhava, Yeshe Tsogyal's kindness to the land of Tibet and her compassionate activities were no different from that of Guru

Rinpoche. Taking advice from the Lotus Born she wrote them dow: and concealed as precious "Terma" treasures.

Yeshe Tsogyal went into an isolated Meditation Retreat in 79(AD and stayed out until 805 AD. After the death of Trisong Deutsen and the installation of a new king, Padmasambhava left Tibet. After her great Guru had already left Tibet, but when she did finally emerge it was as a fully Enlightened Buddha. She remained in her own country and continued to teach and gather disciples around her. She had written down many of Guru Padmasambhava's teachings. Acting as the compiler of all Guru Rinpoche's words, she visited everywhere in the central and surrounding lands of Tibet and concealed innumerable major and minor termas

In 837 AD, she transcended worldly existence, ascending bodily to the manifested pure field dimension of the Sacred Red Mountain, the luminous sphere of her Guru, the Lord Padmasambhava.

It is said that at present she resides in the indestructible form of the rainbow body in the Palace of Lotus Light on (the continent of) Chamara.

REFERENCES

- A Brief History of Maitreya by *Venerable Lama Thubten Yeshe*, From teachings given at Maitreya Institute, Holland in September, 1981.
- A Buddhist Guide to the Power Places of the Kathmandu Valley by *Venerable Chokey Nyima*.
- A Concise History of Buddhism by *Skilton, Andrew*, Wind horse Pub. London, 2004.
- A Safe Guide for the Practitioner of Hevajra Tantra by *Yogi C. M. Chen*, published by the Oxford University Press.
- A Short Biography of Tsongkhapa by Alexander Berzin, based on a discourse by *Geshe Ngawang Dhargyey Dharamsala*, India August 2003.
- A Short Teaching on the Medicine Buddha by *Geshe Kelsang Gyatso*.
- An Iconography of the Lamaist by *Ferdinand Diederich Lessing*.
- An Introduction to the Kalachakra by *Geshe Wangdrak* (Losang Tenzin) of Namgyal Monastery.
- Arya Avalokitesvara and the Six Syllable Mantra by *Venerable Shangpa Rinpoche, Dhagpo Kagyu Ling*.
- Atisha's Lamp for the Path to Enlightenment by *Geshe Sonam Rinchen*, Snow Lion Publications.

- Becoming Vajrasattva: The Tantric Path of Purification (2004) by *Lama Yeshe*, ISBN-13: 978-0861713899, Wisdom Publications.
- Buddha in the Crown: Avalokitesvara in the Buddhist Traditions of Sri Lanka by *James P. McDermott*, Journal of the American Oriental Society, 1999.
- Cathedral in Peking, Stockholm: The Sino-Swedish Expedition, Publication 18, 1942.
- Chenrezig Lord of Love–Principles and Methods of Deity Meditation by *Bokar Rinpoche* (1991), San Francisco, California: Clear point Press, pp 15. ISBN 09630371-0-2.
- Concealed Essence of the Hevajra Tantra, by *Farrow & Menon*, Motilal, HC, 303pp.
- Congress of the Holy, the anti-erotic yab-yum iconography of Tibet, Holy Mountain Trading Company.
- Dakini's Warm Breath: The Feminine Principle in Tibetan Buddhism by *Judith Simmer-Brown* (2002) p.110.
- Dictionary of Buddhist Iconography by *Chandra, Lokesh* (2002), Delhi, Aditya Prakashan.
- Early Buddhism - A New Approach: by *Sue Hamilton* (2000) p.121.
- Encyclopedia of Gods by *Jordan, Michael*, New York, Facts On File, Inc. 1993, pp. 9-10.
- Encyclopedia of Religion. By *Jones, Lindsay* (Ed. in Chief), 2005, 2nd Ed, Volume 14.
- Enlightened Courage by *Dilgo Khyentse*, Snow Lion 1993, ISBN 1-55939-023-9.
- Four Buddhist Siddhas, published by *State University of New York Press*, 1985.
- Great Kagyu Masters: The Golden Lineage Treasury by *Khenpo Konchog Gyaltsen*, Snow Lion Publications.
- Guide to Dakini Land by Venerable Geshe Kelsang Gyatso, published by *Duldzin Buddhist Center*, United Kingdom.

- Hevajra Tantra: A Critical Study by *D.L. Snellgrove* 2 Volumes. (1959).

- Hevajra Tantra: A Critical Study by S*nellgrove, D. L.*. 2 Vols. London: Oxford University Press, 1959. Reprint. 1980.

- Indian Esoteric Buddhism: A Social History of the Tantric Movement. Davidson, by *Ronald M.* (2003). Columbia University Press. ISBN 81-208-1991-8.

- Life of Tilopa by *Ven. Khenpo Karthar Rinpoche* at KTD, Woodstock, NY, March 25-30, 1986.

- Mahakala by *Ven. Geshé Damchö Yönten*, published by Dharma Therapy Trust under UK, Jan. 1994.

- Masters of Mahamudra Songs and Histories of the Eighty-four Siddhas by *Keith Dowman.*

- Meeting the Buddhas, by *Vessantara,* Wind horse Publications 2003, chapter 9.

- Oracles and Demons of Tibet by *Rene De Nebesky-*Wojokowitz, The Hague, Mouton and Co, 1956.

- Pawo Tsuklak Trengwa's Feast for Scholars (chos 'byung mkhas pa'i dg'a ston), Beijing edition, vol. 2, pp. 913-918.

- Simhamukha: Wrathful Lion-Headed Dakini by *Reynolds, John Myrdhin.*

- Sky Dancer, the Secret Life and Songs o f the Lady Yeshe Tsogyal, by *K. Dowman, Snow Lion,* NY.

- Teachings from the Vajrasattva Retreat (1999) by *Lama Thubten Zopa,* ISBN-13: 978-1891868047, *Lama Yeshe Wisdom Archive.*

- The Concealed Essence of the Hevajra Tantra with the Commentary Yogaratnamala by *Farrow G. W.,* and *Menon,* I. Delhi: 1992.

- The Concealed Essence of the hevajra-tantra by *Farrow, G.W. & Menon* I.(1992). Delhi: Motilal Banarasidas.

- The Cult of Tara by Beyer, *Stephen* (1973). University of California Press. ISBN 0-520-03635-2.

- The Cult of Tara: Magic and Ritual in Tibet (Hermeneutics: Studies in the History of Religions) by *Stephan Beyer* (1978) p.154.

- The Deeper Dimension of Yoga: Theory and Practice by George Feuerstein (2003) p.369.

- The Encyclopedia of Tibetan Symbols and Motifs (Hardcover) by *Beer, Robert* (1999). Shambhala. ISBN-10: 157062416X, ISBN-13: 978-1570624162.

- The Encyclopedia of Tibetan Symbols and Motifs by *Robert Beer* (1999) p.23.

- The Hevajra Tantra: A Critical Study by *Snellgrove*, D.L. (1959). (London Oriental Series, Vol. 6) London: Oxford University Press.

- The Life of Marpa was given by *Khenpo Karthar Rinpoche* at KTD, Woodstock, NY, on March 25-30, 1986.

- The Lineage of His Holiness Sakya Trizin Ngawang-Kunga by *Penny-Dimri, Sandra*. The Tibet Journal, Vol. XX No. 4, Winter 1995, pp. 71-73.

- The Mandala of Heruka by *Pott, P.H.* (1969). in CIBA Journal No. 50, 1969.

- The Origins of Om Manipadme Hum by *Alexander Studholme*: Albany NY: State University of New York Press, 2002 ISBN 0-7914-5389-8.

- The Practice Of Vajrakilaya by *Khenpo Namdrol* Rinpoche (1999). Snow Lion Publications. ISBN-10: 1559391030 & ISBN-13: 978-1559391030.

- The Ri-Me Philosophy of Jamgon Kongtrul the Great: A Study of the Buddhist Lineages of Tibet by *Ringu Tulku*, ISBN 1-59030-286-9, Shambhala Publications.

- The Tantric Path of Purification: The Yoga Method of Heruka Vajrasattva (1994) by *Lama Thubten Yeshe*, ISBN-13: 978-0861710201, Wisdom Publications.

- The Teaching on Vajradhara, by *Khenpo Karthar Rinpoche* at

KTD, Woodstock, March 25-30, 1986, translated by *Chojor Radha*, and edited by Tina Armond.

- The Temples of Western Tibet and Their Artistic Symbolism by *Giuseppe Tucci*, ed. Lokesh Chandra (New Delhi: Aditya Prakashan, 1988), p. 152.
- The Vajrakilaya Sadhana: An Euro American Experience of a Nyingma Ritual by *Cleland, Elizabeth* (2001).
- The Wheel of Great Compassion by *Lorne Ladner and Lama Zopa Rinpoche* (2001) p.28.
- Tibetan Painted Scrolls by *Guiseppe Tucci*, Rome: La Liberia Dello Stato, 1949.
- Tibetan Renaissance: Tantric Buddhism in the Rebirth of Tibetan Culture. Davidson, by *Ronald M.* (2005). Columbia University Press. ISBN 0-231-13471-1.
- Treasures of Tibetan Art by *Barbara Lipton*, Nimu Dorjee Rajnubs. Oxford University Press, 1996.
- Vaisravana/Kuvera in The Sino-Japanese Tradition* By *Dr. Lokesh Chandra*, From Cultural Horizons of India, Volume II, pp. 137-147.
- Vajrayogini, Her Visualizations, Rituals and Forms, A Study of the Cult of Vajrayogini in India by *Elizabeth English*, Wisdom 2002.
- Vajrayogini: Her Visualizations, Rituals, & Forms by *Elizabeth* (2002). Boston: Wisdom Publications. ISBN 0-86171-329-X.
- What the Buddha Taught, by *The Dzogchen Ponlop Rinpoche*, Shambhala Sun, May 2006.
- Wisdom and Compassion by *Rhie, Marylin and Robert A.F. Thurman*. New York: Harry N. Abrams, Inc., Publishers, 1991.
- Wisdom and Compassion: The Sacred Art of Tibet. By *Marylin M. Rhie and Robert A. F. Thurman*. 1991: Asian Art Museum of San Francisco and Tibet House of New York in association with Harry N. Abrams, Inc., New York.

WEB SITES CONSULTED

http://arobuddhism.org/
http://buddhism.about.com/
http://ccbs.ntu.edu.tw/
http://en.wikipedia.org/
http://kaladarshan.arts.ohic-state.edu/
http://members.fortunecity.com/
http://members.tripod.com/
http://museum.oglethorpe.edu/
http://quietmountain.org/
http://rywiki.tsadra.org/
http://shunya.typepad.com/
http://vajranatha.com/
http://web.ukonline.co.uk/buddhism/
http://www.abuddhistlibrary.com/Buddhism/
http://www.ackland.org/art/exhibitions/buddhistart/
http://www.akashavana.org/
http://www.amarilloart.org/
http://www.angelfire.com/
http://www.animalliberationfront.com/
http://www.answers.com/
http://www.asianart.com/
http://www.atiling.org/
http://www.avalokiteshvara2005.org/index2.htm
http://www.berzinarchives.com/web/en/archives/approaching_
    buddhism/
http://www.Buddhafiguren.de
http://www.buddhamuseum.com/old-gilt-mahakala_27.html
http://www.buddhanature.com/buddha/aval.html
http://www.buddhanet.net/e-learning/
http://www.buddhist-artwork.com/statues-buddhism/
http://www.clipclip.org/clips/detail/
http://www.craftgarden.biz/nepal/crafts/Statues+Crafts/

http://www.drukpa.com/drukpa_lineage/
http://www.e-sangha.com/
http://www.fengshuibestbuy.com/
http://www.gakkaionline.net/
http://www.geocities.com/directx_user/gallery/
http://www.geocities.com/ekchew.geo/buddha-lineage.html
http://www.himalayanart.org/image.cfm/531.html
http://www.himalayanmart.com/
http://www.hindupaintings.com/
http://www.holymtn.com/gods/TantricGods.htm
http://www.iep.utm.edu/n/nagarjun.htm
http://www.iloveulove.com/buddhistdeities.htm
http://www.iol.ie/~taeger/tengabio/
http://www.kagyu.org/kagyulineage/lineage/kag06.php
http://www.kagyuoffice.org/
http://www.kailashzone.org/pages/dolpo/crystal.html
http://www.kalachakra.com/home/content/myth.html
http://www.khandro.net/
http://www.lamayeshe.com/otherteachers/hhdl/yoga_method.shtml
http://www.medicinebuddha.org/
http://www.meditationinliverpool.org.uk/
http://www.nagarjunainstitute.com/newararticles/
http://www.namsebangdzo.com/
http://www.natural-tribal-designs.com/
http://www.onmarkproductions.com/html/
http://www.rangjung.com/authors/
http://www.rigdzin.com/
http://www.rossirossi.com/gallery2/19.html
http://www.sacred-texts.com/journals/jras/ns06-14.htm
http://www.simhas.org/kl2.html
http://www.slam.org/exhibits/2005_01_03/asian_01.html
http://www.souledout.org/healing/healingdeities/
http://www.spiritual-teachers.com/

http://www.taraco.com/ref.asp

http://www.taraling.org/id1.html

http://www.tbsn.org/english2/article.php?id=335

http://www.thangka.ru/history/he_padmadsat_3.html

http://www.tharpa.com/us/

http://www.thezensite.com/ZenTeachings/Miscellaneous/

http://www.thirdworldcraft.com/EN/100021938.html

http://www.tibet.com/Buddhism/kala.html

http://www.tientai.net/teachings/dharma/6realms/4kings.htm

http://www.travel-nepal.com/samayak/index.html

http://www.trocadero.com/pmorse/items/483553/item483553
    store.html

http://www.unc.edu/~kalman/mahakala/

http://www.asianart.com/exhibitions/nies/15.html

http://www.yogichen.org/chenian/bk078.html

http://www.yoniversum.nl/dakini/tthevajra.html

http://www2.bremen.de/info/nepal/Icono/EVajrapa.htm

http://z14.invisionfree.com/taoism_singapore/ar/t1115.htm

SANSKRIT WORDS
AND GLOSSARY

Abhaya-mudra : 'Fear not' or 'protection', posture of hands wherein the palm is kept open and facing in front, fingers extended and hand kept at the level of chest

Abhirati : Name of Eastern Pure land where Akshobhya Buddha resides.

Ah : Mantra seed syllable symbolizing great emptiness from which all forms arise, the speech of all the Buddhas, or the *"Vajra* Speech of the Buddhas."

Amoghapasa : Infallible noose usually held by Deities to bring forth what is desired.

Anuttarayoga : It refers to the highest of the four levels of *Vajrayana* teachings. The three lower *tantra* classifications are *Kriya*, *Carya* and *Yoga* (the three Outer Tantras of the Nyingma School).

Astami vrata : Observance of worshipping rituals with fasting during half moon days.

Asuras : Sentient beings, belonging to one of the six realms, usually evil beings who can interact with the human realm, causing major and minor problems in people's lives.

Bhikshu : Monk, One of the four primary classes of Buddhist disciples, the male who has taken the monastic precepts.

Bija : Mantra seed syllables, sounds that are symbols that enlightened beings use to communicate to Dharma practitioners, who also visualize them.

Bodhichitta : Awakened heart, awakened mind, enlightened thought.

Bodhisattvas : Awakened Being, Shakyamuni Buddha used this term to describe himself when he was seeking enlightenment. Bodhi means "Enlightenment" and Sattva means "sentient" or "conscious.

Buddhaksetra : Buddhaland. In Mahayana, the realm acquired by one who reaches perfect enlightenment, where he instructs all beings born there, preparing them for enlightenment, e.g. Amitabha in Sukhavati-Dewachen (Western Paradise); Bhaisajyaguru (Medicine Master Buddha) in Pure Land of Lapus Lazuli Light (Eastern Paradise).

Bumisparsha mudra : The posture which is also called touching the earth. The right arm is pendent over the right knee. The hand with the palm turned inward and all the fingers extended downward with the finger touching the base.

Chintamani : Wish fulfilling.

Chod : The charnal ground practice in which the practitioners sever attachment to his or her corporeal form. This practice always begins with Phowa in which the consciousness of the practitioner is visualized as leaving the body through the crown *chakra* and taking the form of the female deity *Vajrayogini*.

Chorten : Stupa, Symbolic representation of the Buddha's mind, Chortens often have a wide, square base, rounded mid-section, and a tall conical upper section. They usually hold relics of enlightened beings and may vary in size from small clay models to big, multi-storied structures.

Dakinis : These are accomplished female spirits, who have attained the Clear Light and assist practitioners in removing physical hindrances and spiritual obstacles. They are companions of

Buddhas and meditators who can transmit special understanding when the recipient is properly prepared.

Damaru : Musical instrument, played during worshipping. It has two strings with a striking material in each and makes sound after beating through oscillating movement by hand.

Dana : The practice of generosity or charity; one of the Paramitas.

Devas : Beings living in the higher astral plane, in a subtle, non-physical body. Deva is also used in scripture to mean "god or deity" in the class of the least painful existence of *samsara*.

Dharani : Short sutras of symbolic syllables.

Dharma : The teachings of the Buddha (Buddha-Dharma) and the underlying meaning of the teachings.

Dharmakaya : The primordial core of a fully enlightened one, which is free of all conceptions, One of the three bodies of a Buddha (others being *sambhogakaya* and *nirmanakaya*).

Dharmapala : Protector of the Dharma, Special Buddha aspect, both male and female, usually fierce in appearance, purposed to assist practitioners in overcoming obstacles encountered along the way to enlightenment.

Gandharvas : Celestial musicians who are nourished by odours, the name which designates a category of gods in the sphere of desire.

Garuda : Bird just like falcon.

Gompa : Gompa is the actual pursuit of meditational practice, Buddhist monastery, temple, or dharma hall.

Guru : A being of good qualities, great knowledge and skill.

Hum : Mantra seed syllable known as the seal of the "vajra mind" of all buddhas, symbolizing the integration of the universal, absolute and divine within the particular individual, this syllable mantra is regarded as the quintessence of all Buddhas.

Japa : Recitation, Practice of repeating a mantra with concentration, usually followed by use of a mala. It fills the mind with divine syllables, awakening the divine essence of spiritual energies.

It is recommended as a cure for pride and arrogance, anger and jealousy, fear and confusion.

Jaathaka Kathas : Sutras narrating the birth stories of Shakyamuni Buddha in past lives, and effects related to the past and the present lives.

Kalpa : An aeon, world cycle—vast stretch of time.

Kapala : Skull Cup.

Karmamudra : This has been concisely defined as "the practice performed with a maiden possessing the physical attributes of a woman, such as beautiful hair and so forth, with whom one has a strong karmic link" - written by Gendun Drub, the First Dalai Lama (one of Tsongkhapa's direct disciples). Je Tsongkhapa says that both oneself and the yogic "partner" must have received initiation, keep all the vows and pledges, and have mastery of all the 64 arts described in the Indian *Kamasutra*. As well, Tsongkhapa says: "All the authoritative tantric scriptures and treatises point out that the practice of *Karmamudra* is only to be performed by those who are qualified. To engage in it on any other basis, only opens the door to the lower realms. The practice itself should be learned from a qualified master holding the authentic oral tradition." The physical application of sexual practice was largely internalized in adapting to the primarily monastic traditions of Tibet.

Kartika : A special weapon like thing.

Karuna : Compassion, the will to free others from suffering, based on an empathetic sensitivity to that suffering.

Kayas : The three bodies of the Buddha: the *nirmanakaya, sambhogakaya* and *dharmakaya*.

Khatvanga : A special weapon like trident.

Kotis : Lakhs.

Ksanti : Patience or forbearance, one of the six Paramitas.

Madhyamika : Middle Way. A philosophical school based on the Prajnaparamita Sutras and their doctrine of Emptiness; the

Middle Way philosophy expounded by Nagarjuna. The *Madhyamika* is concerned both with the transcendence of logical affirmation and negation, and stresses the dependent origination of all things and the limitations of rational constructs.

Mahamudra : Great Seal or Symbol. The highest meditative transmission/teaching in the Tibetan Kagyu school as is "Dzogchen" or Great Perfection in the Nyingma school. The Mahamudra Sutra emphasizes dwelling in tranquility and insight, and progressing along the Five Paths (which starts with the beginning of Dharma practice and the accumulation of merit and ends with complete Enlightenment).

Mala : A string of beads for counting prayers and other spiritual practices. The ideal number of beads is said to be 108.

Mandala : Circle; sacred space. A support for a meditating person, a mystical diagram of energy within which deities or their emblems are portrayed in a symmetrically arrange diagram arranged in a basically circular pattern.

Mantra : Sanskrit words signifying a sacred word, verse or syllable which embodies in sound the energy of some specific deity or primordial power. A series of syllables invoking a spiritual power or blessing; a creative sound expressing the innermost essence of understandings.

Mara : The Evil One who "takes" away the wisdom-life of all living beings.

Mudra : Hand gestures which express specific energies or powers. Usually accompanied by precise visualizations, *mudras* are a vital element of ritual worship, dance and yoga.

Nagas : *Naga* goddesses and gods are a mystical, primitive race of divine serpent people that play an important role in religion, mythology, and fairy tales worldwide.

Nirmanakaya : The Creation Body, the worldly form of a Buddha or other enlightened being.

Nirvana : Transcendence of suffering; cessation of birth in Samsara.

Om : Mantra seed syllable, "the *Vajra* body of all Buddhas." It invokes the power of universal creativity and resonates with current of the all-pervading divine energy of being, thus, is used at the beginning of many mantras.

Paramita : Perfection. The paramitas are the framework of the bodhisattva's religious practice, usually consisting of six categories.

Phurba : A phurba is a three-edged knife with a handle often in the shape of half of a dorje or bearing the images of the countenance of a wrathful deity. The use of the phurba was introduced into the practice of Tibetan Buddhism by Padmasambhava. Phurbas are used in tantric ceremonies to exorcise demons (physical and psychological obstacles) or as a spiritual nail to pin down the distractions of greed, desire and envy.

Prajna : Fundamental wisdom or insight; the sixth Paramita.

Preta : Hungry ghost; a lower dimensional being subject to intense suffering being plagued by deep attachments.

Sadhana : Method of accomplishment. 1. Religious or spiritual disciplines, such as puja, yoga, meditation, japa, fasting and austerity. The effect of sadhana is the building of willpower, concentration, faith and confidence in oneself and in the guru. 2. A highly structured technical text focussing on Deity Yoga using various meditation and recitation techniques.

Samadhi : Deep meditation. State of profound mental absorption."Sameness; evenness, contemplation; union, wholeness; completion, accomplishment." Samadhi is the state of true yoga, in which the meditator and the object of meditation are one.

Sambhogakaya : The Sambhogakâya is the supramundane form that a fully enlightened Buddha appears in following the completion of their career as a Bodhisattva. It is also called body of enjoyment. Sambhogakâya body appears is an extra-cosmic realm and can be seen or felt only by bodhisattvas.

Samsara : Going round in circles. The phenomenal world experienced dualistically, from the viewpoint of ego-clinging. Transmigratory existence, fraught with emotional reactivity, deluding notions, impermanence and change. The cycle of birth, death and rebirth.

Sanskara : Learnt through traditional practice.

Siddha : "Perfected one" or accomplished yogi, a person of great spiritual attainment or powers.

Siddhi : Power, accomplishment; perfection; blessing.

Sila : Morality, ethics. The mind-set of doing no harm, either to oneself or to others. Often accompanied by precepts and vows for practical purposes. These number 5, 8, 10, 250 or 350. Also, one of the Paramitas.

Skandhas : The five aggregates that constitute the personality: form, sensation, perception (recognition), mental formations, and conciousness.

Sravaka : Listener, hearer. Early main branch of Buddhism. These people chose to base their practice on doctrines that were believed by everyone to be the public teachings of the Buddha to his monks and lay disciples.

Stupa : Chorten. Sacred structure built to physically embody and preserve the spiritual power of a great lama. It is a physical representation of perfect enlightenment. It symbolizes the transformation of all emotions and elements into the five enlightened wisdoms associated with the five Buddha families. Its symmetrical form is usually filled with relics, mantras, etc.

Sudarshan-chakra : Whirling circular thing held by Deities symbolizing his/her means of power display.

Sukhavati : Western Pure land of Amitabha Buddha.

Sunyata : "Emptiness, Void"; A central notion of Buddha's Dharma. Ancient Buddhism recognized that all composite things are empty, impermanent, devoid of an essence, characterized by psycho-physical suffering, decay and death.

Sutra : An aphoristic verse; the literary style consisting of such maxims. A discourse by the Buddha or one of his major disciples.

Swayambhu Purana : Document elaborating the origin of Kathmandu valley and *Swayambhunath* temple.

Tantra : Tantra means continuum, transmission, and secret teaching, a sacred text of that tradition.

Tarpana mudra : Hand postures wherein both palm are open and fingers all stretched in front as if offering to someone at front.

Uposadha Vrata : Observance of worshipping rituals with fasting during full moon days and no-moon days of lunar calendar.

Ushnisa : A diadem.

Uttarabodhi mudra : Posture of hand wherein hands are held near chest, index fingers on both hands are raised, touching each other, remaining fingers are crossed and folded down, and thumbs are crossed and folded.

Vajra : The *Vajra* is the quintessential symbol of Vajrayana Buddhism. The *Vajra* means 'the hard or mighty one', and its Tibetan equivalent of dorje, which means an indestructible hardness and brilliance like the diamond, which cannot be cut or broken. The *Vajra* essentially symbolizes the indestructible state of enlightenment or Buddhahood. In tantric rituals, the *Vajra* symbolizes the male principle, which represents *method* in the right hand and the Bell symbolizes the female principle, which represents wisdom in the left hand.

Varada-mudra : Hand posture wherein the palm is open and pointing downward with all fingers straight and clinging, it depicts boon giving.

Vayu : Wind.

Vijnana : Consciousness.

Vina : Musical instrument.

Vinaya : Cause and effect (karma), guidelines for action.

Vishva-vajra : Two *Vajras* kept crossed with each other, it symbolizes that a certain deity is consecrated and thus sealed. It is also the symbol of Buddha Amoghasiddhi.

Yakshas : A class of beings mentioned in the Buddhist Canon who are divine in nature and possess supernatural powers.

Yogi : A devoted practitioner of religion.

TIBETAN NAMES

Tibetan Name	Sanskrit/Nepali Name
Mi yo wa	Achala
Mikyop	Akshobhya Buddha
Opame	Amitâbha Buddha
Donyo Drupa	Amoghasiddhi Buddha
Tse-pameh	Aparmita
Chenrezig	Avalokiteshvara, Kharkseri
Korlo Demchog	Chakrasamvara
Yul khor srung	Dhritarashtra
Mi slob	Dipankara Buddha
Dorje Legpa	Vajrasadhu
Tse-chik-ma, Ral-chik-ma	Ekajati
Pagma Drolma	Green Tara
Sangwa-dupa	Guhyasamaja
Kye Dorje	Hevajra
Jambala	Kubera, Vaishravana
Rigjyedma	Kurukula
Gonpo Phyag	Mahakala
Jampa	Maitreya Bodhisattva
lha lcam dkar mo	Mandarava
Jampelyang	Manjushree

Tibetan Name	Sanskrit/Nepali Name
Öser Chenma	Marichi
Sangye Menla	Bhaisajyaguru
Klu Sgrub	Nagarjuna
Dagmena	Nairatma
Tsug Tor Nam Par Gyelma or *Namgyalma*	Ushnishavijaya
Pema Jungne	Guru Padmasambhava
Palden Lhamo	Shri Devi
Yum Chenmo	Prajnaparamita
kyab jug	Rahula
Rinchen Jung ne	Ratnasambhava Buddha
Kuntu zangpo	Samantabhadra
Seng-gdong-ma	Simhamukha
Dukar	Ushnisha-Sitatapatra
rNam-par-snang mdzad	Buddha Vairocana
Dorje Chang	Vajradhara
Dorje Purba	Vajrakilaya
Chana Dorje	Vajrapani
Dorje sempa	Vajrasattva
Dorje Phagmo	Vajravarahi
Dorje Naljorma	Vajrayogini
Pag pi kye bo	Virudhaka
Sgrol-dkar	White Tara
Shinjeshe, Dorje Jig-je	Yamantaka,
Tsongkhapa	Je Rinpoche

ALTERNATIVE NAMES OF THE SAME DEITY OR MASTER

Prevailed Name	Other Names of the same deity
Achala ·	Acala, Achalanath, Chandamaharosana, and Krodaraja, Shankata
Aparmita	Amitayus
Avalokiteshvara	Chenrezig, Kharkseri
Chundi	Cundi
Kubera	Vaishravana, Jambala
Karma Pakshi	Second Gyalwa Karmapa
Marichi	Marici
Medicine Buddha	Bhaisajyaguru
Namgyalma	Ushnishavijaya
Padmasambhava	Guru Rinpoche, Padmakara, Lotus-born
Palden Lhamo	Shri Devi, Chhwasakamani Devi,
Rangjung Rigpe Dorje	Sixteenth Gyalwa Karmapa

Prevailed Name	Other Names of the same deity
Sakyamuni Gautama Buddha	Buddha, Tathagata, Sakyamuni Buddha, Siddhartha Gautama (childhood name)
Thousand-armed Avalokiteshvara	Sahastrabhuja Lokeshvara
Tsongkhapa	Je Rinpoche
Ushnisha-Sitatapatra	Sitapatra, White parasol
Vajrapani	Dharmavajra, Vajra Garba
White Tara	Saptalocana Tara
Yamantaka	Vajrabhairava, Mega-samvara,

INDEX